NEVERMORE

A GRAPHIC ADAPTATION OF EDGAR ALLAN POE'S SHORT STORIES

STERLING

New York / London

www.sterlingpublishing.com

Published by Sterling Publishing Co., Inc.
387 Park Avenue South, New York, NY 10016

© 2008 SelfMadeHero

First published 2008
by SelfMadeHero
A division of Metro Media Ltd
5 Upper Wimpole Street
London W1G 6BP
www.selfmadehero.com

Editor: Dan Whitehead
Cover Designer: Jeff Willis
Designer: Andy Huckle
Originating Publisher: Emma Hayley

Distributed in Canada by Sterling Publishing
C/o Canadian Manda Group, 165 Dufferin Street,
Toronto, Ontario, Canada M6K 3H6

Library of Congress Cataloging-in-Publication Data

Nevermore: A graphic adaptation of Edgar Allan Poe's short stories.
    p. cm.—(Illustrated Classics)
  ISBN-13: 978-1-4114-1592-8 (pbk.)
  ISBN-10: 1-4114-1592-2 (pbk.)
    1. Poe, Edgar Allan, 1809-1849—Adaptations. I. Poe, Edgar Allan, 1809-1849.
PN6726.N47 2008
741.5'973—dc22

2007060596

Printed in the United States

10 9 8 7 6 5 4 3 2 1

For information about custom editions, special sales, premium and corporate
purchases, please contact Sterling Special Sales Department at 800-805-5489 or
specialsales@sterlingpub.com.

CONTENTS

The timeless quality of Edgar Allan Poe's work has once again inspired a new generation of talented writers and artists to come up with fresh interpretations of his macabre tales. In this graphic novel anthology, you will find imaginative adaptations of some of Poe's less famous stories, as well as superb adaptations of his most famous tales.

As a long-time admirer of Edgar Allan Poe's gripping stories, I took the opportunity, early in my career, to adapt some of my favorites (such as *The Fall of the House of Usher*, *The Masque of the Red Death*, *The Pit and the Pendulum*, *The Raven*, and *The Tomb of Ligeia*) to film. These were straight period adaptations, full of gothic atmosphere, in many of which I was fortunate enough to work with the brilliant Vincent Price, who brought to these films an understanding of the depth and complexity of Poe's doomed protagonists. This anthology takes a completely different, and highly effective, approach. The writers and artists have recast the tales for a modern audience, applying Poe's themes to contemporary conflicts and moral ambiguities. This is exciting, original work, both from well-known names in the comics industry and from talented new artists and writers, that conceptually and visually gives new, unnerving life to Poe's obsessions.

These versions of Poe's best-loved and less familiar tales are destined to capture the imagination of a generation new to the master of terror, as well as delight long-time admirers of Poe.

– Roger Corman

THE RAVEN

Adapted by Dan Whitehead and Stuart Tipples
Art by Stuart Tipples

First published in January 1845, *The Raven* is arguably Poe's
most famous work and one of the most respected poems in
American literature.

Aching with the desperation of bereavement, the narrative verse
tells the story of a man struggling in the throes of mourning
a lost love when his home is invaded by a mysterious talking
raven. Believing the bird to be a messenger from the underworld,
he desperately questions the creature for news of his lover's
safe arrival in the afterlife. The bird, however, can only give one
response.

He continues his interrogation, even though the bleak outcome is
clearly inevitable.

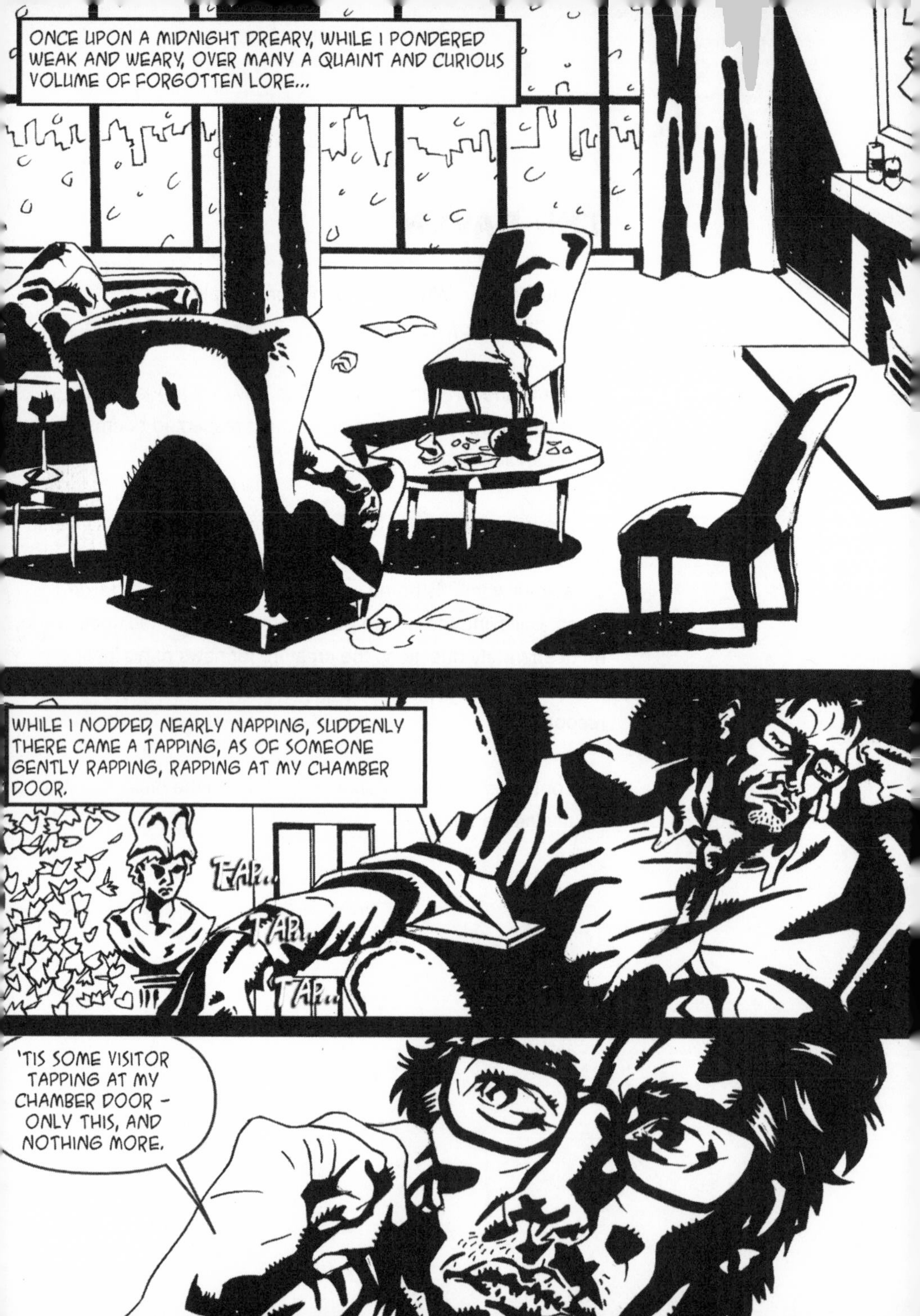
ONCE UPON A MIDNIGHT DREARY, WHILE I PONDERED WEAK AND WEARY, OVER MANY A QUAINT AND CURIOUS VOLUME OF FORGOTTEN LORE...
WHILE I NODDED, NEARLY NAPPING, SUDDENLY THERE CAME A TAPPING, AS OF SOMEONE GENTLY RAPPING, RAPPING AT MY CHAMBER DOOR.
TAP...
TAP...
TAP...
'TIS SOME VISITOR TAPPING AT MY CHAMBER DOOR - ONLY THIS, AND NOTHING MORE.

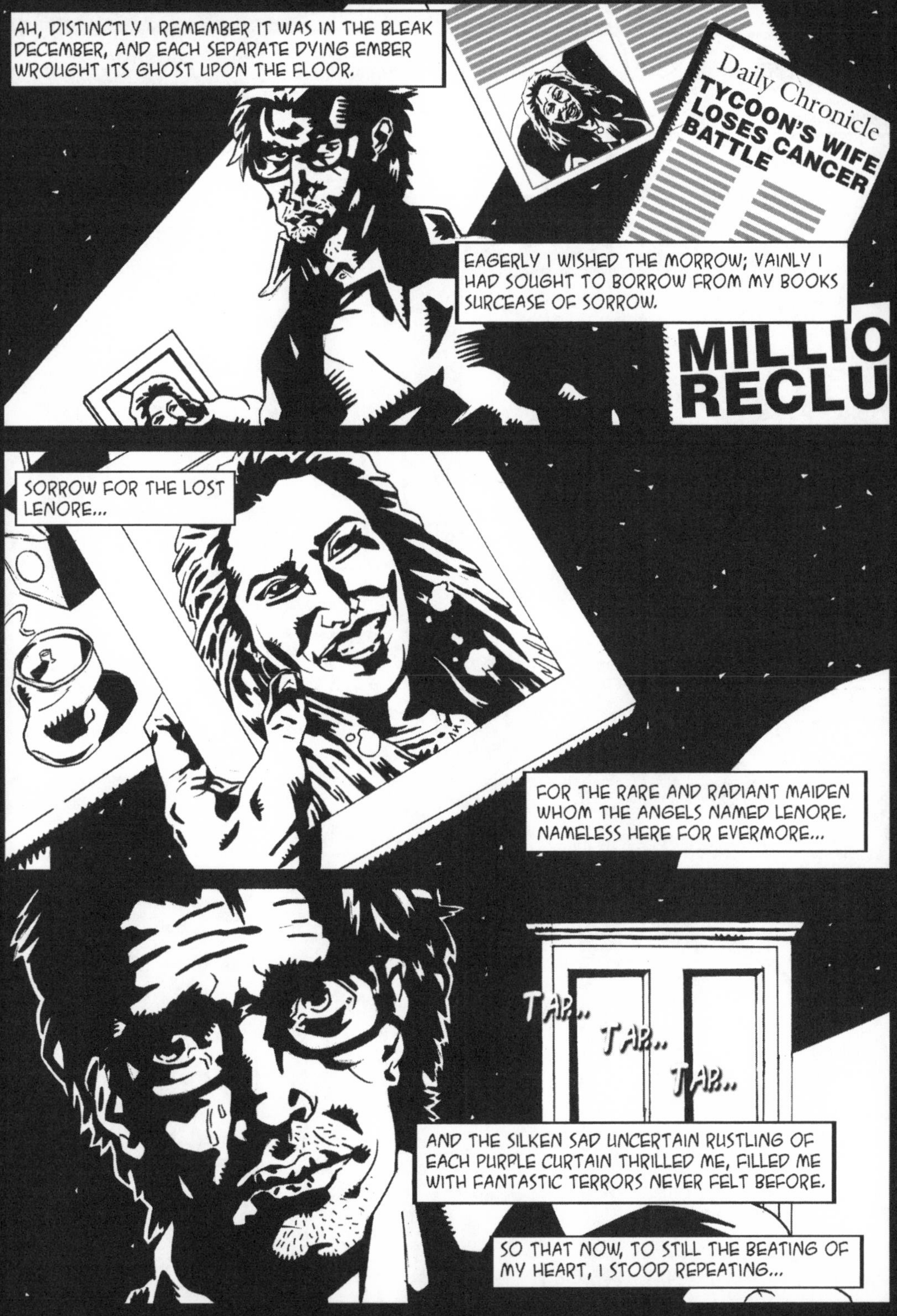
AH, DISTINCTLY I REMEMBER IT WAS IN THE BLEAK DECEMBER, AND EACH SEPARATE DYING EMBER WROUGHT ITS GHOST UPON THE FLOOR.
Daily Chronicle
TYCOON'S WIFE LOSES BATTLE CANCER
EAGERLY I WISHED THE MORROW; VAINLY I HAD SOUGHT TO BORROW FROM MY BOOKS SURCEASE OF SORROW.
MILLIO
RECLU
SORROW FOR THE LOST LENORE...
FOR THE RARE AND RADIANT MAIDEN WHOM THE ANGELS NAMED LENORE. NAMELESS HERE FOR EVERMORE...
TAP...
TAP...
TAP...
AND THE SILKEN SAD UNCERTAIN RUSTLING OF EACH PURPLE CURTAIN THRILLED ME, FILLED ME WITH FANTASTIC TERRORS NEVER FELT BEFORE.
SO THAT NOW, TO STILL THE BEATING OF MY HEART, I STOOD REPEATING...

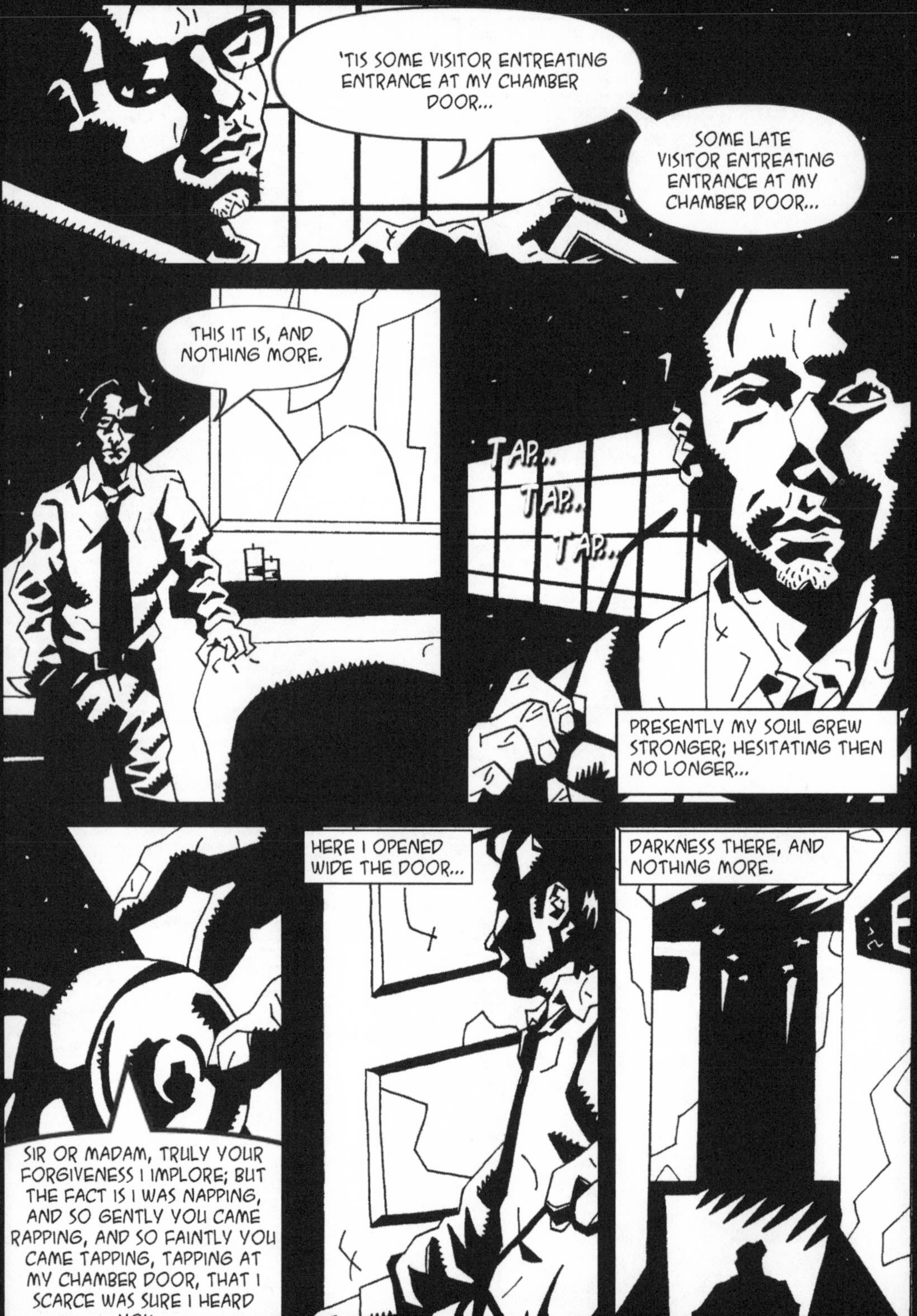
'TIS SOME VISITOR ENTREATING ENTRANCE AT MY CHAMBER DOOR...
SOME LATE VISITOR ENTREATING ENTRANCE AT MY CHAMBER DOOR...
THIS IT IS, AND NOTHING MORE.
TAP... TAP... TAP...
PRESENTLY MY SOUL GREW STRONGER; HESITATING THEN NO LONGER...
SIR OR MADAM, TRULY YOUR FORGIVENESS I IMPLORE; BUT THE FACT IS I WAS NAPPING, AND SO GENTLY YOU CAME RAPPING, AND SO FAINTLY YOU CAME TAPPING, TAPPING AT MY CHAMBER DOOR, THAT I SCARCE WAS SURE I HEARD YOU...
HERE I OPENED WIDE THE DOOR...
DARKNESS THERE, AND NOTHING MORE.

DEEP INTO THAT DARKNESS PEERING, LONG I STOOD THERE, WONDERING, FEARING, DOUBTING, DREAMING DREAMS NO MORTAL EVER DARED TO DREAM BEFORE.

THIS I WHISPERED, AND AN ECHO MURMURED BACK THE WORD...

TAP...

TAP...

TAP...

LENORE...

BUT THE SILENCE WAS UNBROKEN, AND THE DARKNESS GAVE NO TOKEN, AND THE ONLY WORD THERE SPOKEN WAS THE WHISPERED WORD, "LENORE"!

MERELY THIS AND NOTHING MORE.

BACK INTO THE CHAMBER TURNING, ALL MY SOUL WITHIN ME BURNING, SOON AGAIN I HEARD A TAPPING SOMEWHAT LOUDER THAN BEFORE.

LET MY HEART BE STILL A MOMENT AND THIS MYSTERY EXPLORE...

'TIS THE WIND AND NOTHING MORE!

OPEN HERE I FLUNG THE SHUTTER, WHEN, WITH MANY A FLIRT AND FLUTTER, IN THERE STEPPED A STATELY RAVEN OF THE SAINTLY DAYS OF YORE.

SURELY THAT IS SOMETHING AT MY WINDOW LATTICE; LET ME SEE THEN, WHAT THEREAT IS AND THIS MYSTERY EXPLORE...

NOT THE LEAST OBEISANCE MADE HE; NOT A MINUTE STOPPED OR STAYED HE; BUT, WITH MIEN OF LORD OR LADY, PERCHED ABOVE MY CHAMBER DOOR...

PERCHED UPON A BUST OF PALLAS JUST ABOVE MY CHAMBER DOOR...

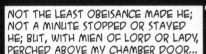

PERCHED, AND SAT, AND NOTHING MORE.

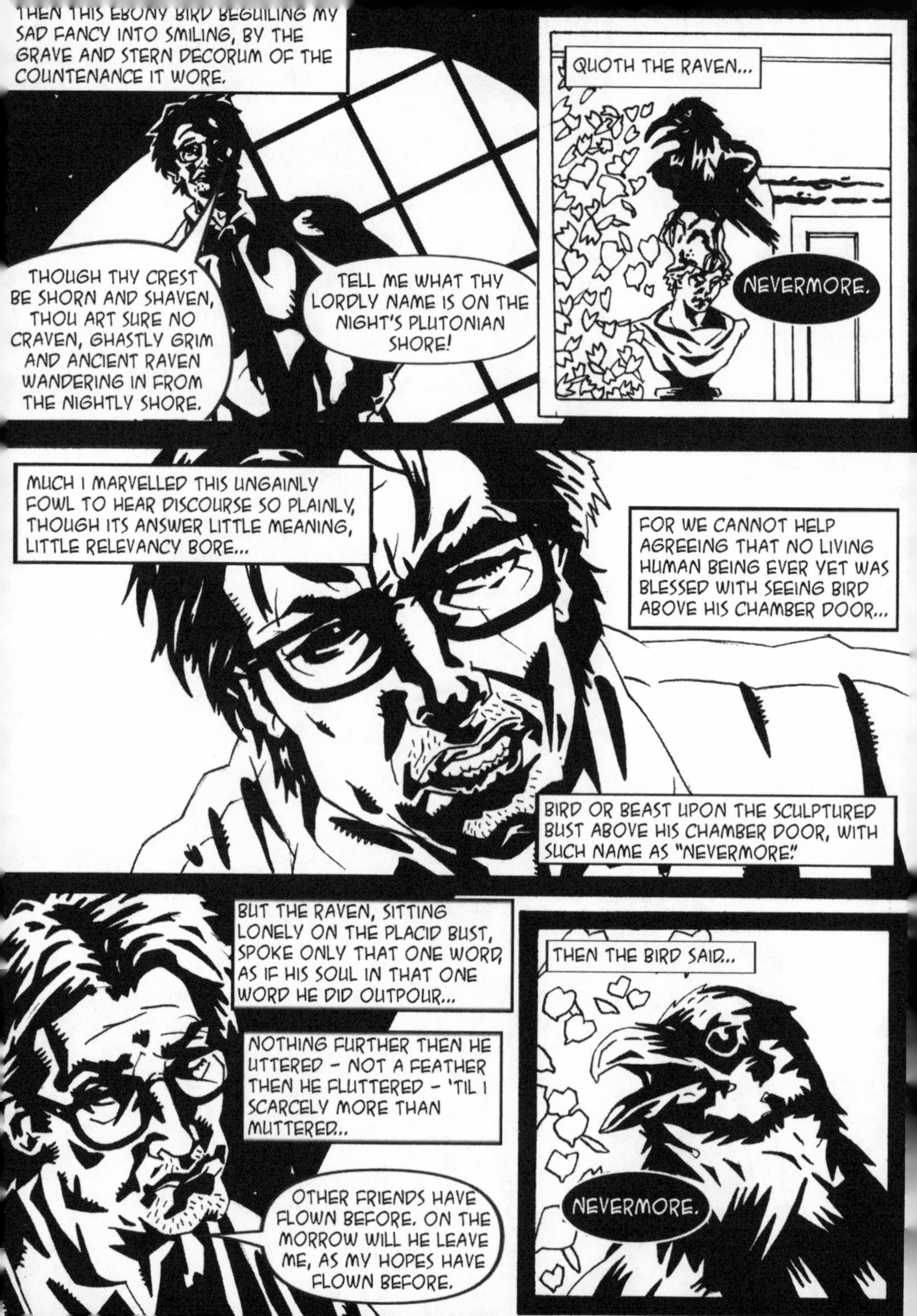

THEN THIS EBONY BIRD BEGUILING MY SAD FANCY INTO SMILING, BY THE GRAVE AND STERN DECORUM OF THE COUNTENANCE IT WORE.
THOUGH THY CREST BE SHORN AND SHAVEN, THOU ART SURE NO CRAVEN, GHASTLY GRIM AND ANCIENT RAVEN WANDERING IN FROM THE NIGHTLY SHORE.
TELL ME WHAT THY LORDLY NAME IS ON THE NIGHT'S PLUTONIAN SHORE!
QUOTH THE RAVEN...
NEVERMORE.
MUCH I MARVELLED THIS UNGAINLY FOWL TO HEAR DISCOURSE SO PLAINLY, THOUGH ITS ANSWER LITTLE MEANING, LITTLE RELEVANCY BORE...
FOR WE CANNOT HELP AGREEING THAT NO LIVING HUMAN BEING EVER YET WAS BLESSED WITH SEEING BIRD ABOVE HIS CHAMBER DOOR...
BIRD OR BEAST UPON THE SCULPTURED BUST ABOVE HIS CHAMBER DOOR, WITH SUCH NAME AS "NEVERMORE."
BUT THE RAVEN, SITTING LONELY ON THE PLACID BUST, SPOKE ONLY THAT ONE WORD, AS IF HIS SOUL IN THAT ONE WORD HE DID OUTPOUR...
NOTHING FURTHER THEN HE UTTERED - NOT A FEATHER THEN HE FLUTTERED - 'TIL I SCARCELY MORE THAN MUTTERED...
OTHER FRIENDS HAVE FLOWN BEFORE. ON THE MORROW WILL HE LEAVE ME, AS MY HOPES HAVE FLOWN BEFORE.
THEN THE BIRD SAID...
NEVERMORE.

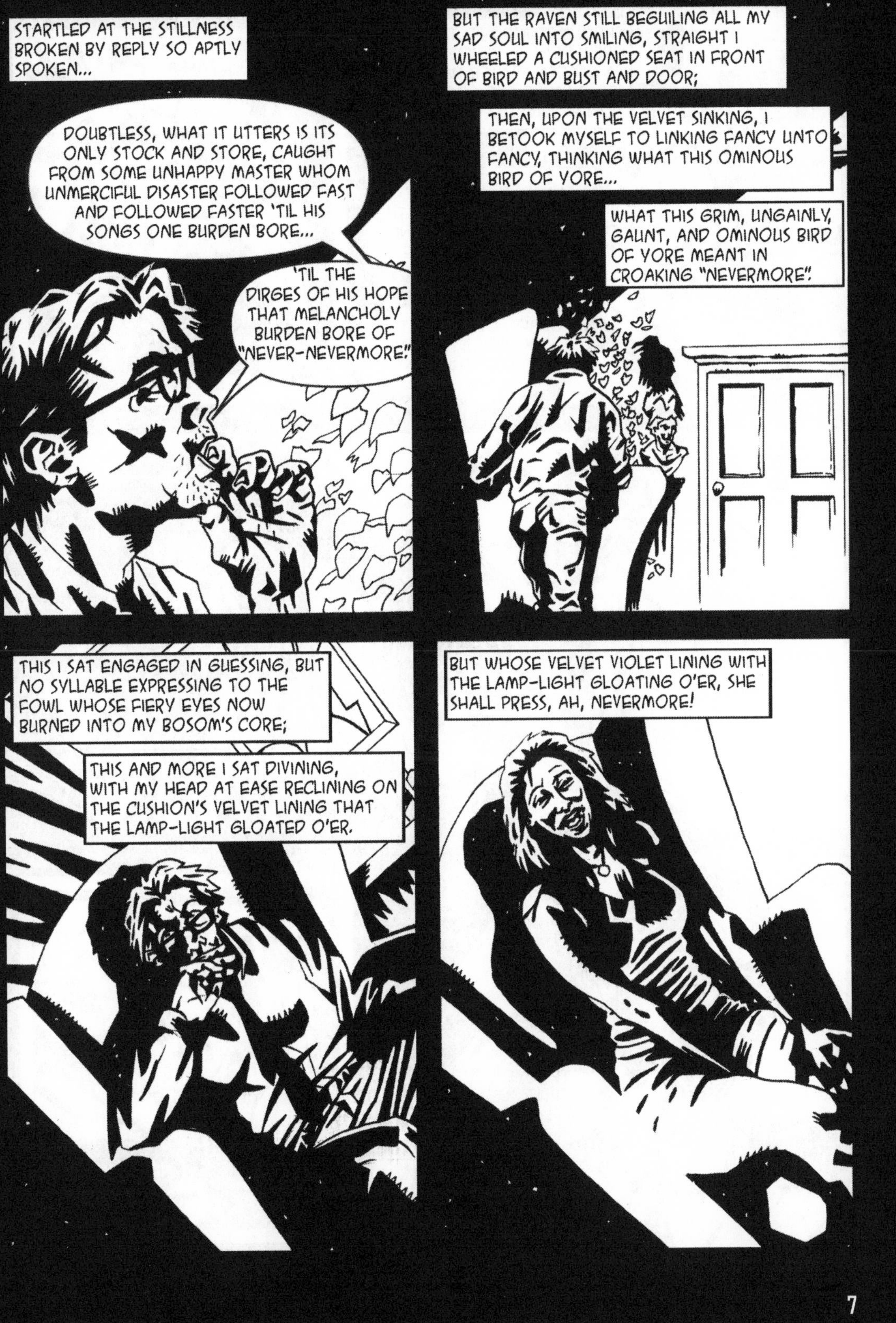
STARTLED AT THE STILLNESS BROKEN BY REPLY SO APTLY SPOKEN...
DOUBTLESS, WHAT IT UTTERS IS ITS ONLY STOCK AND STORE, CAUGHT FROM SOME UNHAPPY MASTER WHOM UNMERCIFUL DISASTER FOLLOWED FAST AND FOLLOWED FASTER 'TIL HIS SONGS ONE BURDEN BORE...
'TIL THE DIRGES OF HIS HOPE THAT MELANCHOLY BURDEN BORE OF "NEVER-NEVERMORE."
BUT THE RAVEN STILL BEGUILING ALL MY SAD SOUL INTO SMILING, STRAIGHT I WHEELED A CUSHIONED SEAT IN FRONT OF BIRD AND BUST AND DOOR;
THEN, UPON THE VELVET SINKING, I BETOOK MYSELF TO LINKING FANCY UNTO FANCY, THINKING WHAT THIS OMINOUS BIRD OF YORE...
WHAT THIS GRIM, UNGAINLY, GAUNT, AND OMINOUS BIRD OF YORE MEANT IN CROAKING "NEVERMORE".
THIS I SAT ENGAGED IN GUESSING, BUT NO SYLLABLE EXPRESSING TO THE FOWL WHOSE FIERY EYES NOW BURNED INTO MY BOSOM'S CORE;
THIS AND MORE I SAT DIVINING, WITH MY HEAD AT EASE RECLINING ON THE CUSHION'S VELVET LINING THAT THE LAMP-LIGHT GLOATED O'ER.
BUT WHOSE VELVET VIOLET LINING WITH THE LAMP-LIGHT GLOATING O'ER, SHE SHALL PRESS, AH, NEVERMORE!

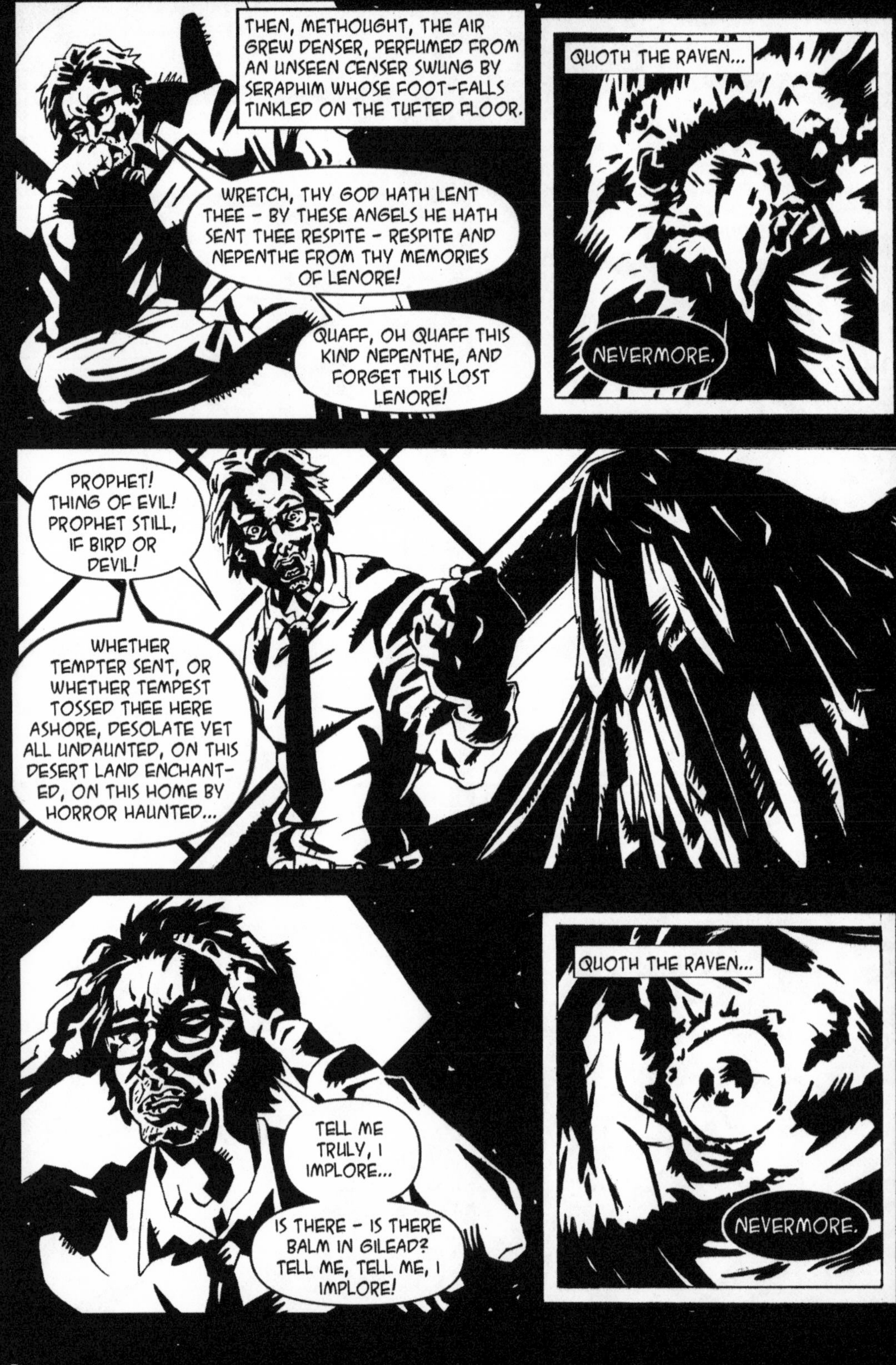
THEN, METHOUGHT, THE AIR GREW DENSER, PERFUMED FROM AN UNSEEN CENSER SWUNG BY SERAPHIM WHOSE FOOT-FALLS TINKLED ON THE TUFTED FLOOR.
WRETCH, THY GOD HATH LENT THEE - BY THESE ANGELS HE HATH SENT THEE RESPITE - RESPITE AND NEPENTHE FROM THY MEMORIES OF LENORE!
QUAFF, OH QUAFF THIS KIND NEPENTHE, AND FORGET THIS LOST LENORE!
QUOTH THE RAVEN...
NEVERMORE.
PROPHET! THING OF EVIL! PROPHET STILL, IF BIRD OR DEVIL!
WHETHER TEMPTER SENT, OR WHETHER TEMPEST TOSSED THEE HERE ASHORE, DESOLATE YET ALL UNDAUNTED, ON THIS DESERT LAND ENCHANTED, ON THIS HOME BY HORROR HAUNTED...
TELL ME TRULY, I IMPLORE...
IS THERE - IS THERE BALM IN GILEAD? TELL ME, TELL ME, I IMPLORE!
QUOTH THE RAVEN...
NEVERMORE.

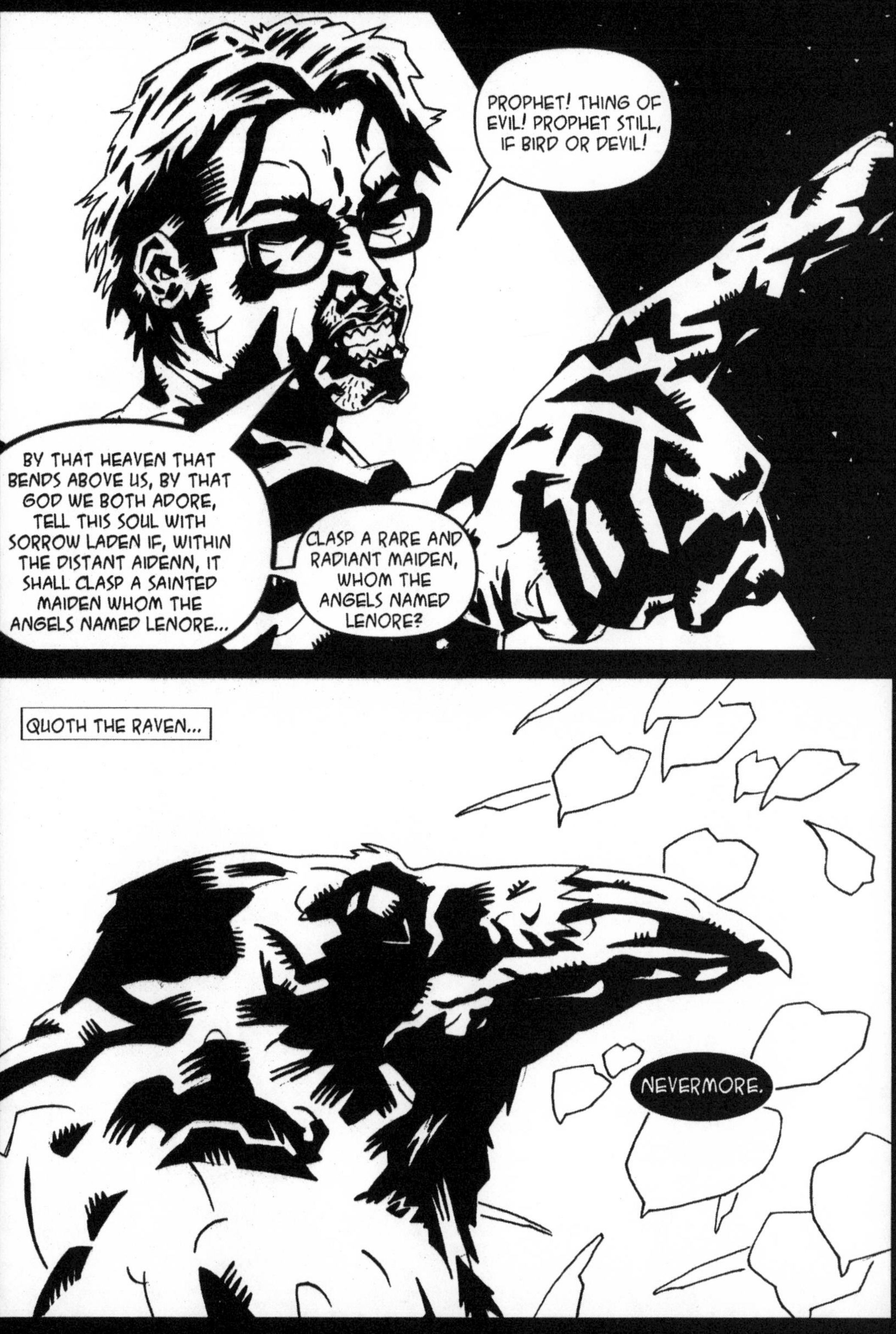
PROPHET! THING OF EVIL! PROPHET STILL, IF BIRD OR DEVIL!
BY THAT HEAVEN THAT BENDS ABOVE US, BY THAT GOD WE BOTH ADORE, TELL THIS SOUL WITH SORROW LADEN IF, WITHIN THE DISTANT AIDENN, IT SHALL CLASP A SAINTED MAIDEN WHOM THE ANGELS NAMED LENORE...
CLASP A RARE AND RADIANT MAIDEN, WHOM THE ANGELS NAMED LENORE?
QUOTH THE RAVEN...
NEVERMORE.

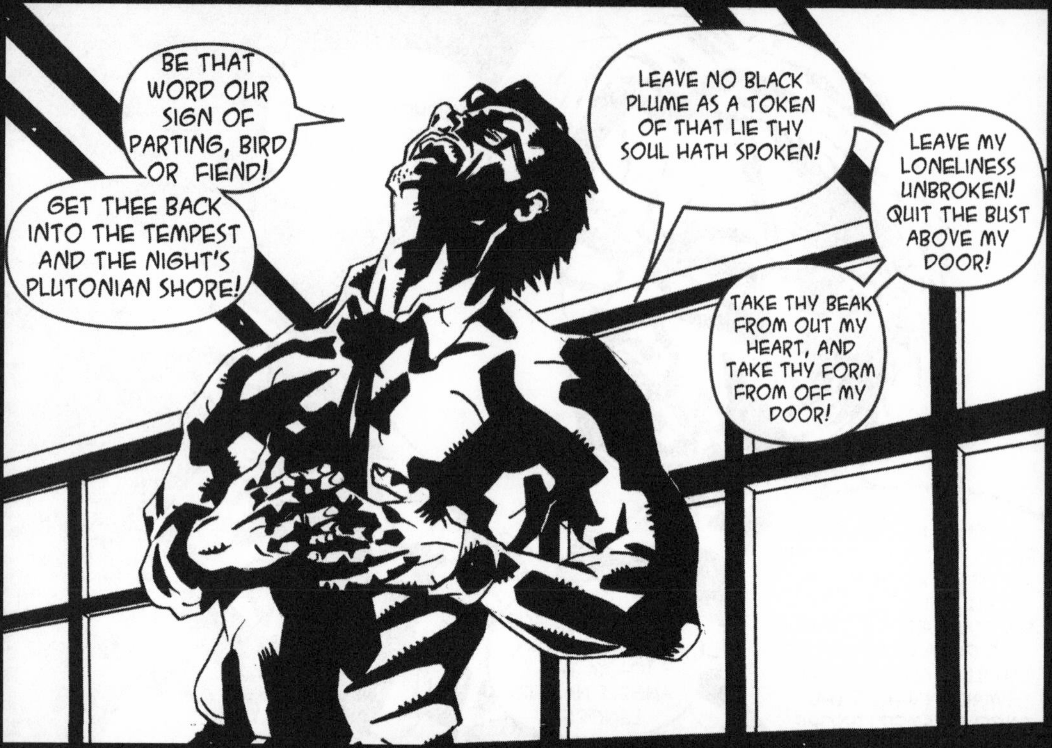
BE THAT WORD OUR SIGN OF PARTING, BIRD OR FIEND!
GET THEE BACK INTO THE TEMPEST AND THE NIGHT'S PLUTONIAN SHORE!
LEAVE NO BLACK PLUME AS A TOKEN OF THAT LIE THY SOUL HATH SPOKEN!
LEAVE MY LONELINESS UNBROKEN! QUIT THE BUST ABOVE MY DOOR!
TAKE THY BEAK FROM OUT MY HEART, AND TAKE THY FORM FROM OFF MY DOOR!

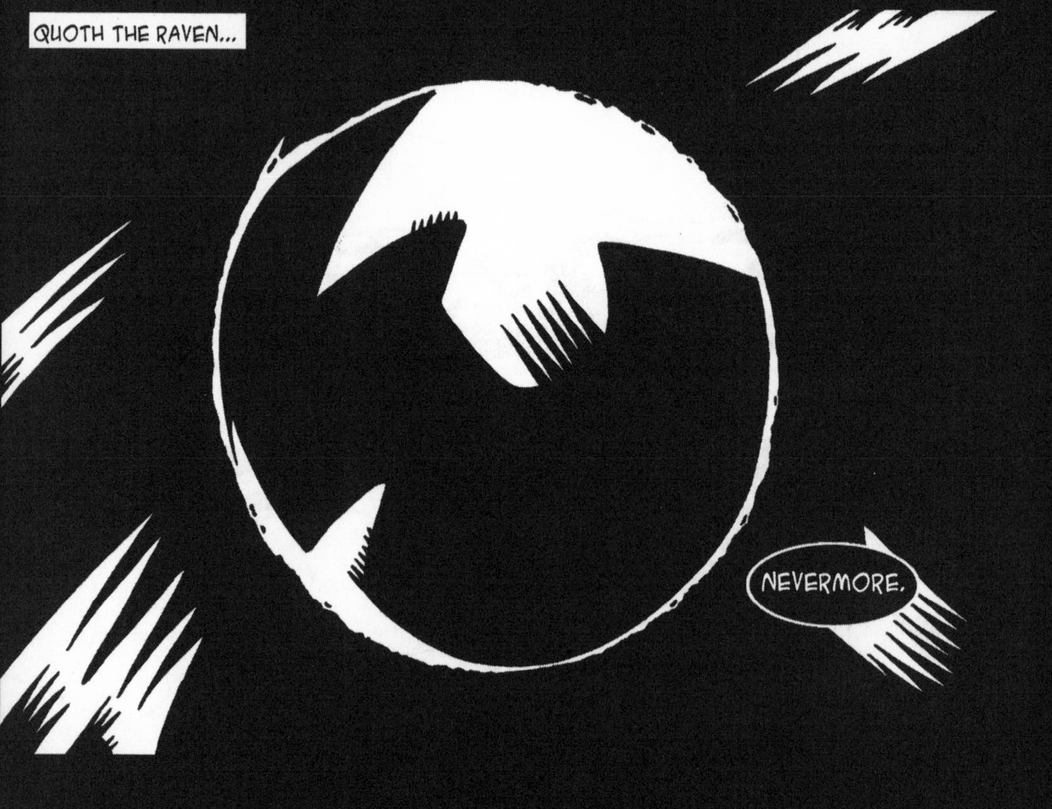
QUOTH THE RAVEN...
NEVERMORE.

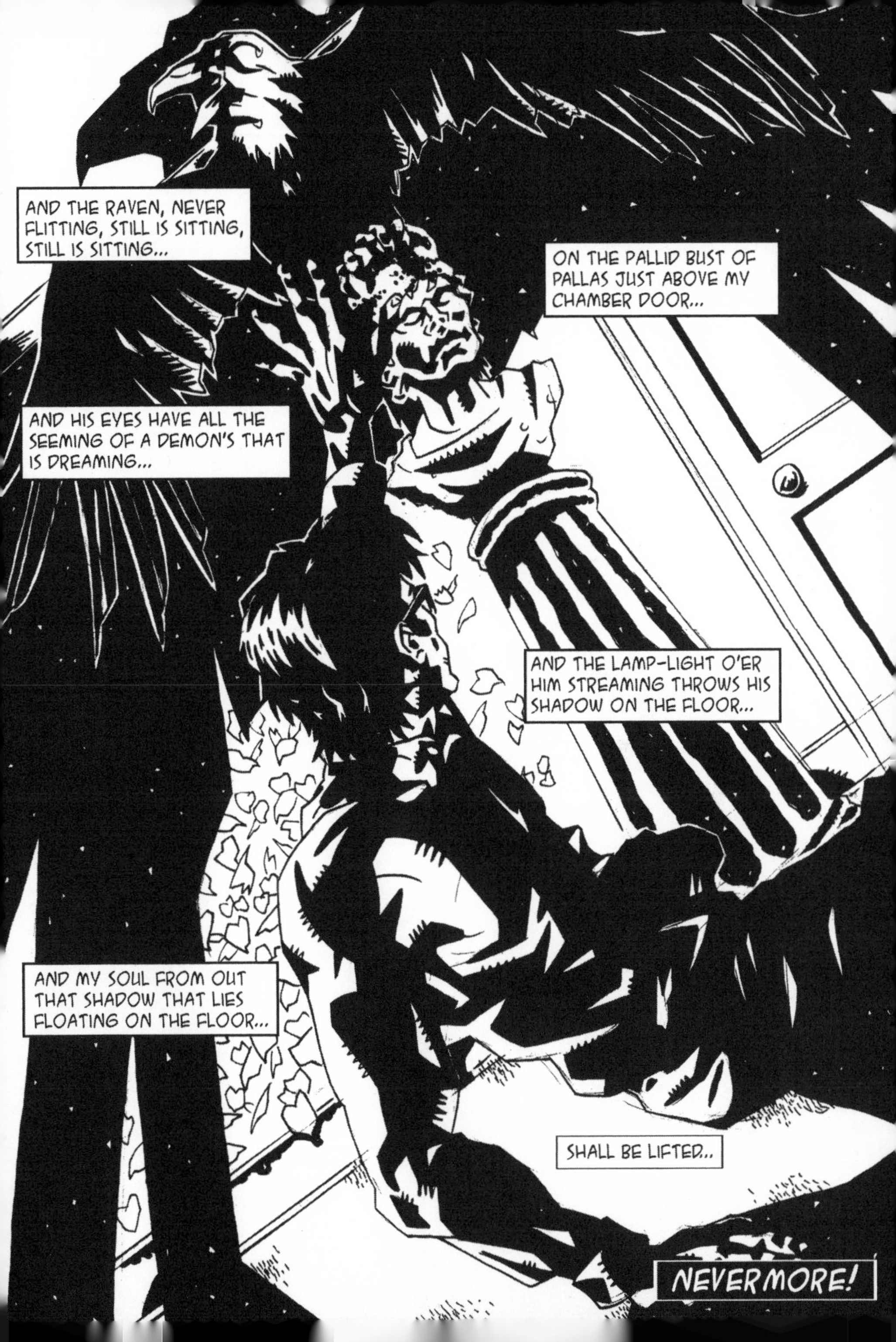
AND THE RAVEN, NEVER FLITTING, STILL IS SITTING, STILL IS SITTING...
ON THE PALLID BUST OF PALLAS JUST ABOVE MY CHAMBER DOOR...
AND HIS EYES HAVE ALL THE SEEMING OF A DEMON'S THAT IS DREAMING...
AND THE LAMP-LIGHT O'ER HIM STREAMING THROWS HIS SHADOW ON THE FLOOR...
AND MY SOUL FROM OUT THAT SHADOW THAT LIES FLOATING ON THE FLOOR...
SHALL BE LIFTED...
NEVERMORE!

THE PIT AND THE PENDULUM

Adapted by Jamie Delano
Art by Steve Pugh

Poe's most notorious story, published in 1842, tackles themes
that remain sadly relevant even today. Originally set during the
Spanish Inquisition, this grueling exploration of judicial corruption,
degradation, and torture, both physical and mental, resonates
even more strongly today.

Although its methods remain justifiably notorious, there is no
historical evidence for the Spanish Inquisition using the sort
of elaborate torture devices made famous by Poe's
grisly description.

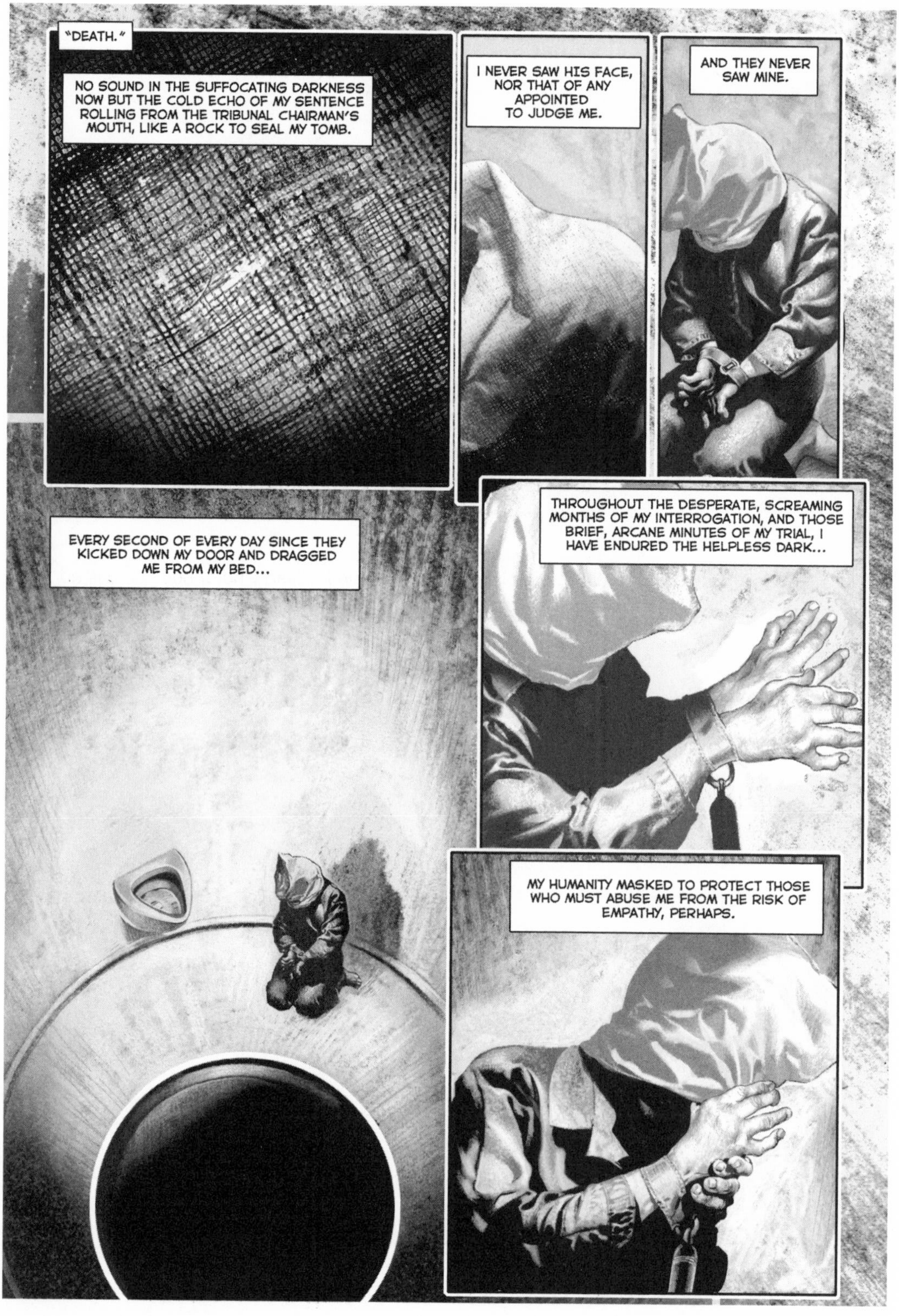
"DEATH."
NO SOUND IN THE SUFFOCATING DARKNESS NOW BUT THE COLD ECHO OF MY SENTENCE ROLLING FROM THE TRIBUNAL CHAIRMAN'S MOUTH, LIKE A ROCK TO SEAL MY TOMB.
I NEVER SAW HIS FACE, NOR THAT OF ANY APPOINTED TO JUDGE ME.
AND THEY NEVER SAW MINE.
EVERY SECOND OF EVERY DAY SINCE THEY KICKED DOWN MY DOOR AND DRAGGED ME FROM MY BED...
THROUGHOUT THE DESPERATE, SCREAMING MONTHS OF MY INTERROGATION, AND THOSE BRIEF, ARCANE MINUTES OF MY TRIAL, I HAVE ENDURED THE HELPLESS DARK...
MY HUMANITY MASKED TO PROTECT THOSE WHO MUST ABUSE ME FROM THE RISK OF EMPATHY, PERHAPS.

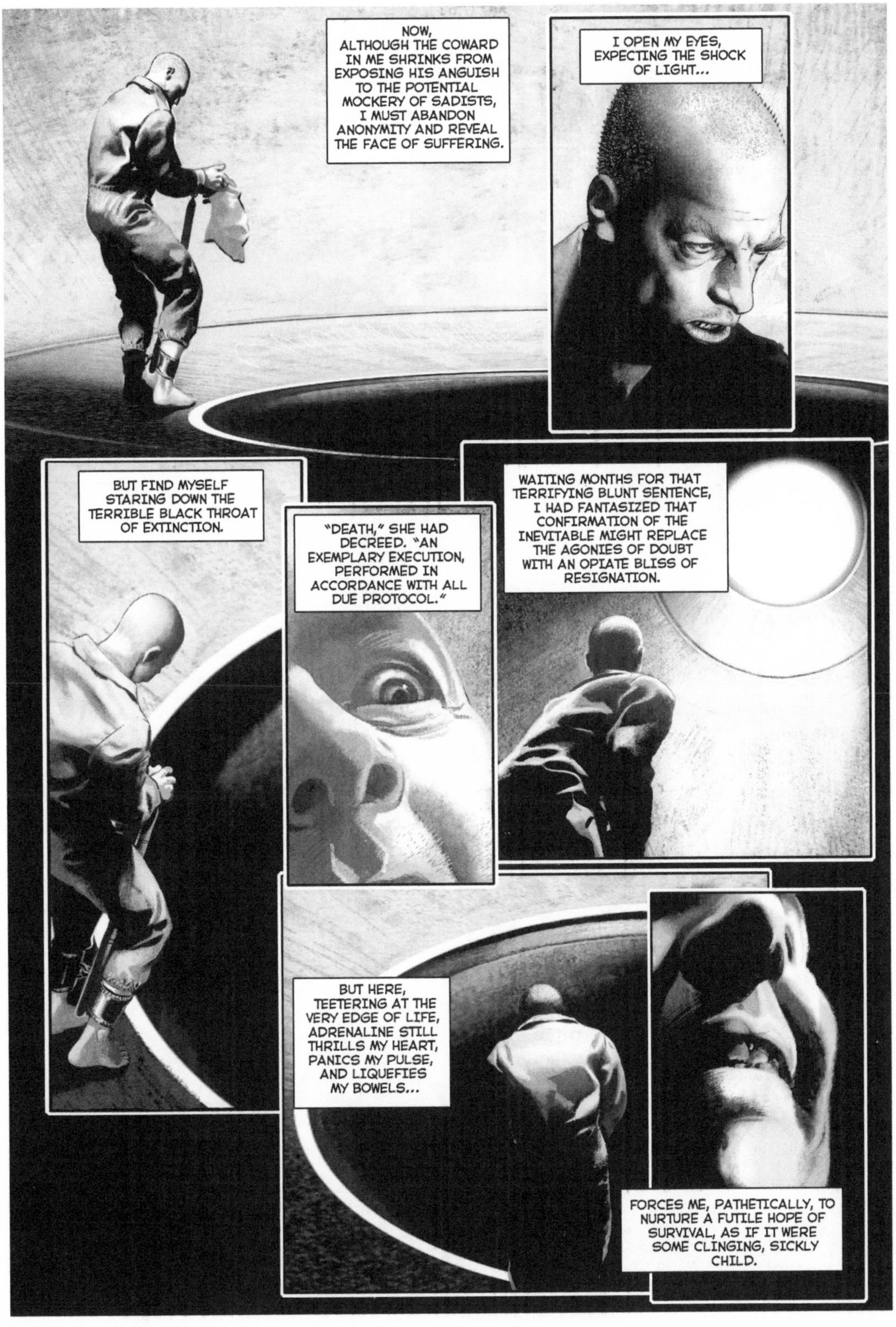
NOW, ALTHOUGH THE COWARD IN ME SHRINKS FROM EXPOSING HIS ANGUISH TO THE POTENTIAL MOCKERY OF SADISTS, I MUST ABANDON ANONYMITY AND REVEAL THE FACE OF SUFFERING.
I OPEN MY EYES, EXPECTING THE SHOCK OF LIGHT...
BUT FIND MYSELF STARING DOWN THE TERRIBLE BLACK THROAT OF EXTINCTION.
"DEATH," SHE HAD DECREED. "AN EXEMPLARY EXECUTION, PERFORMED IN ACCORDANCE WITH ALL DUE PROTOCOL."
WAITING MONTHS FOR THAT TERRIFYING BLUNT SENTENCE, I HAD FANTASIZED THAT CONFIRMATION OF THE INEVITABLE MIGHT REPLACE THE AGONIES OF DOUBT WITH AN OPIATE BLISS OF RESIGNATION.
BUT HERE, TEETERING AT THE VERY EDGE OF LIFE, ADRENALINE STILL THRILLS MY HEART, PANICS MY PULSE, AND LIQUEFIES MY BOWELS...
FORCES ME, PATHETICALLY, TO NURTURE A FUTILE HOPE OF SURVIVAL, AS IF IT WERE SOME CLINGING, SICKLY CHILD.

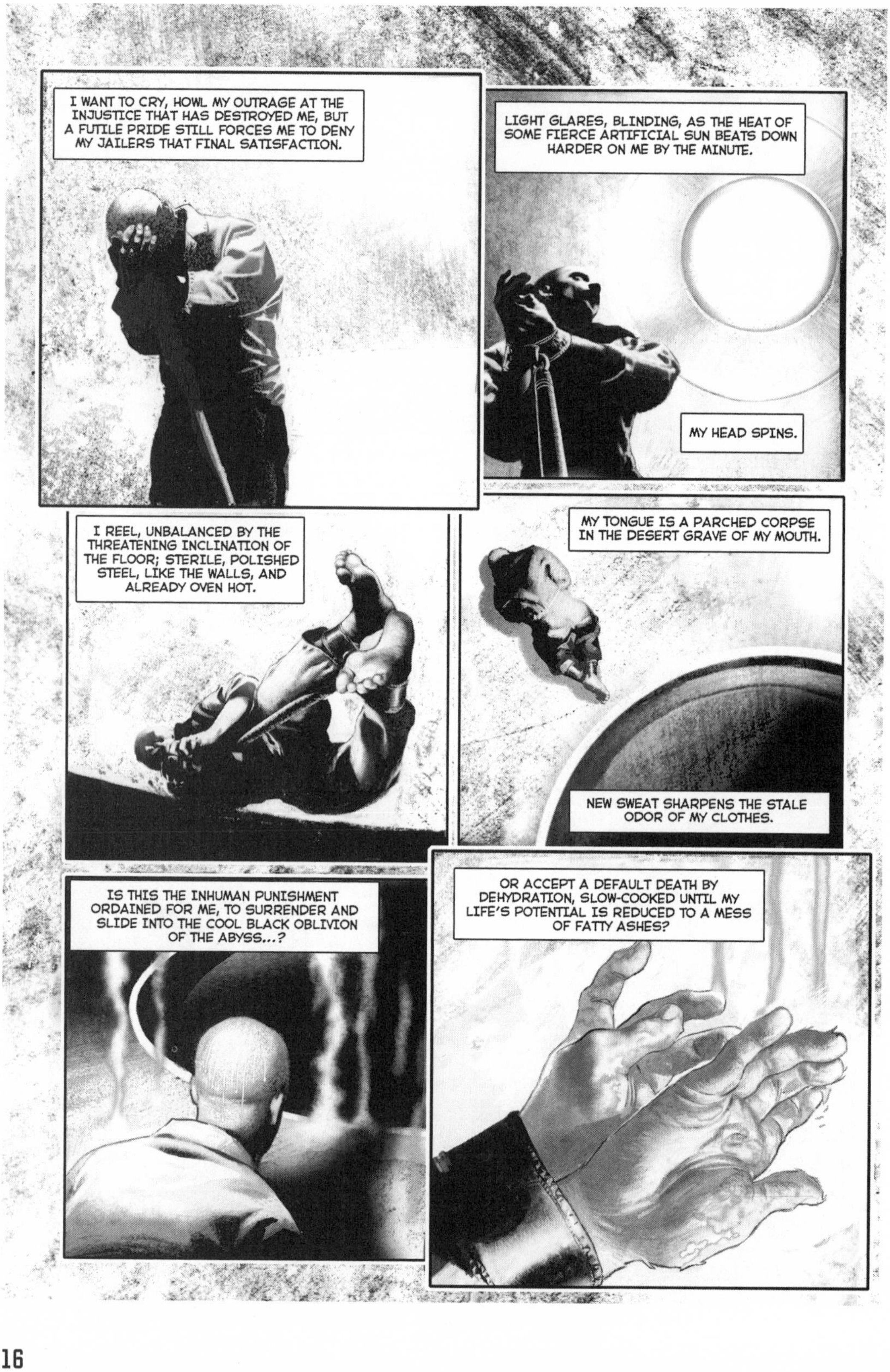
I WANT TO CRY, HOWL MY OUTRAGE AT THE INJUSTICE THAT HAS DESTROYED ME, BUT A FUTILE PRIDE STILL FORCES ME TO DENY MY JAILERS THAT FINAL SATISFACTION.
LIGHT GLARES, BLINDING, AS THE HEAT OF SOME FIERCE ARTIFICIAL SUN BEATS DOWN HARDER ON ME BY THE MINUTE.
MY HEAD SPINS.
I REEL, UNBALANCED BY THE THREATENING INCLINATION OF THE FLOOR; STERILE, POLISHED STEEL, LIKE THE WALLS, AND ALREADY OVEN HOT.
MY TONGUE IS A PARCHED CORPSE IN THE DESERT GRAVE OF MY MOUTH.
NEW SWEAT SHARPENS THE STALE ODOR OF MY CLOTHES.
IS THIS THE INHUMAN PUNISHMENT ORDAINED FOR ME, TO SURRENDER AND SLIDE INTO THE COOL BLACK OBLIVION OF THE ABYSS...?
OR ACCEPT A DEFAULT DEATH BY DEHYDRATION, SLOW-COOKED UNTIL MY LIFE'S POTENTIAL IS REDUCED TO A MESS OF FATTY ASHES?

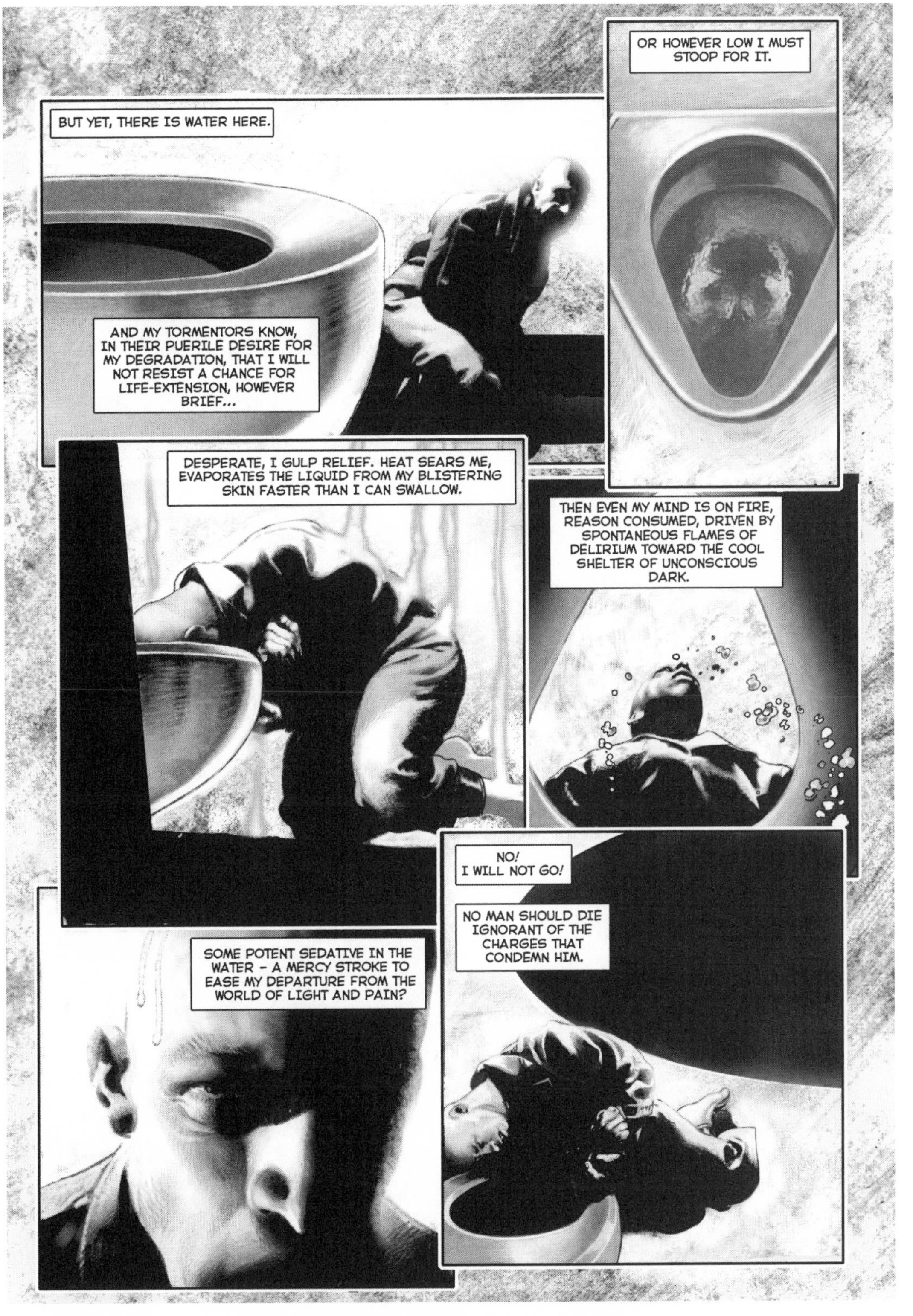
BUT YET, THERE IS WATER HERE.
AND MY TORMENTORS KNOW, IN THEIR PUERILE DESIRE FOR MY DEGRADATION, THAT I WILL NOT RESIST A CHANCE FOR LIFE-EXTENSION, HOWEVER BRIEF...
OR HOWEVER LOW I MUST STOOP FOR IT.
DESPERATE, I GULP RELIEF. HEAT SEARS ME, EVAPORATES THE LIQUID FROM MY BLISTERING SKIN FASTER THAN I CAN SWALLOW.
THEN EVEN MY MIND IS ON FIRE, REASON CONSUMED, DRIVEN BY SPONTANEOUS FLAMES OF DELIRIUM TOWARD THE COOL SHELTER OF UNCONSCIOUS DARK.
SOME POTENT SEDATIVE IN THE WATER - A MERCY STROKE TO EASE MY DEPARTURE FROM THE WORLD OF LIGHT AND PAIN?
NO! I WILL NOT GO!
NO MAN SHOULD DIE IGNORANT OF THE CHARGES THAT CONDEMN HIM.

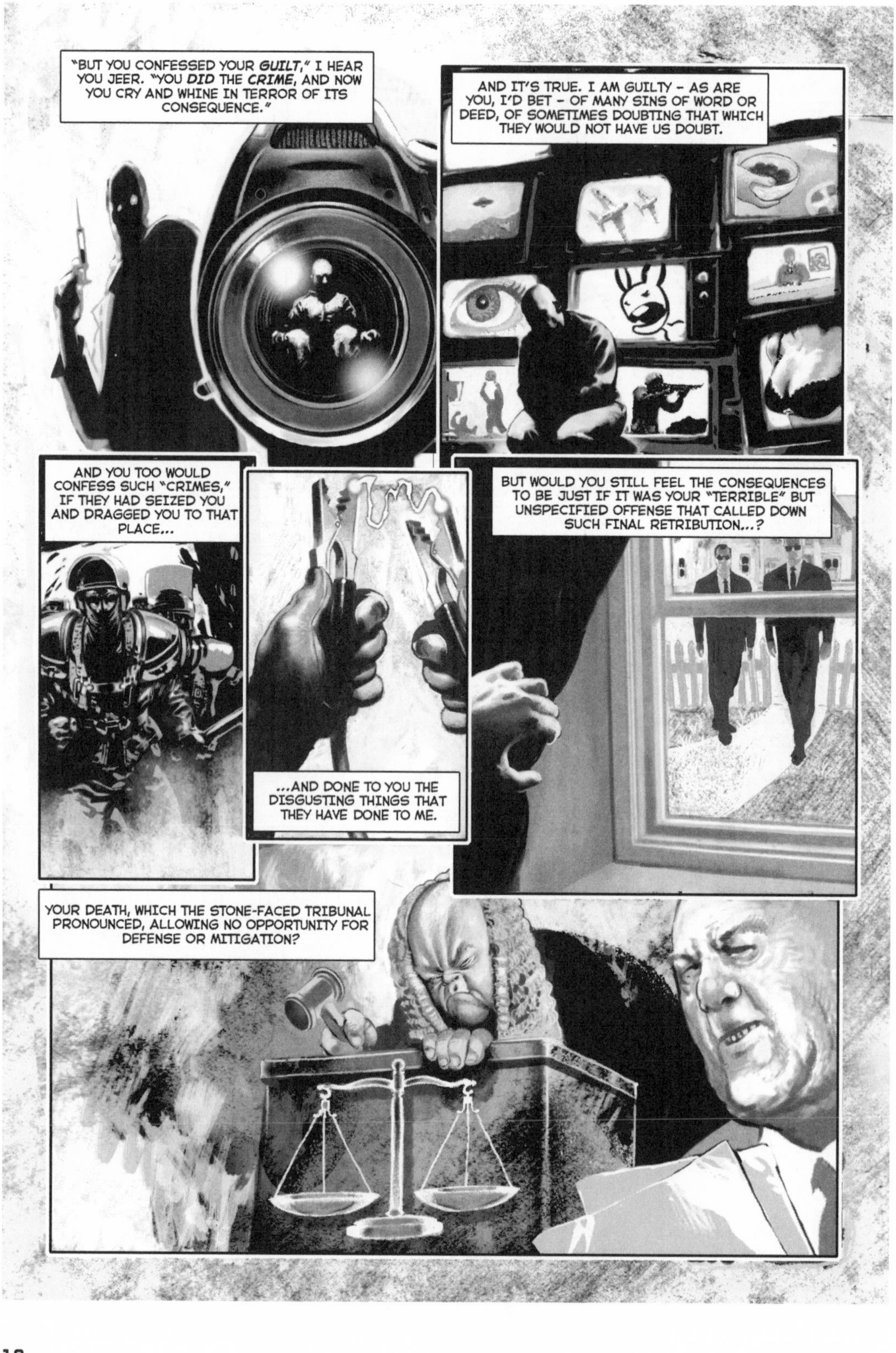
"BUT YOU CONFESSED YOUR GUILT," I HEAR YOU JEER. "YOU DID THE CRIME, AND NOW YOU CRY AND WHINE IN TERROR OF ITS CONSEQUENCE."
AND IT'S TRUE. I AM GUILTY - AS ARE YOU, I'D BET - OF MANY SINS OF WORD OR DEED, OF SOMETIMES DOUBTING THAT WHICH THEY WOULD NOT HAVE US DOUBT.
AND YOU TOO WOULD CONFESS SUCH "CRIMES," IF THEY HAD SEIZED YOU AND DRAGGED YOU TO THAT PLACE...
...AND DONE TO YOU THE DISGUSTING THINGS THAT THEY HAVE DONE TO ME.
BUT WOULD YOU STILL FEEL THE CONSEQUENCES TO BE JUST IF IT WAS YOUR "TERRIBLE" BUT UNSPECIFIED OFFENSE THAT CALLED DOWN SUCH FINAL RETRIBUTION...?
YOUR DEATH, WHICH THE STONE-FACED TRIBUNAL PRONOUNCED, ALLOWING NO OPPORTUNITY FOR DEFENSE OR MITIGATION?

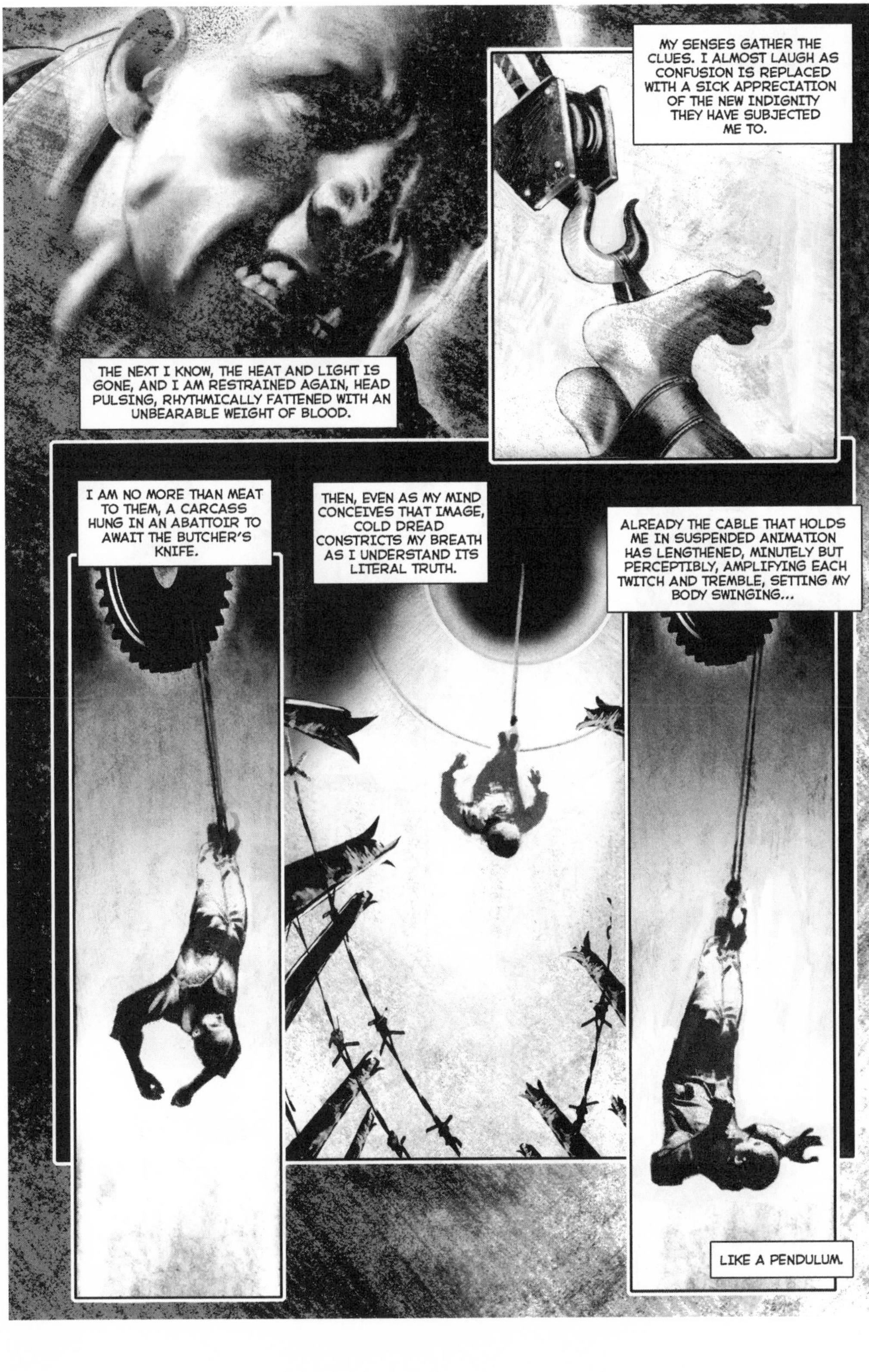
MY SENSES GATHER THE CLUES. I ALMOST LAUGH AS CONFUSION IS REPLACED WITH A SICK APPRECIATION OF THE NEW INDIGNITY THEY HAVE SUBJECTED ME TO.
THE NEXT I KNOW, THE HEAT AND LIGHT IS GONE, AND I AM RESTRAINED AGAIN, HEAD PULSING, RHYTHMICALLY FATTENED WITH AN UNBEARABLE WEIGHT OF BLOOD.
I AM NO MORE THAN MEAT TO THEM, A CARCASS HUNG IN AN ABATTOIR TO AWAIT THE BUTCHER'S KNIFE.
THEN, EVEN AS MY MIND CONCEIVES THAT IMAGE, COLD DREAD CONSTRICTS MY BREATH AS I UNDERSTAND ITS LITERAL TRUTH.
ALREADY THE CABLE THAT HOLDS ME IN SUSPENDED ANIMATION HAS LENGTHENED, MINUTELY BUT PERCEPTIBLY, AMPLIFYING EACH TWITCH AND TREMBLE, SETTING MY BODY SWINGING...
LIKE A PENDULUM.

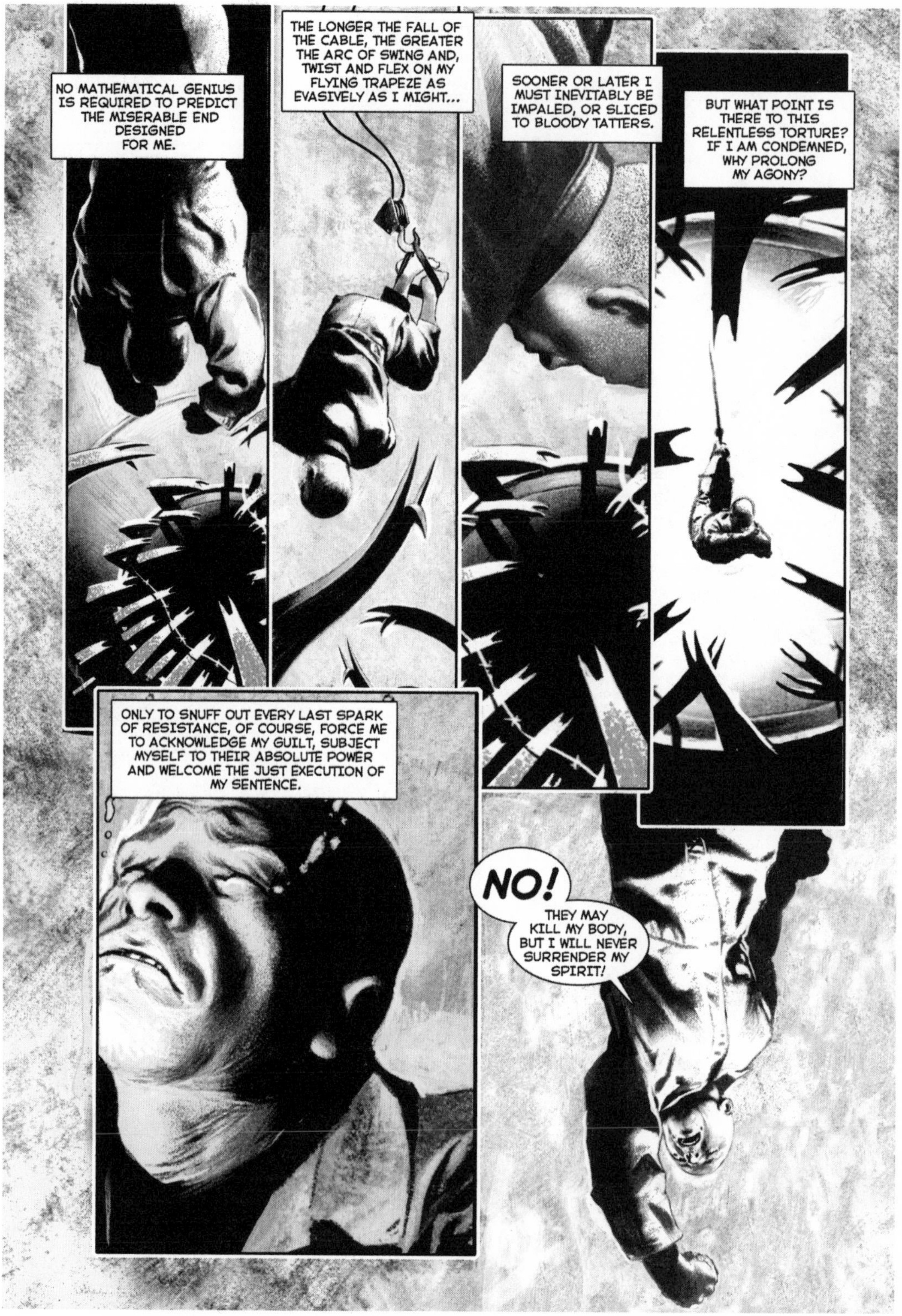
NO MATHEMATICAL GENIUS IS REQUIRED TO PREDICT THE MISERABLE END DESIGNED FOR ME.
THE LONGER THE FALL OF THE CABLE, THE GREATER THE ARC OF SWING AND, TWIST AND FLEX ON MY FLYING TRAPEZE AS EVASIVELY AS I MIGHT...
SOONER OR LATER I MUST INEVITABLY BE IMPALED, OR SLICED TO BLOODY TATTERS.
BUT WHAT POINT IS THERE TO THIS RELENTLESS TORTURE? IF I AM CONDEMNED, WHY PROLONG MY AGONY?
ONLY TO SNUFF OUT EVERY LAST SPARK OF RESISTANCE, OF COURSE, FORCE ME TO ACKNOWLEDGE MY GUILT, SUBJECT MYSELF TO THEIR ABSOLUTE POWER AND WELCOME THE JUST EXECUTION OF MY SENTENCE.
NO! THEY MAY KILL MY BODY, BUT I WILL NEVER SURRENDER MY SPIRIT!

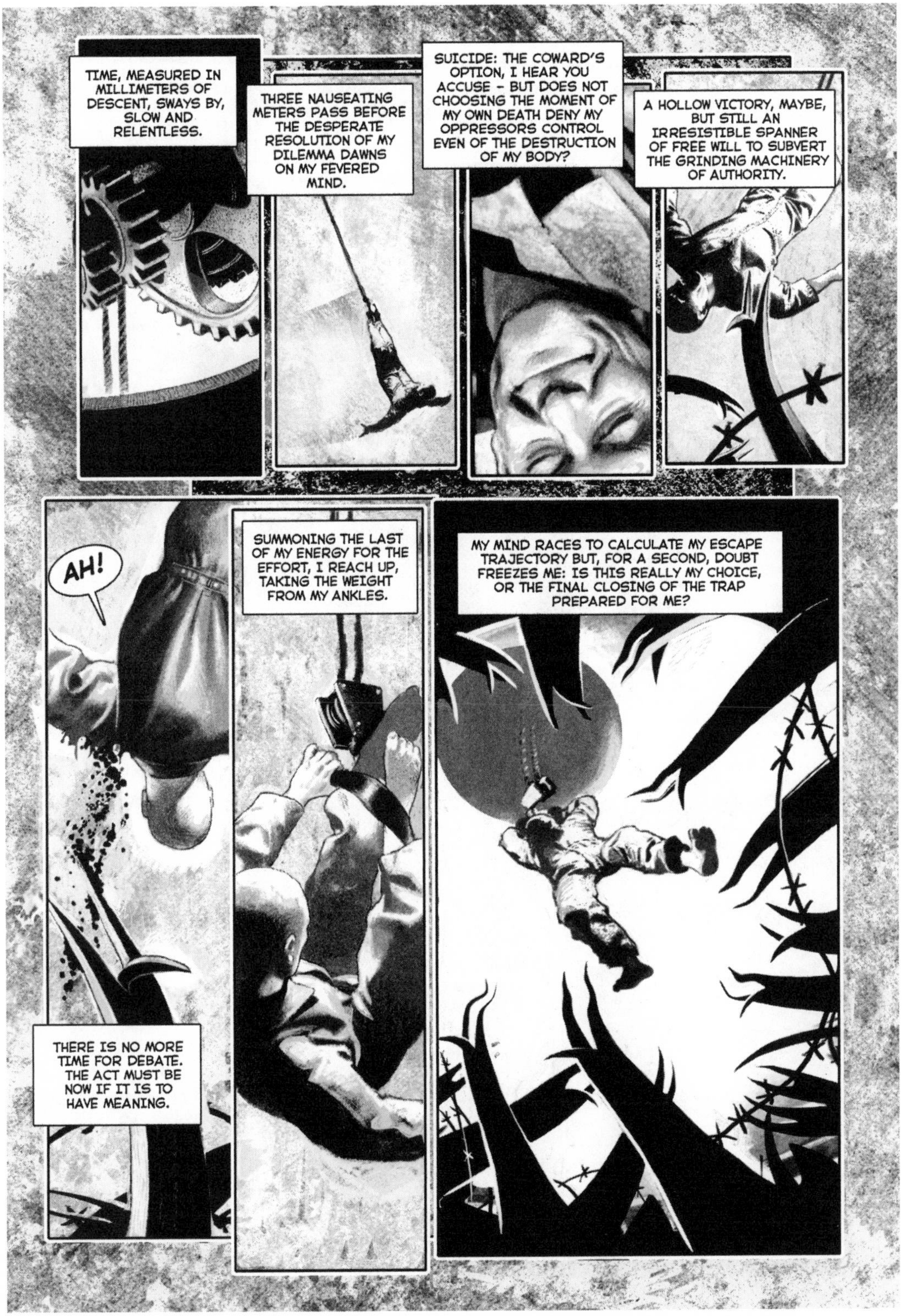
TIME, MEASURED IN MILLIMETERS OF DESCENT, SWAYS BY, SLOW AND RELENTLESS.
THREE NAUSEATING METERS PASS BEFORE THE DESPERATE RESOLUTION OF MY DILEMMA DAWNS ON MY FEVERED MIND.
SUICIDE: THE COWARD'S OPTION, I HEAR YOU ACCUSE - BUT DOES NOT CHOOSING THE MOMENT OF MY OWN DEATH DENY MY OPPRESSORS CONTROL EVEN OF THE DESTRUCTION OF MY BODY?
A HOLLOW VICTORY, MAYBE, BUT STILL AN IRRESISTIBLE SPANNER OF FREE WILL TO SUBVERT THE GRINDING MACHINERY OF AUTHORITY.
AH!
THERE IS NO MORE TIME FOR DEBATE. THE ACT MUST BE NOW IF IT IS TO HAVE MEANING.
SUMMONING THE LAST OF MY ENERGY FOR THE EFFORT, I REACH UP, TAKING THE WEIGHT FROM MY ANKLES.
MY MIND RACES TO CALCULATE MY ESCAPE TRAJECTORY BUT, FOR A SECOND, DOUBT FREEZES ME: IS THIS REALLY MY CHOICE, OR THE FINAL CLOSING OF THE TRAP PREPARED FOR ME?

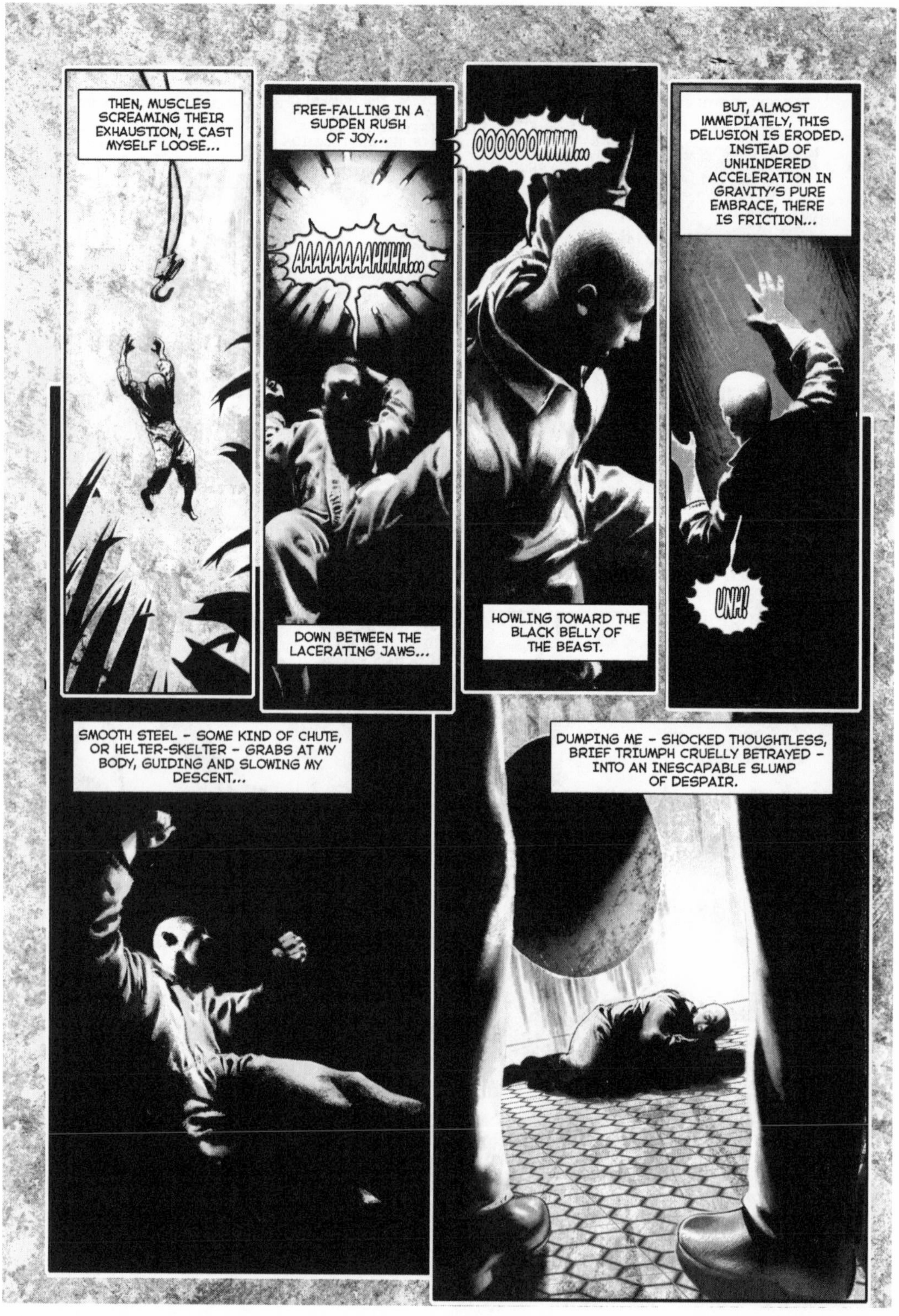
THEN, MUSCLES SCREAMING THEIR EXHAUSTION, I CAST MYSELF LOOSE...
FREE-FALLING IN A SUDDEN RUSH OF JOY...
AAAAAAAAHHHH...
DOWN BETWEEN THE LACERATING JAWS...
OOOOOOWWWW...
HOWLING TOWARD THE BLACK BELLY OF THE BEAST.
BUT, ALMOST IMMEDIATELY, THIS DELUSION IS ERODED. INSTEAD OF UNHINDERED ACCELERATION IN GRAVITY'S PURE EMBRACE, THERE IS FRICTION...
UNH!
SMOOTH STEEL - SOME KIND OF CHUTE, OR HELTER-SKELTER - GRABS AT MY BODY, GUIDING AND SLOWING MY DESCENT...
DUMPING ME - SHOCKED THOUGHTLESS, BRIEF TRIUMPH CRUELLY BETRAYED - INTO AN INESCAPABLE SLUMP OF DESPAIR.

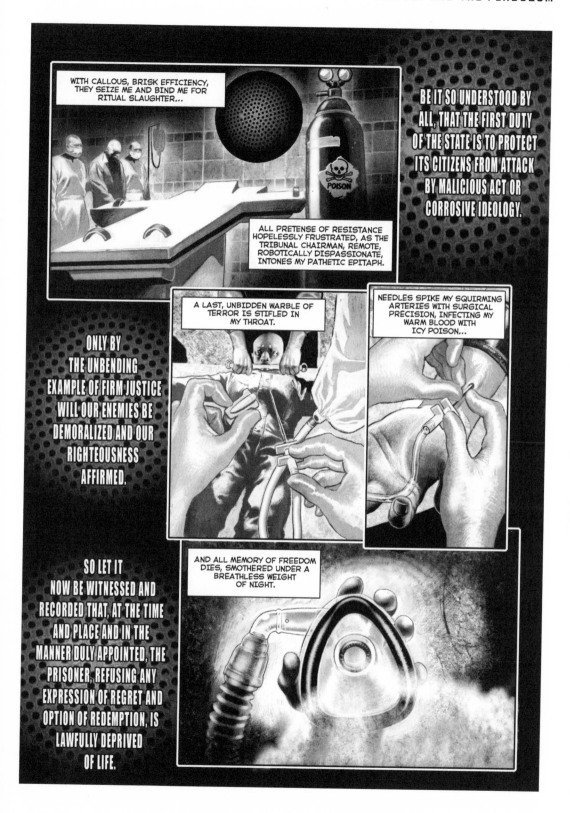

WITH CALLOUS, BRISK EFFICIENCY, THEY SEIZE ME AND BIND ME FOR RITUAL SLAUGHTER...

POISON

BE IT SO UNDERSTOOD BY ALL, THAT THE FIRST DUTY OF THE STATE IS TO PROTECT ITS CITIZENS FROM ATTACK BY MALICIOUS ACT OR CORROSIVE IDEOLOGY.

ALL PRETENSE OF RESISTANCE HOPELESSLY FRUSTRATED, AS THE TRIBUNAL CHAIRMAN, REMOTE, ROBOTICALLY DISPASSIONATE, INTONES MY PATHETIC EPITAPH.

A LAST, UNBIDDEN WARBLE OF TERROR IS STIFLED IN MY THROAT.

NEEDLES SPIKE MY SQUIRMING ARTERIES WITH SURGICAL PRECISION, INFECTING MY WARM BLOOD WITH ICY POISON...

ONLY BY THE UNBENDING EXAMPLE OF FIRM JUSTICE WILL OUR ENEMIES BE DEMORALIZED AND OUR RIGHTEOUSNESS AFFIRMED.

AND ALL MEMORY OF FREEDOM DIES, SMOTHERED UNDER A BREATHLESS WEIGHT OF NIGHT.

SO LET IT NOW BE WITNESSED AND RECORDED THAT, AT THE TIME AND PLACE AND IN THE MANNER DULY APPOINTED, THE PRISONER, REFUSING ANY EXPRESSION OF REGRET AND OPTION OF REDEMPTION, IS LAWFULLY DEPRIVED OF LIFE.

THE FACTS IN THE CASE OF MR. VALDEMAR

Adapted by Jeremy Slater
Art by John McCrea

When this tale was originally published, appearing in both
the *American Review* and *Broadway Journal* in December 1845,
Poe deliberately neglected to identify it as a work of fiction.

The gruesome description of a soul trapped in limbo by the
misapplication of mesmerism, and the effect this spiritual
dislocation has on the physical body, horrified many astonished
readers who believed it to be a factual account.

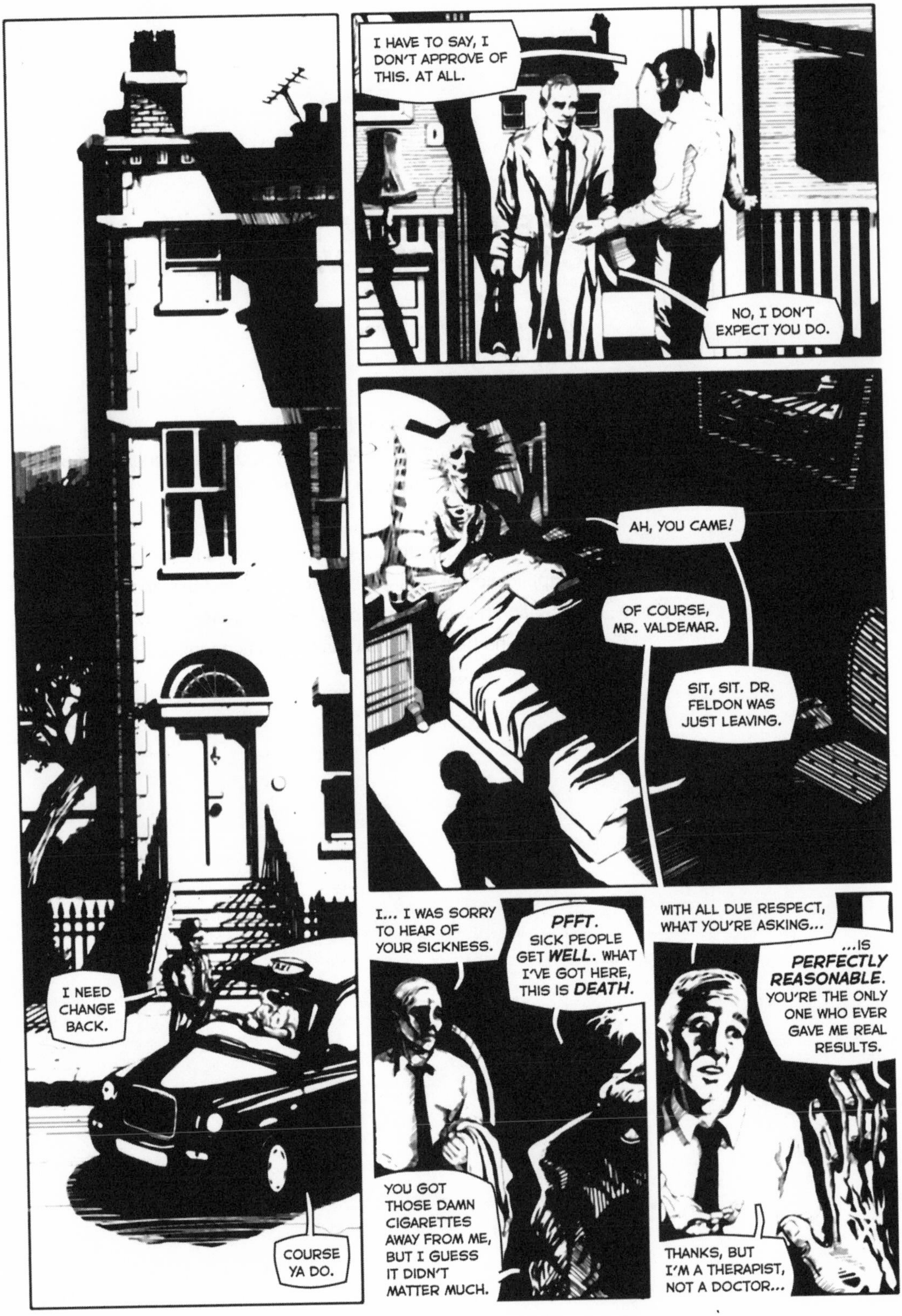
I NEED CHANGE BACK.
COURSE YA DO.
I HAVE TO SAY, I DON'T APPROVE OF THIS. AT ALL.
NO, I DON'T EXPECT YOU DO.
AH, YOU CAME!
OF COURSE, MR. VALDEMAR.
SIT, SIT. DR. FELDON WAS JUST LEAVING.
I... I WAS SORRY TO HEAR OF YOUR SICKNESS.
PFFT. SICK PEOPLE GET WELL. WHAT I'VE GOT HERE, THIS IS DEATH.
YOU GOT THOSE DAMN CIGARETTES AWAY FROM ME, BUT I GUESS IT DIDN'T MATTER MUCH.
WITH ALL DUE RESPECT, WHAT YOU'RE ASKING...
...IS PERFECTLY REASONABLE. YOU'RE THE ONLY ONE WHO EVER GAVE ME REAL RESULTS.
THANKS, BUT I'M A THERAPIST, NOT A DOCTOR...

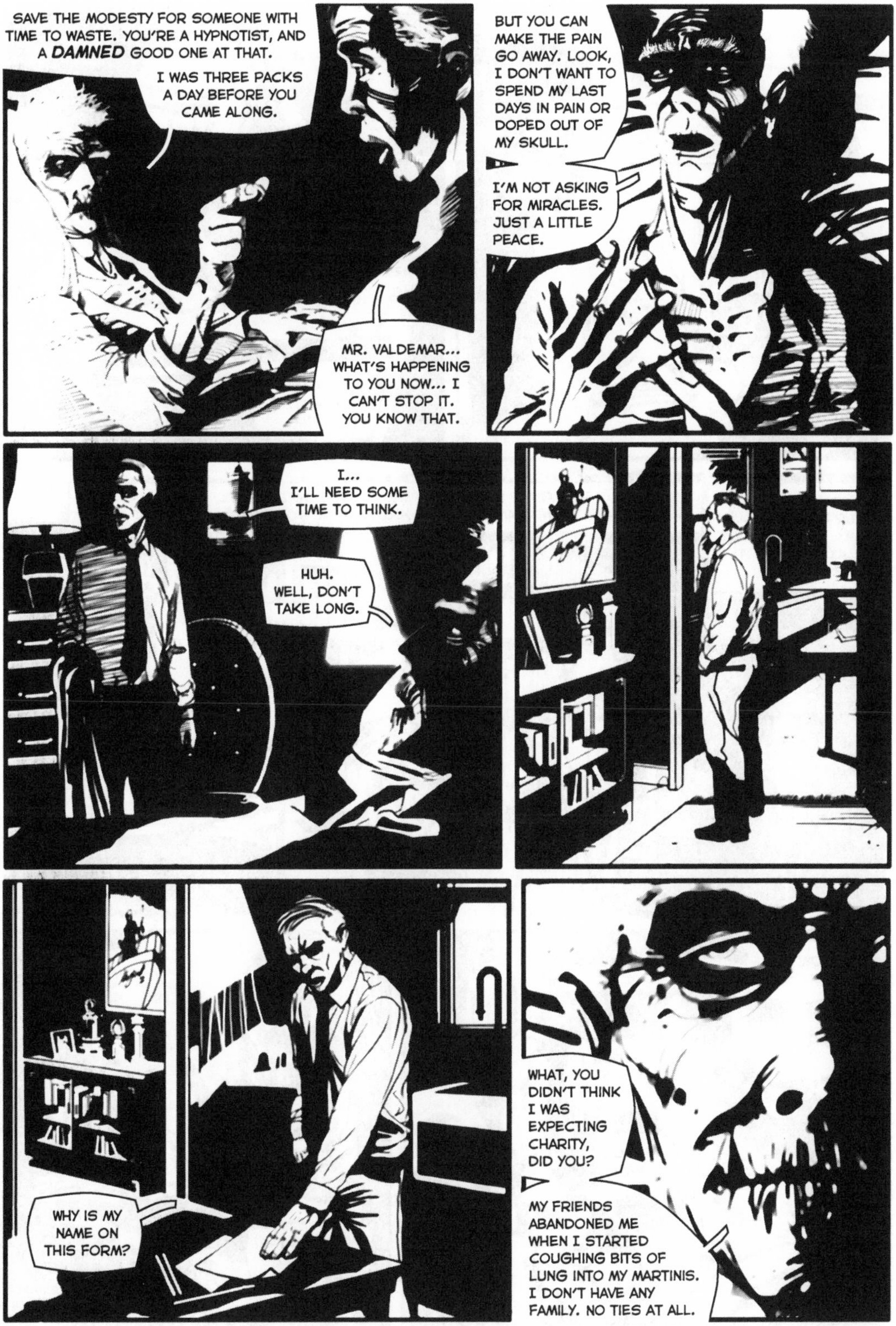
SAVE THE MODESTY FOR SOMEONE WITH TIME TO WASTE. YOU'RE A HYPNOTIST, AND A *DAMNED* GOOD ONE AT THAT.
I WAS THREE PACKS A DAY BEFORE YOU CAME ALONG.
MR. VALDEMAR... WHAT'S HAPPENING TO YOU NOW... I CAN'T STOP IT. YOU KNOW THAT.
BUT YOU CAN MAKE THE PAIN GO AWAY. LOOK, I DON'T WANT TO SPEND MY LAST DAYS IN PAIN OR DOPED OUT OF MY SKULL.
I'M NOT ASKING FOR MIRACLES. JUST A LITTLE PEACE.
I... I'LL NEED SOME TIME TO THINK.
HUH. WELL, DON'T TAKE LONG.
WHY IS MY NAME ON THIS FORM?
WHAT, YOU DIDN'T THINK I WAS EXPECTING CHARITY, DID YOU?
MY FRIENDS ABANDONED ME WHEN I STARTED COUGHING BITS OF LUNG INTO MY MARTINIS. I DON'T HAVE ANY FAMILY. NO TIES AT ALL.

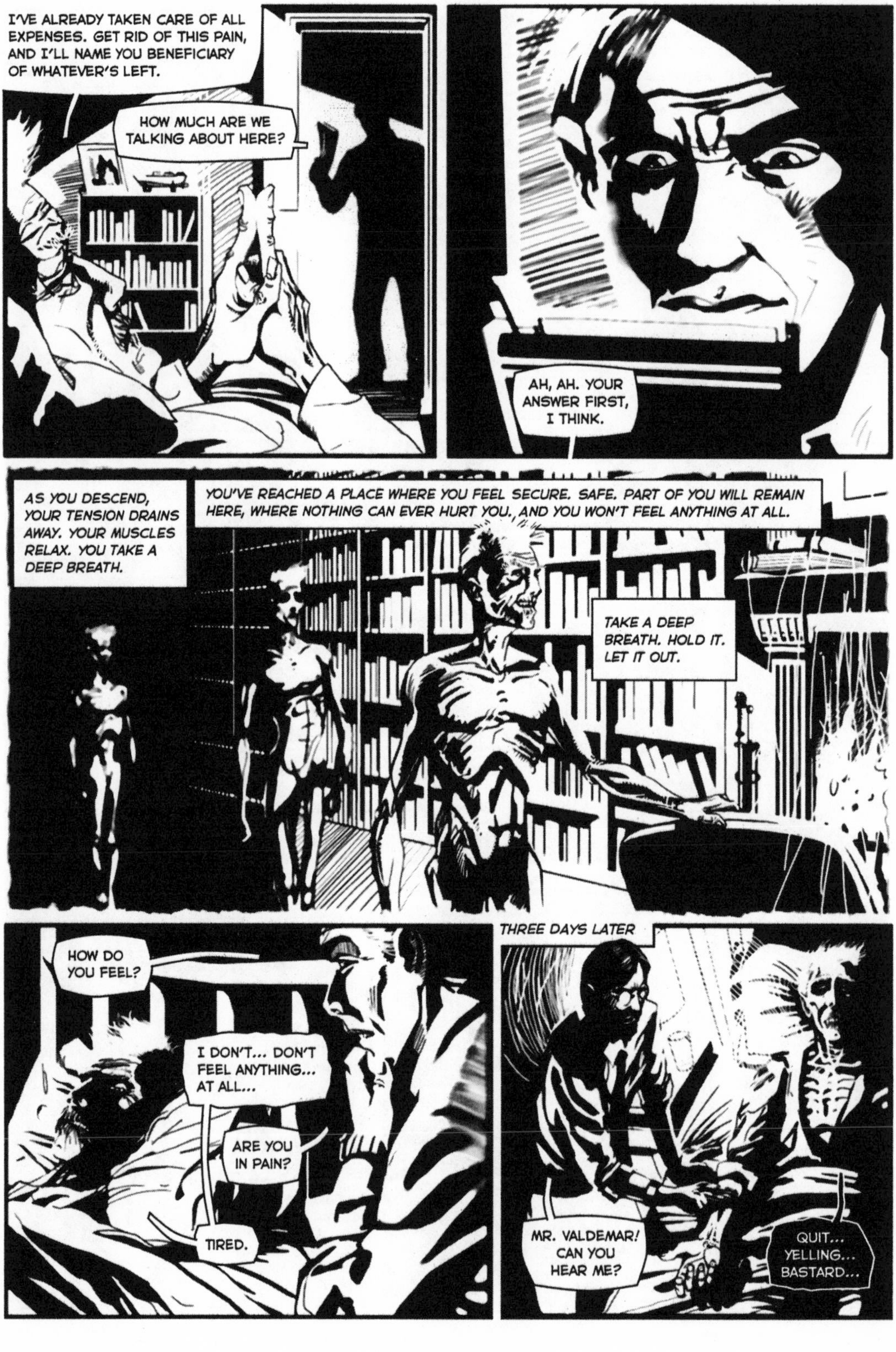
I'VE ALREADY TAKEN CARE OF ALL EXPENSES. GET RID OF THIS PAIN, AND I'LL NAME YOU BENEFICIARY OF WHATEVER'S LEFT.
HOW MUCH ARE WE TALKING ABOUT HERE?
AH, AH. YOUR ANSWER FIRST, I THINK.
AS YOU DESCEND, YOUR TENSION DRAINS AWAY. YOUR MUSCLES RELAX. YOU TAKE A DEEP BREATH.
YOU'VE REACHED A PLACE WHERE YOU FEEL SECURE. SAFE. PART OF YOU WILL REMAIN HERE, WHERE NOTHING CAN EVER HURT YOU, AND YOU WON'T FEEL ANYTHING AT ALL.
TAKE A DEEP BREATH. HOLD IT. LET IT OUT.
HOW DO YOU FEEL?
I DON'T... DON'T FEEL ANYTHING... AT ALL...
ARE YOU IN PAIN?
TIRED.
THREE DAYS LATER
MR. VALDEMAR! CAN YOU HEAR ME?
QUIT... YELLING... BASTARD...

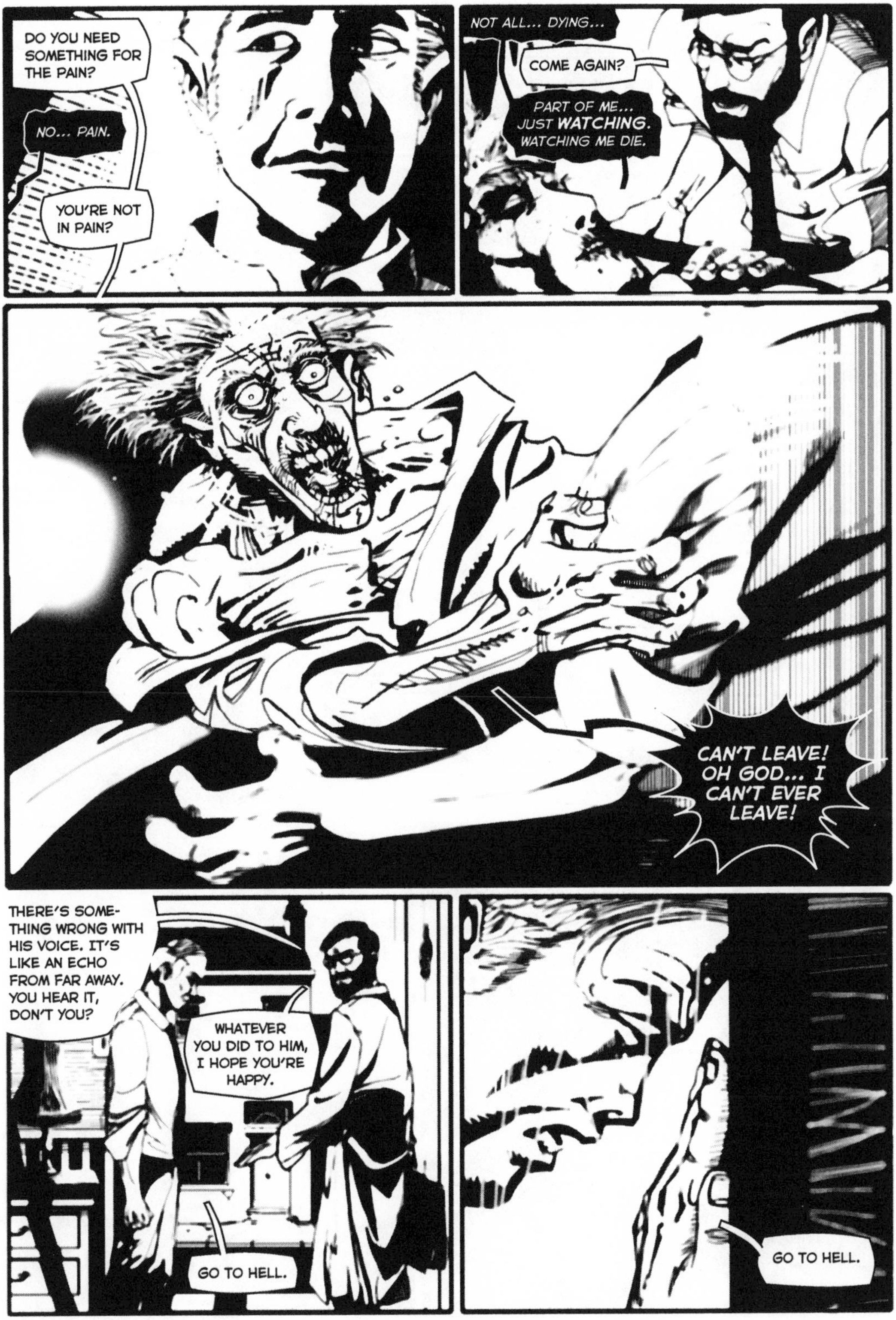
DO YOU NEED SOMETHING FOR THE PAIN?
NO... PAIN.
YOU'RE NOT IN PAIN?
NOT ALL... DYING...
COME AGAIN?
PART OF ME... JUST WATCHING. WATCHING ME DIE.
CAN'T LEAVE! OH GOD... I CAN'T EVER LEAVE!
THERE'S SOMETHING WRONG WITH HIS VOICE. IT'S LIKE AN ECHO FROM FAR AWAY. YOU HEAR IT, DON'T YOU?
WHATEVER YOU DID TO HIM, I HOPE YOU'RE HAPPY.
GO TO HELL.
GO TO HELL.

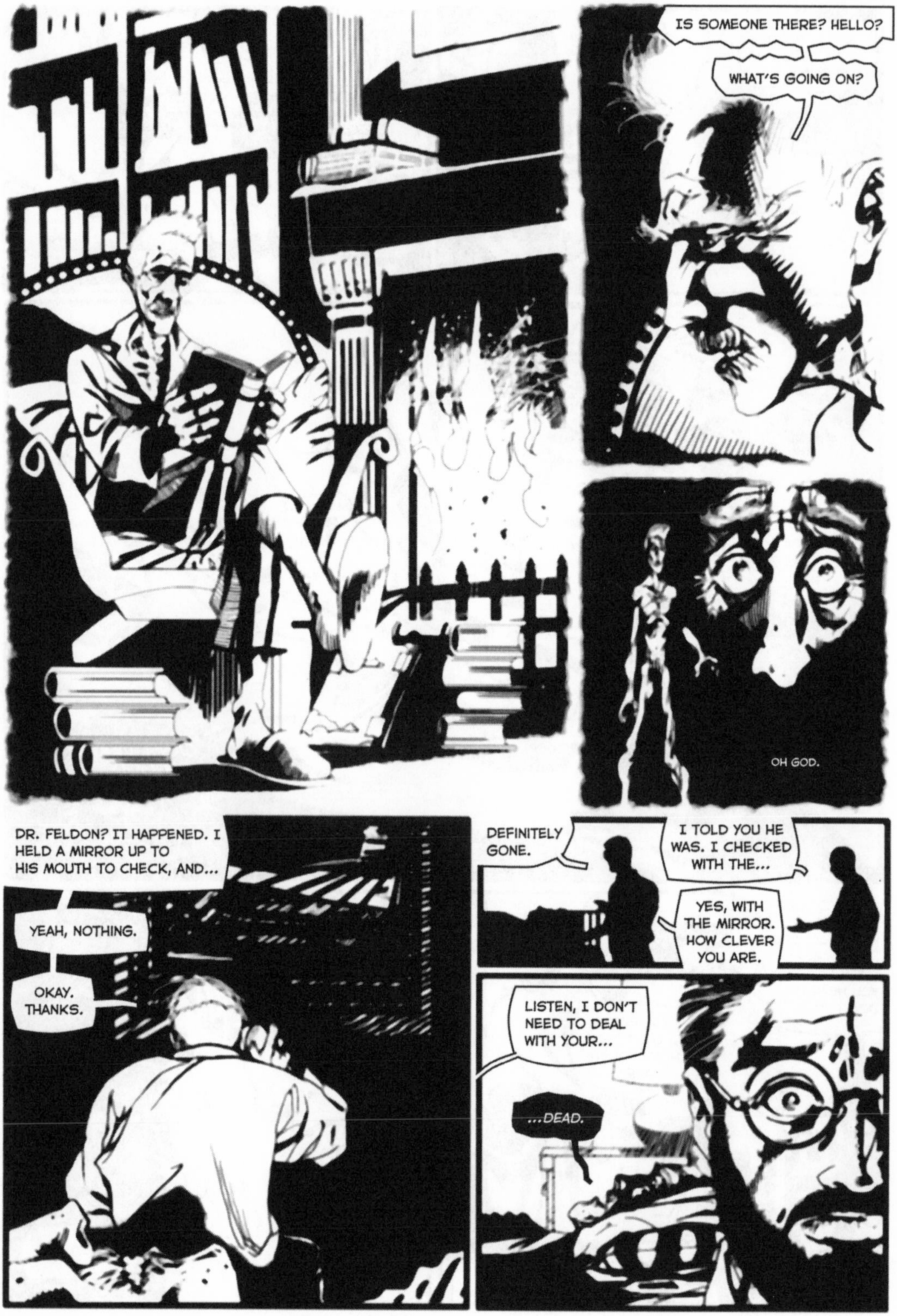
IS SOMEONE THERE? HELLO?
WHAT'S GOING ON?
OH GOD.
DR. FELDON? IT HAPPENED. I HELD A MIRROR UP TO HIS MOUTH TO CHECK, AND...
YEAH, NOTHING.
OKAY. THANKS.
DEFINITELY GONE.
I TOLD YOU HE WAS. I CHECKED WITH THE...
YES, WITH THE MIRROR. HOW CLEVER YOU ARE.
LISTEN, I DON'T NEED TO DEAL WITH YOUR...
...DEAD.

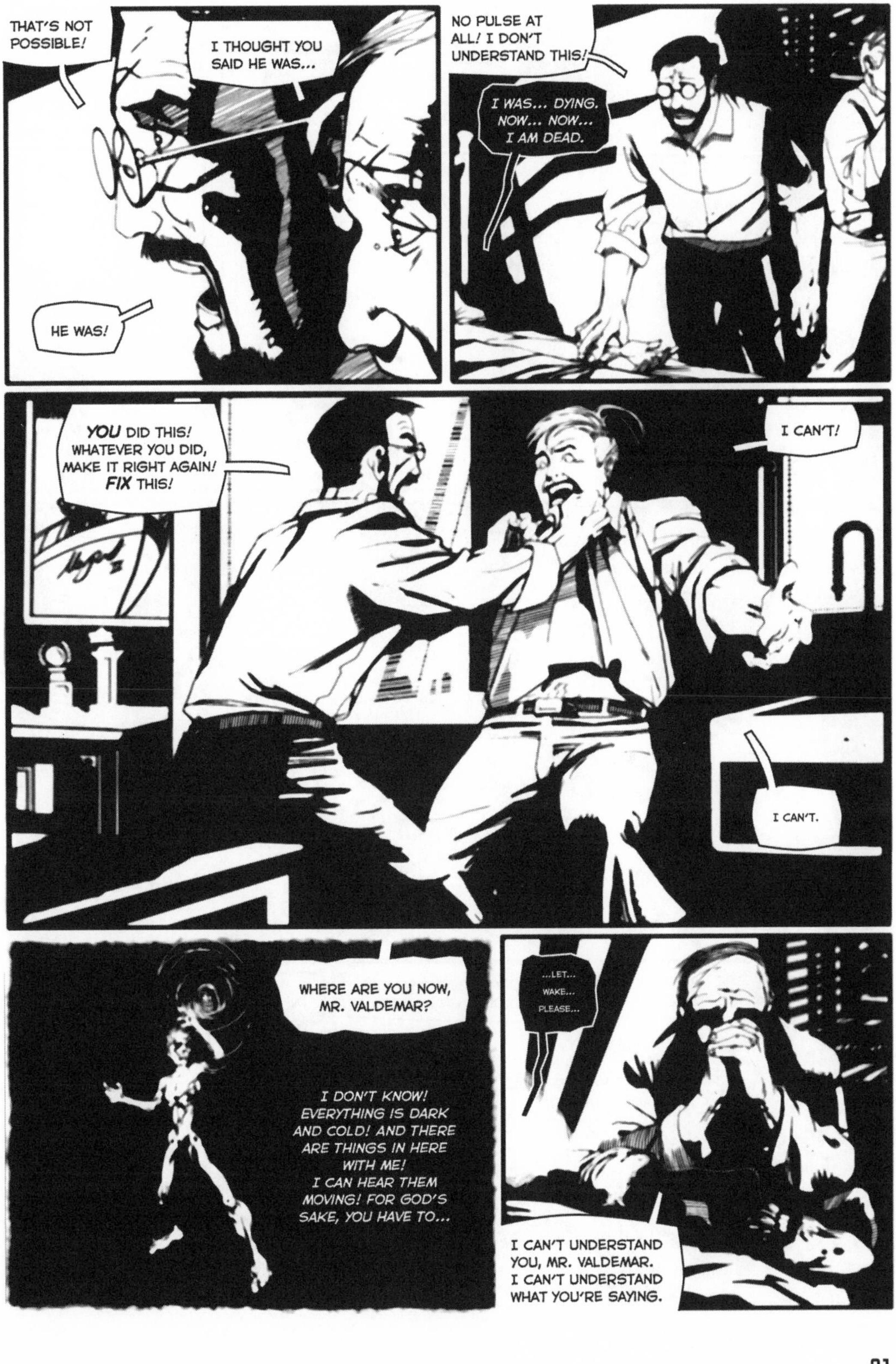
THAT'S NOT POSSIBLE!
I THOUGHT YOU SAID HE WAS...
HE WAS!
NO PULSE AT ALL! I DON'T UNDERSTAND THIS!
I WAS... DYING. NOW... NOW... I AM DEAD.
YOU DID THIS! WHATEVER YOU DID, MAKE IT RIGHT AGAIN! FIX THIS!
I CAN'T!
I CAN'T.
WHERE ARE YOU NOW, MR. VALDEMAR?
I DON'T KNOW! EVERYTHING IS DARK AND COLD! AND THERE ARE THINGS IN HERE WITH ME! I CAN HEAR THEM MOVING! FOR GOD'S SAKE, YOU HAVE TO...
...LET... WAKE... PLEASE...
I CAN'T UNDERSTAND YOU, MR. VALDEMAR. I CAN'T UNDERSTAND WHAT YOU'RE SAYING.

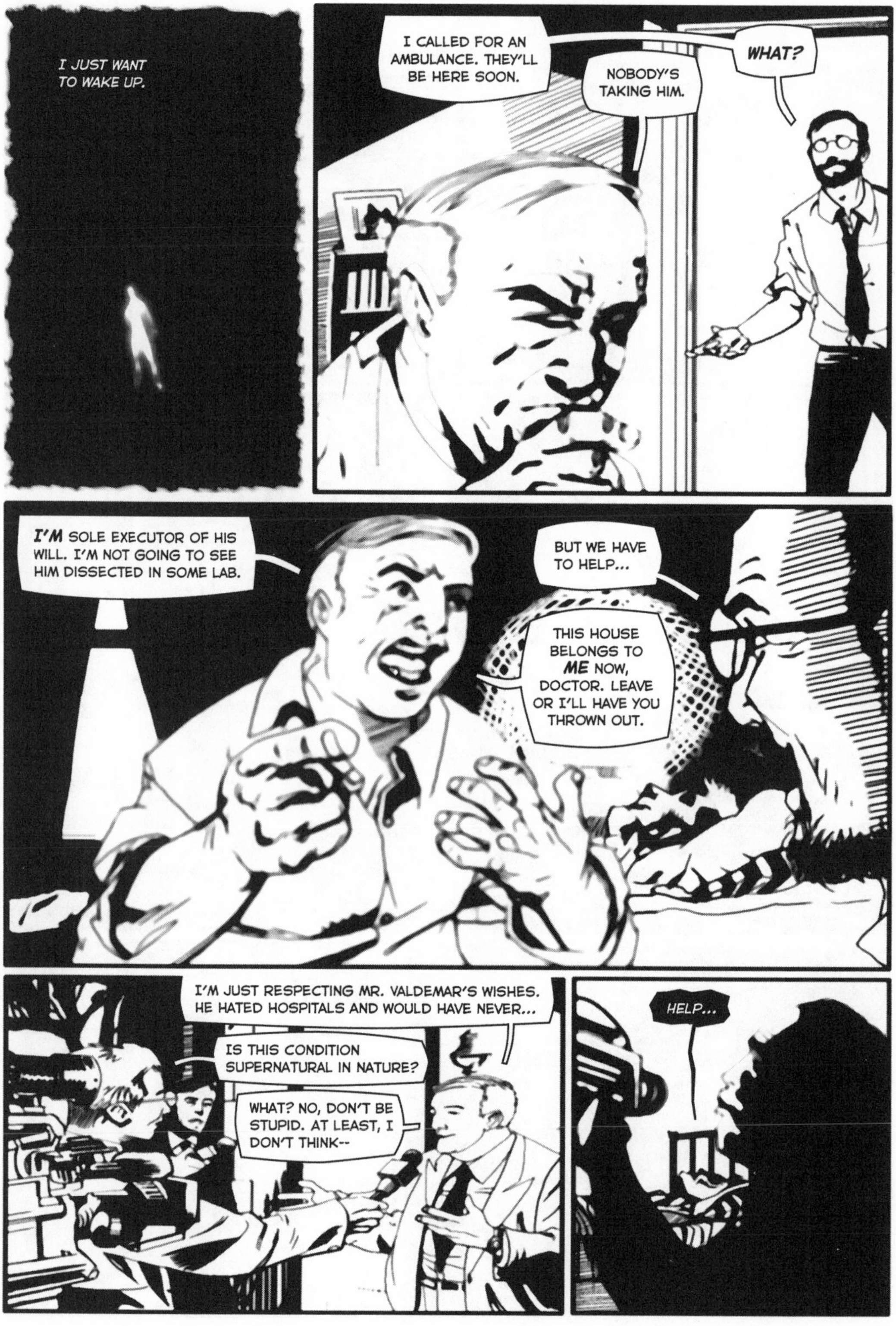
I JUST WANT TO WAKE UP.
I CALLED FOR AN AMBULANCE. THEY'LL BE HERE SOON.
WHAT?
NOBODY'S TAKING HIM.
I'M SOLE EXECUTOR OF HIS WILL. I'M NOT GOING TO SEE HIM DISSECTED IN SOME LAB.
BUT WE HAVE TO HELP...
THIS HOUSE BELONGS TO ME NOW, DOCTOR. LEAVE OR I'LL HAVE YOU THROWN OUT.
I'M JUST RESPECTING MR. VALDEMAR'S WISHES. HE HATED HOSPITALS AND WOULD HAVE NEVER...
IS THIS CONDITION SUPERNATURAL IN NATURE?
WHAT? NO, DON'T BE STUPID. AT LEAST, I DON'T THINK--
HELP...

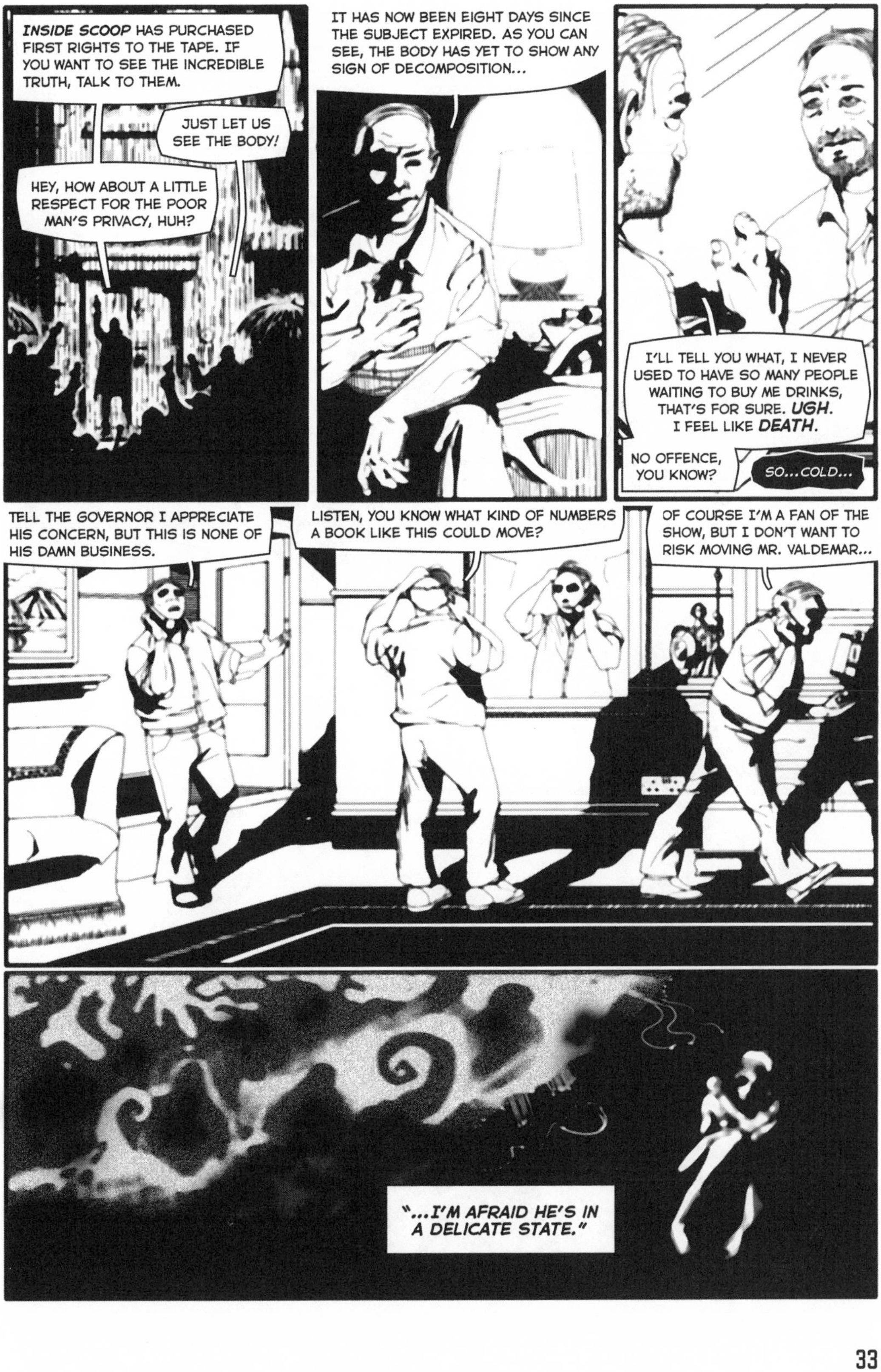
INSIDE SCOOP HAS PURCHASED FIRST RIGHTS TO THE TAPE. IF YOU WANT TO SEE THE INCREDIBLE TRUTH, TALK TO THEM.
JUST LET US SEE THE BODY!
HEY, HOW ABOUT A LITTLE RESPECT FOR THE POOR MAN'S PRIVACY, HUH?
IT HAS NOW BEEN EIGHT DAYS SINCE THE SUBJECT EXPIRED. AS YOU CAN SEE, THE BODY HAS YET TO SHOW ANY SIGN OF DECOMPOSITION...
I'LL TELL YOU WHAT, I NEVER USED TO HAVE SO MANY PEOPLE WAITING TO BUY ME DRINKS, THAT'S FOR SURE. UGH. I FEEL LIKE DEATH.
NO OFFENCE, YOU KNOW?
SO...COLD...
TELL THE GOVERNOR I APPRECIATE HIS CONCERN, BUT THIS IS NONE OF HIS DAMN BUSINESS.
LISTEN, YOU KNOW WHAT KIND OF NUMBERS A BOOK LIKE THIS COULD MOVE?
OF COURSE I'M A FAN OF THE SHOW, BUT I DON'T WANT TO RISK MOVING MR. VALDEMAR...
"...I'M AFRAID HE'S IN A DELICATE STATE."

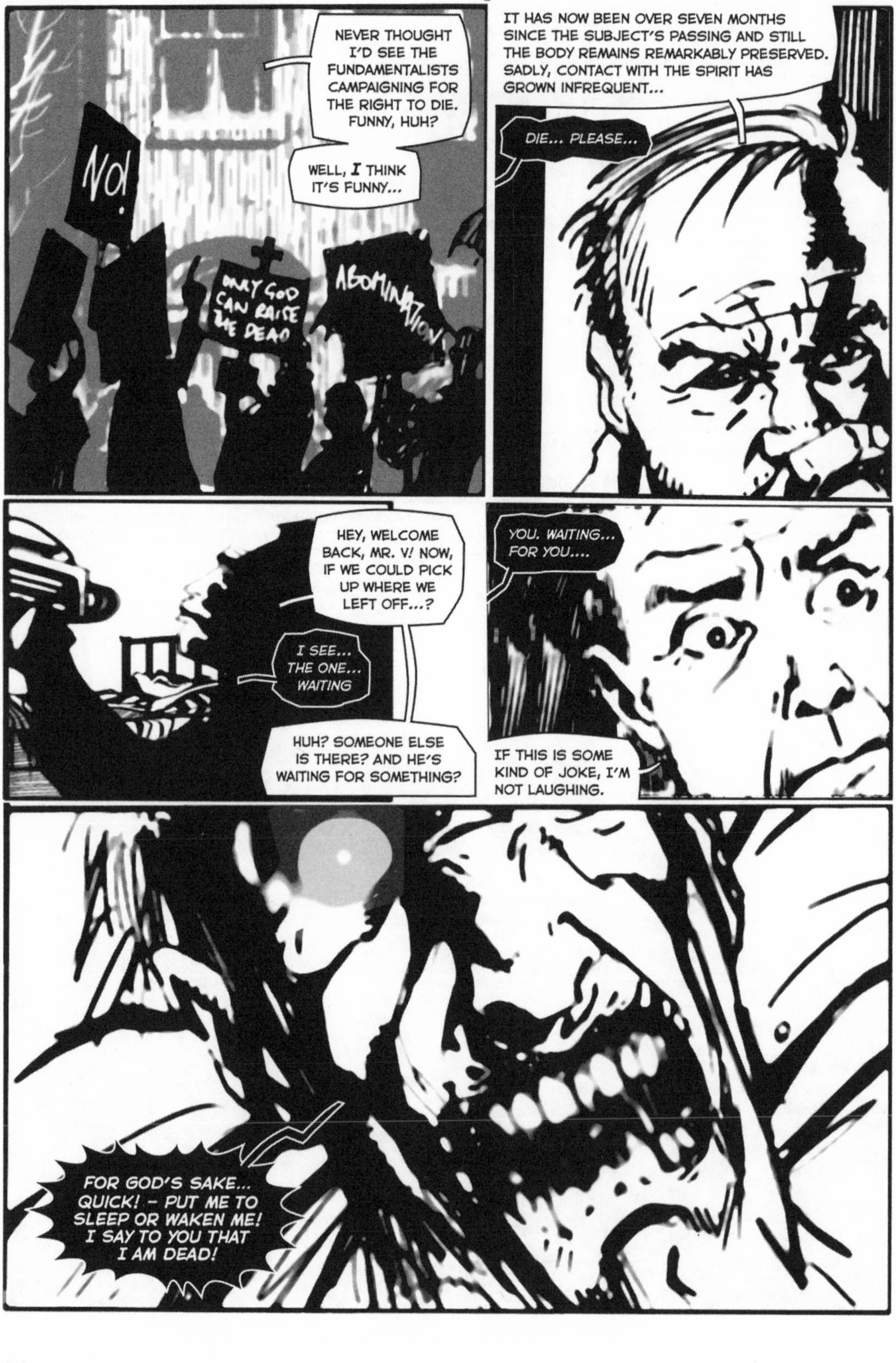
NEVER THOUGHT I'D SEE THE FUNDAMENTALISTS CAMPAIGNING FOR THE RIGHT TO DIE. FUNNY, HUH?
WELL, I THINK IT'S FUNNY...
NO!
ONLY GOD CAN RAISE THE DEAD
ABOMINATION
IT HAS NOW BEEN OVER SEVEN MONTHS SINCE THE SUBJECT'S PASSING AND STILL THE BODY REMAINS REMARKABLY PRESERVED. SADLY, CONTACT WITH THE SPIRIT HAS GROWN INFREQUENT...
DIE... PLEASE...
HEY, WELCOME BACK, MR. V! NOW, IF WE COULD PICK UP WHERE WE LEFT OFF...?
I SEE... THE ONE... WAITING
HUH? SOMEONE ELSE IS THERE? AND HE'S WAITING FOR SOMETHING?
YOU. WAITING... FOR YOU....
IF THIS IS SOME KIND OF JOKE, I'M NOT LAUGHING.
FOR GOD'S SAKE... QUICK! – PUT ME TO SLEEP OR WAKEN ME! I SAY TO YOU THAT I AM DEAD!

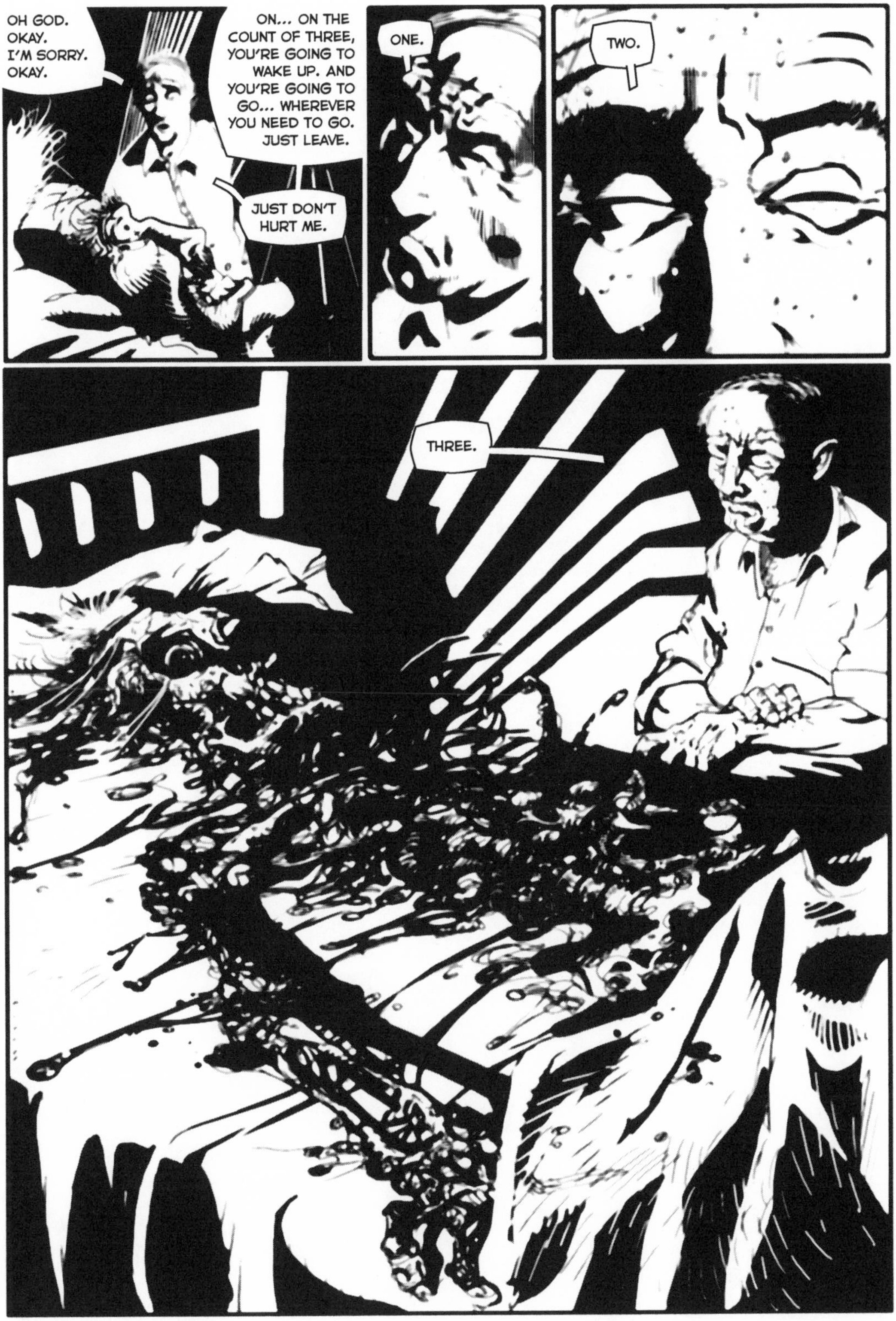
OH GOD. OKAY. I'M SORRY. OKAY.
ON... ON THE COUNT OF THREE, YOU'RE GOING TO WAKE UP. AND YOU'RE GOING TO GO... WHEREVER YOU NEED TO GO. JUST LEAVE.
JUST DON'T HURT ME.
ONE.
TWO.
THREE.

THE MURDERS IN
THE RUE MORGUE

Adapted by Ian Edginton
Art by D'Israeli

Published in 1841, this curious murder mystery is widely
considered to be one of the primary influences on the
development of detective fiction in the years following.
In particular, the character of Auguste Dupin is often cited
as the prototype for Sherlock Holmes.

The Murders in the Rue Morgue is also believed to be one of the
very first fictional "locked room" mysteries, with the seemingly
impossible crime taking place in a sealed chamber with no
obvious means of entry or escape.

Dupin would return in two more Poe stories — *The Mystery
of Marie Roget* (1842) and *The Purloined Letter* (1844).

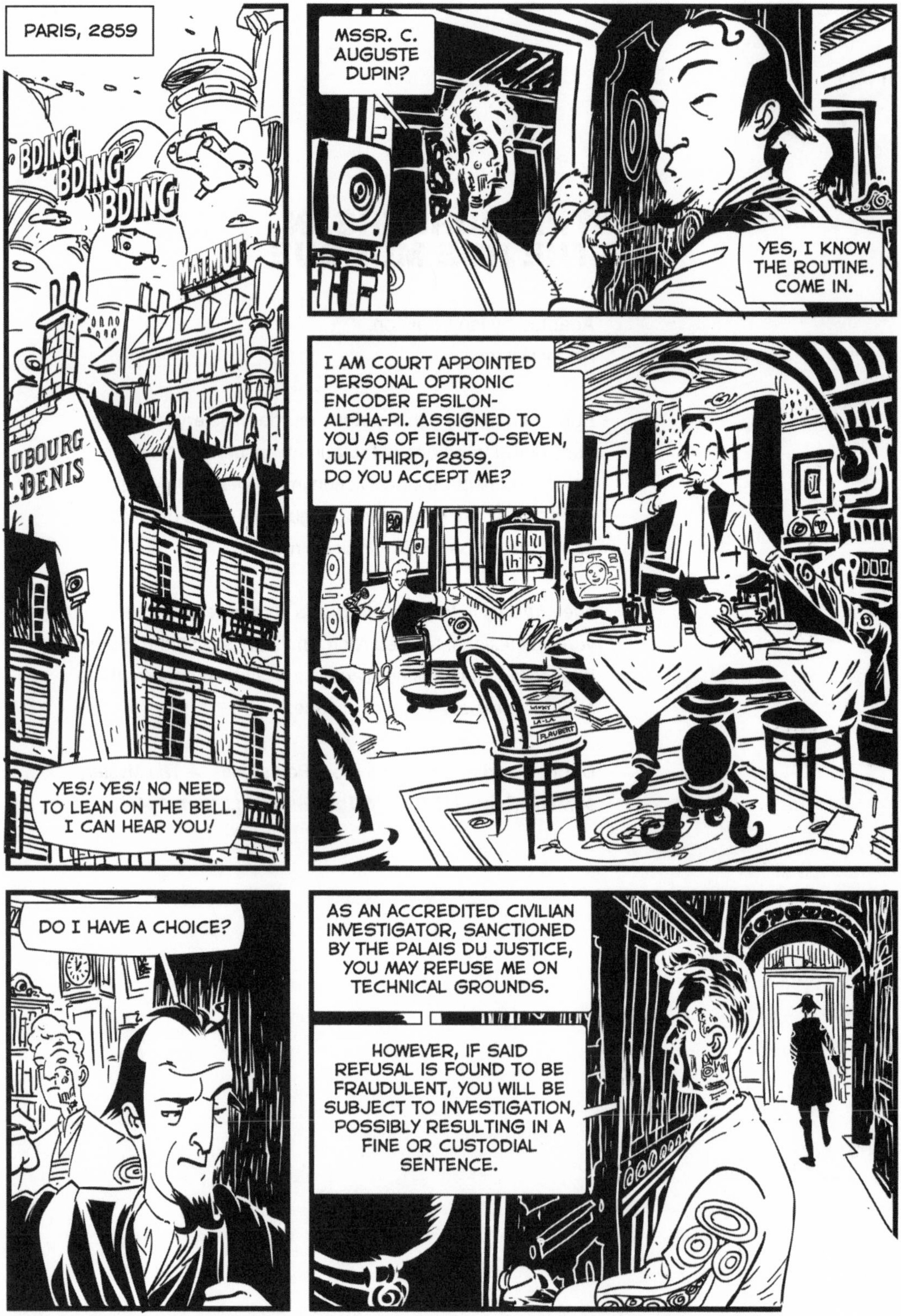
PARIS, 2859
BDING BDING BDING
MATMUT
UBOURG
.DENIS
YES! YES! NO NEED TO LEAN ON THE BELL. I CAN HEAR YOU!
MSSR. C. AUGUSTE DUPIN?
YES, I KNOW THE ROUTINE. COME IN.
I AM COURT APPOINTED PERSONAL OPTRONIC ENCODER EPSILON-ALPHA-PI. ASSIGNED TO YOU AS OF EIGHT-O-SEVEN, JULY THIRD, 2859. DO YOU ACCEPT ME?
FLAUBERT
DO I HAVE A CHOICE?
AS AN ACCREDITED CIVILIAN INVESTIGATOR, SANCTIONED BY THE PALAIS DU JUSTICE, YOU MAY REFUSE ME ON TECHNICAL GROUNDS.
HOWEVER, IF SAID REFUSAL IS FOUND TO BE FRAUDULENT, YOU WILL BE SUBJECT TO INVESTIGATION, POSSIBLY RESULTING IN A FINE OR CUSTODIAL SENTENCE.

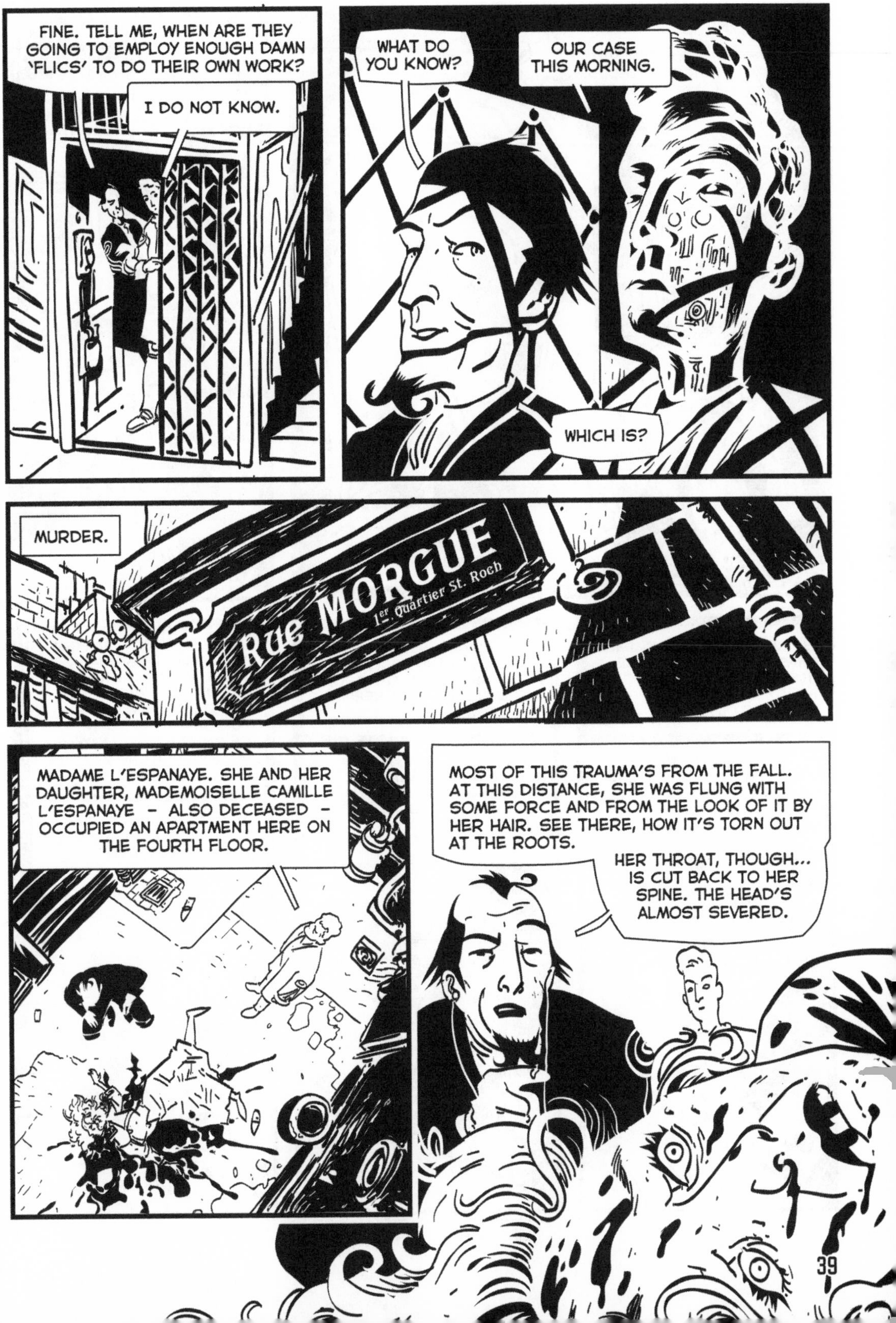
FINE. TELL ME, WHEN ARE THEY GOING TO EMPLOY ENOUGH DAMN 'FLICS' TO DO THEIR OWN WORK?
I DO NOT KNOW.
WHAT DO YOU KNOW?
OUR CASE THIS MORNING.
WHICH IS?
MURDER.
Rue MORGUE
1er Quartier St. Roch
MADAME L'ESPANAYE. SHE AND HER DAUGHTER, MADEMOISELLE CAMILLE L'ESPANAYE – ALSO DECEASED – OCCUPIED AN APARTMENT HERE ON THE FOURTH FLOOR.
MOST OF THIS TRAUMA'S FROM THE FALL. AT THIS DISTANCE, SHE WAS FLUNG WITH SOME FORCE AND FROM THE LOOK OF IT BY HER HAIR. SEE THERE, HOW IT'S TORN OUT AT THE ROOTS.
HER THROAT, THOUGH... IS CUT BACK TO HER SPINE. THE HEAD'S ALMOST SEVERED.

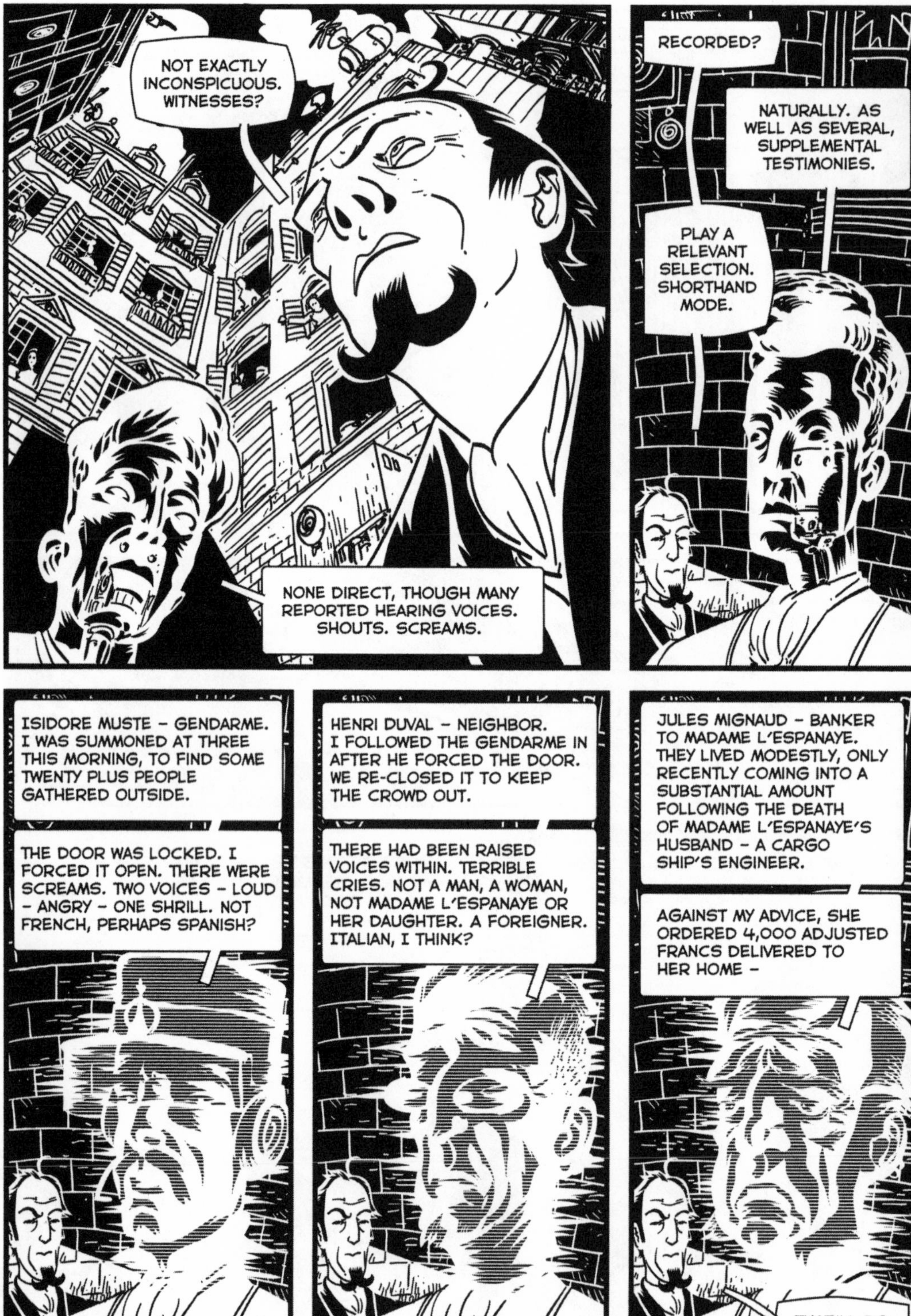
NOT EXACTLY INCONSPICUOUS. WITNESSES?
NONE DIRECT, THOUGH MANY REPORTED HEARING VOICES. SHOUTS. SCREAMS.
RECORDED?
NATURALLY. AS WELL AS SEVERAL, SUPPLEMENTAL TESTIMONIES.
PLAY A RELEVANT SELECTION. SHORTHAND MODE.
ISIDORE MUSTE – GENDARME. I WAS SUMMONED AT THREE THIS MORNING, TO FIND SOME TWENTY PLUS PEOPLE GATHERED OUTSIDE.
THE DOOR WAS LOCKED. I FORCED IT OPEN. THERE WERE SCREAMS. TWO VOICES – LOUD – ANGRY – ONE SHRILL. NOT FRENCH, PERHAPS SPANISH?
HENRI DUVAL – NEIGHBOR. I FOLLOWED THE GENDARME IN AFTER HE FORCED THE DOOR. WE RE-CLOSED IT TO KEEP THE CROWD OUT.
THERE HAD BEEN RAISED VOICES WITHIN. TERRIBLE CRIES. NOT A MAN, A WOMAN, NOT MADAME L'ESPANAYE OR HER DAUGHTER. A FOREIGNER. ITALIAN, I THINK?
JULES MIGNAUD – BANKER TO MADAME L'ESPANAYE. THEY LIVED MODESTLY, ONLY RECENTLY COMING INTO A SUBSTANTIAL AMOUNT FOLLOWING THE DEATH OF MADAME L'ESPANAYE'S HUSBAND – A CARGO SHIP'S ENGINEER.
AGAINST MY ADVICE, SHE ORDERED 4,000 ADJUSTED FRANCS DELIVERED TO HER HOME –
THAT'LL DO.

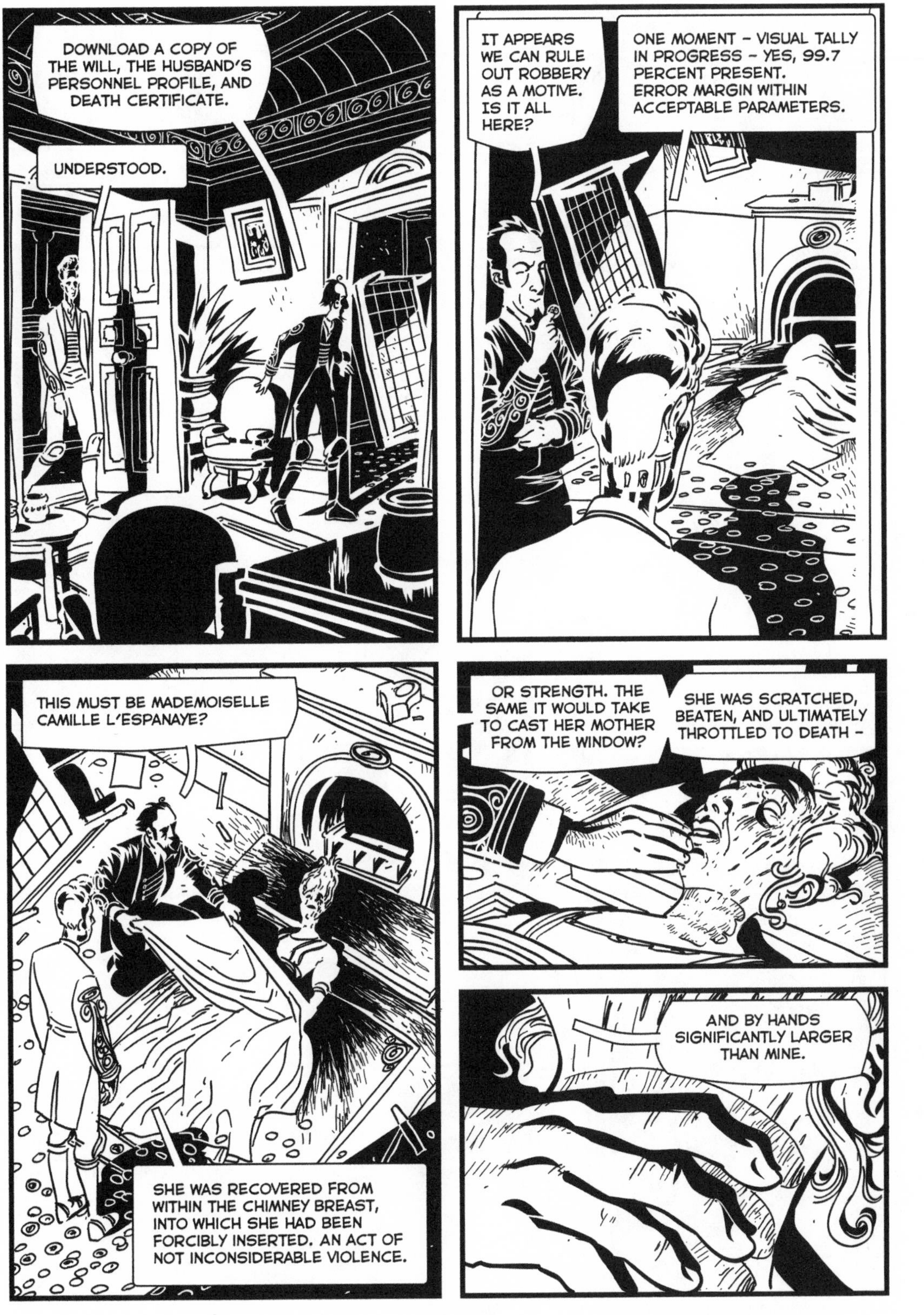
DOWNLOAD A COPY OF THE WILL, THE HUSBAND'S PERSONNEL PROFILE, AND DEATH CERTIFICATE.
UNDERSTOOD.
IT APPEARS WE CAN RULE OUT ROBBERY AS A MOTIVE. IS IT ALL HERE?
ONE MOMENT – VISUAL TALLY IN PROGRESS – YES, 99.7 PERCENT PRESENT. ERROR MARGIN WITHIN ACCEPTABLE PARAMETERS.
THIS MUST BE MADEMOISELLE CAMILLE L'ESPANAYE?
SHE WAS RECOVERED FROM WITHIN THE CHIMNEY BREAST, INTO WHICH SHE HAD BEEN FORCIBLY INSERTED. AN ACT OF NOT INCONSIDERABLE VIOLENCE.
OR STRENGTH. THE SAME IT WOULD TAKE TO CAST HER MOTHER FROM THE WINDOW?
SHE WAS SCRATCHED, BEATEN, AND ULTIMATELY THROTTLED TO DEATH –
AND BY HANDS SIGNIFICANTLY LARGER THAN MINE.

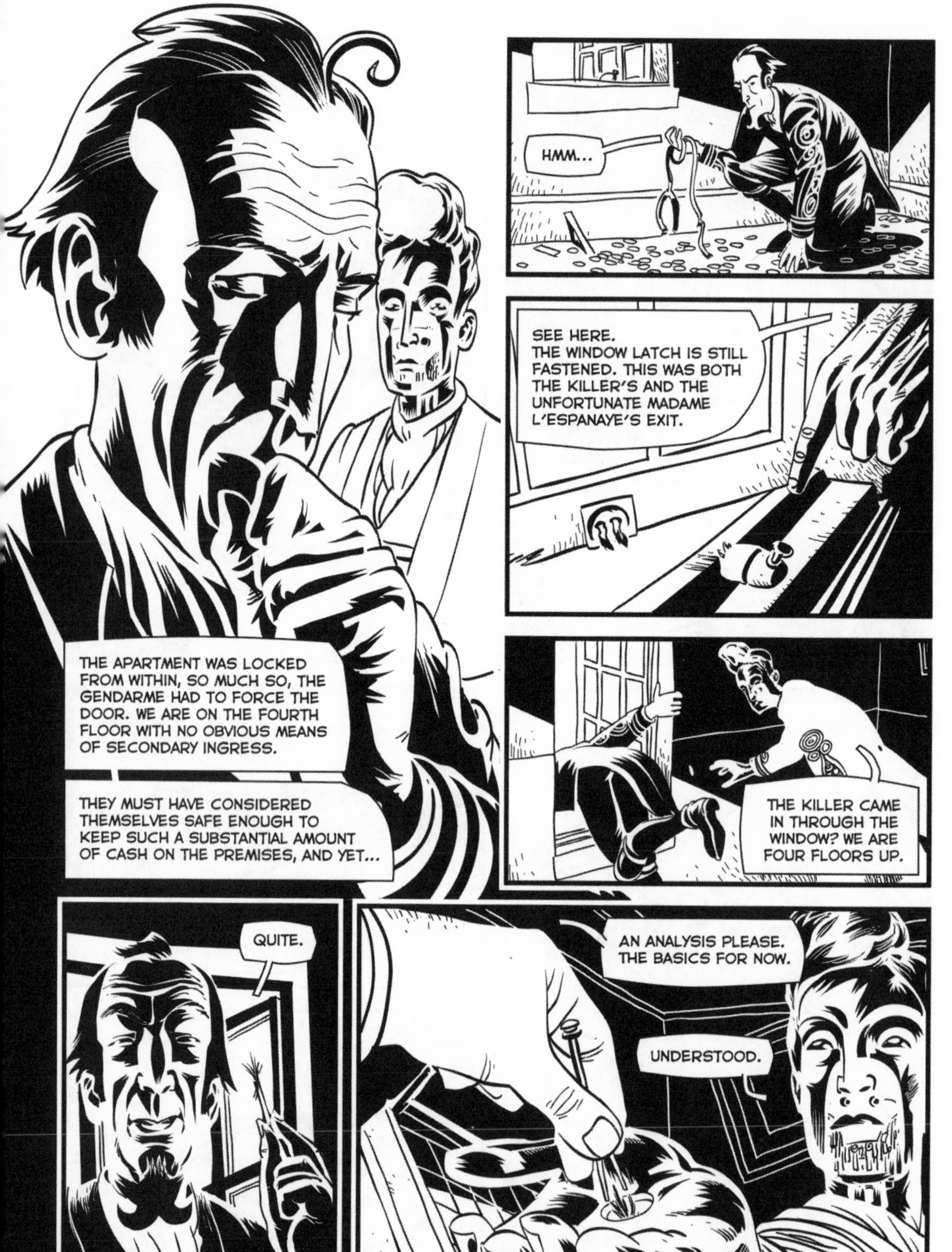
HMM...
SEE HERE. THE WINDOW LATCH IS STILL FASTENED. THIS WAS BOTH THE KILLER'S AND THE UNFORTUNATE MADAME L'ESPANAYE'S EXIT.
THE APARTMENT WAS LOCKED FROM WITHIN, SO MUCH SO, THE GENDARME HAD TO FORCE THE DOOR. WE ARE ON THE FOURTH FLOOR WITH NO OBVIOUS MEANS OF SECONDARY INGRESS.
THEY MUST HAVE CONSIDERED THEMSELVES SAFE ENOUGH TO KEEP SUCH A SUBSTANTIAL AMOUNT OF CASH ON THE PREMISES, AND YET...
THE KILLER CAME IN THROUGH THE WINDOW? WE ARE FOUR FLOORS UP.
QUITE.
AN ANALYSIS PLEASE. THE BASICS FOR NOW.
UNDERSTOOD.

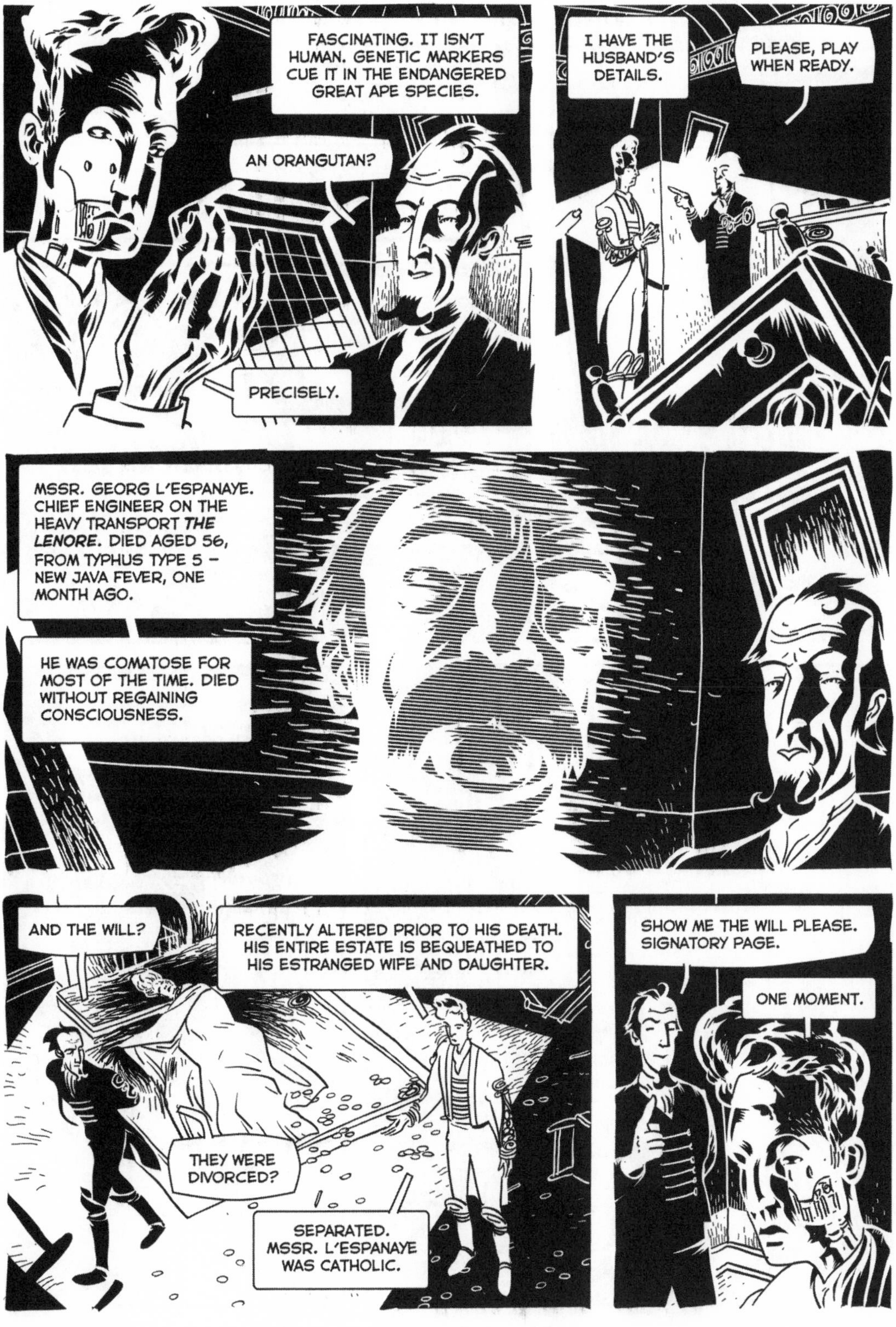
FASCINATING. IT ISN'T HUMAN. GENETIC MARKERS CUE IT IN THE ENDANGERED GREAT APE SPECIES.
AN ORANGUTAN?
PRECISELY.
I HAVE THE HUSBAND'S DETAILS.
PLEASE, PLAY WHEN READY.
MSSR. GEORG L'ESPANAYE. CHIEF ENGINEER ON THE HEAVY TRANSPORT *THE LENORE*. DIED AGED 56, FROM TYPHUS TYPE 5 – NEW JAVA FEVER, ONE MONTH AGO.
HE WAS COMATOSE FOR MOST OF THE TIME. DIED WITHOUT REGAINING CONSCIOUSNESS.
AND THE WILL?
RECENTLY ALTERED PRIOR TO HIS DEATH. HIS ENTIRE ESTATE IS BEQUEATHED TO HIS ESTRANGED WIFE AND DAUGHTER.
THEY WERE DIVORCED?
SEPARATED. MSSR. L'ESPANAYE WAS CATHOLIC.
SHOW ME THE WILL PLEASE. SIGNATORY PAGE.
ONE MOMENT.

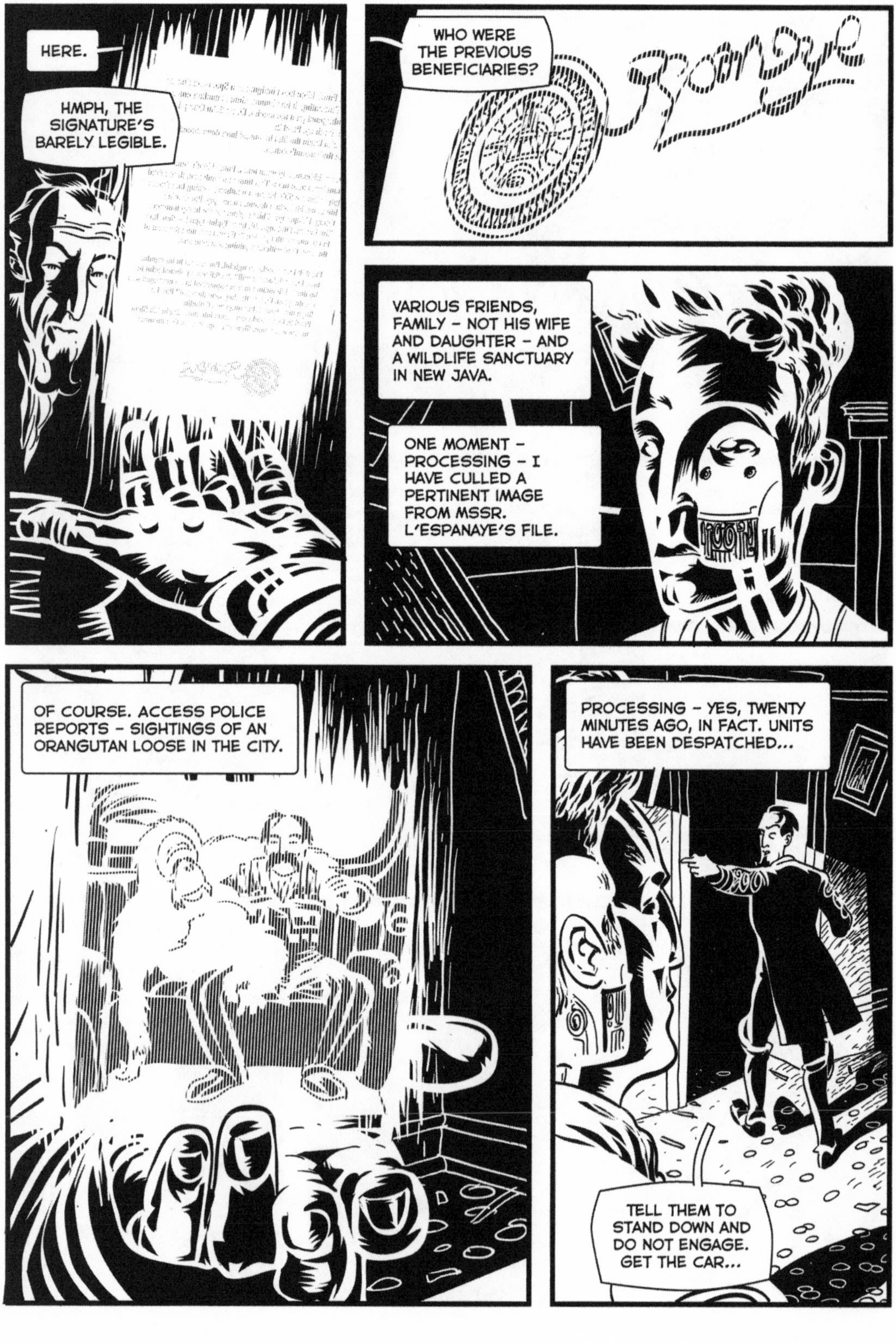
HERE.
HMPH, THE SIGNATURE'S BARELY LEGIBLE.
WHO WERE THE PREVIOUS BENEFICIARIES?
VARIOUS FRIENDS, FAMILY – NOT HIS WIFE AND DAUGHTER – AND A WILDLIFE SANCTUARY IN NEW JAVA.
ONE MOMENT – PROCESSING – I HAVE CULLED A PERTINENT IMAGE FROM MSSR. L'ESPANAYE'S FILE.
OF COURSE. ACCESS POLICE REPORTS – SIGHTINGS OF AN ORANGUTAN LOOSE IN THE CITY.
PROCESSING – YES, TWENTY MINUTES AGO, IN FACT. UNITS HAVE BEEN DESPATCHED...
TELL THEM TO STAND DOWN AND DO NOT ENGAGE. GET THE CAR...

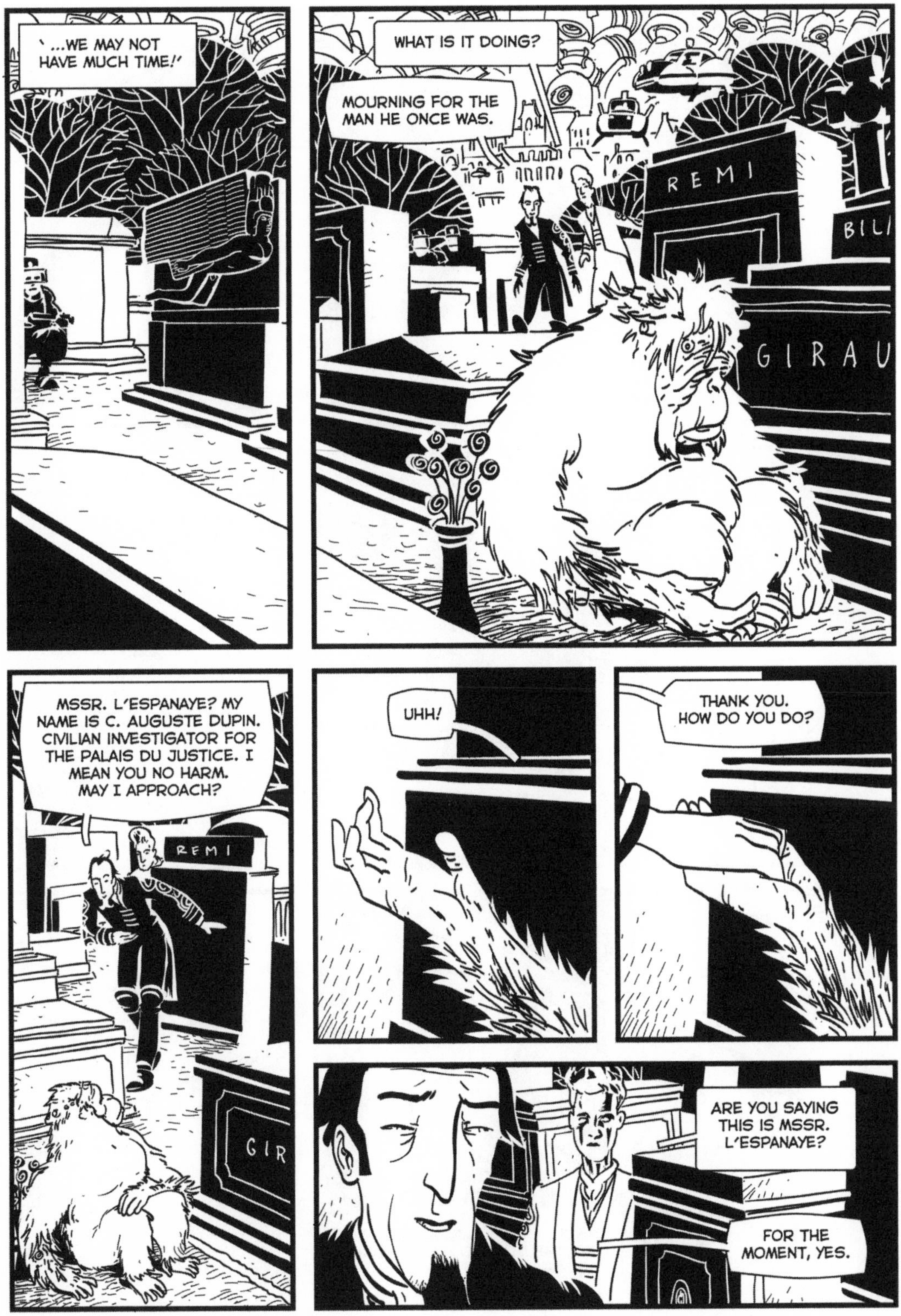
'...WE MAY NOT HAVE MUCH TIME!'
WHAT IS IT DOING?
MOURNING FOR THE MAN HE ONCE WAS.
REMI
BIL
GIRAU
MSSR. L'ESPANAYE? MY NAME IS C. AUGUSTE DUPIN. CIVILIAN INVESTIGATOR FOR THE PALAIS DU JUSTICE. I MEAN YOU NO HARM. MAY I APPROACH?
REMI
GIR
UHH!
THANK YOU. HOW DO YOU DO?
ARE YOU SAYING THIS IS MSSR. L'ESPANAYE?
FOR THE MOMENT, YES.

MSSR. L'ESPANAYE, DO YOU KNOW WHY WE ARE HERE?

THIS APE... THIS BODY YOU ARE IN, WAS A PET ONCE? ACQUIRED ON YOUR TRAVELS?

MSSR. L'ESPANAYE, ANSWER ME TRUTHFULLY. DID YOU MURDER YOUR WIFE AND DAUGHTER?

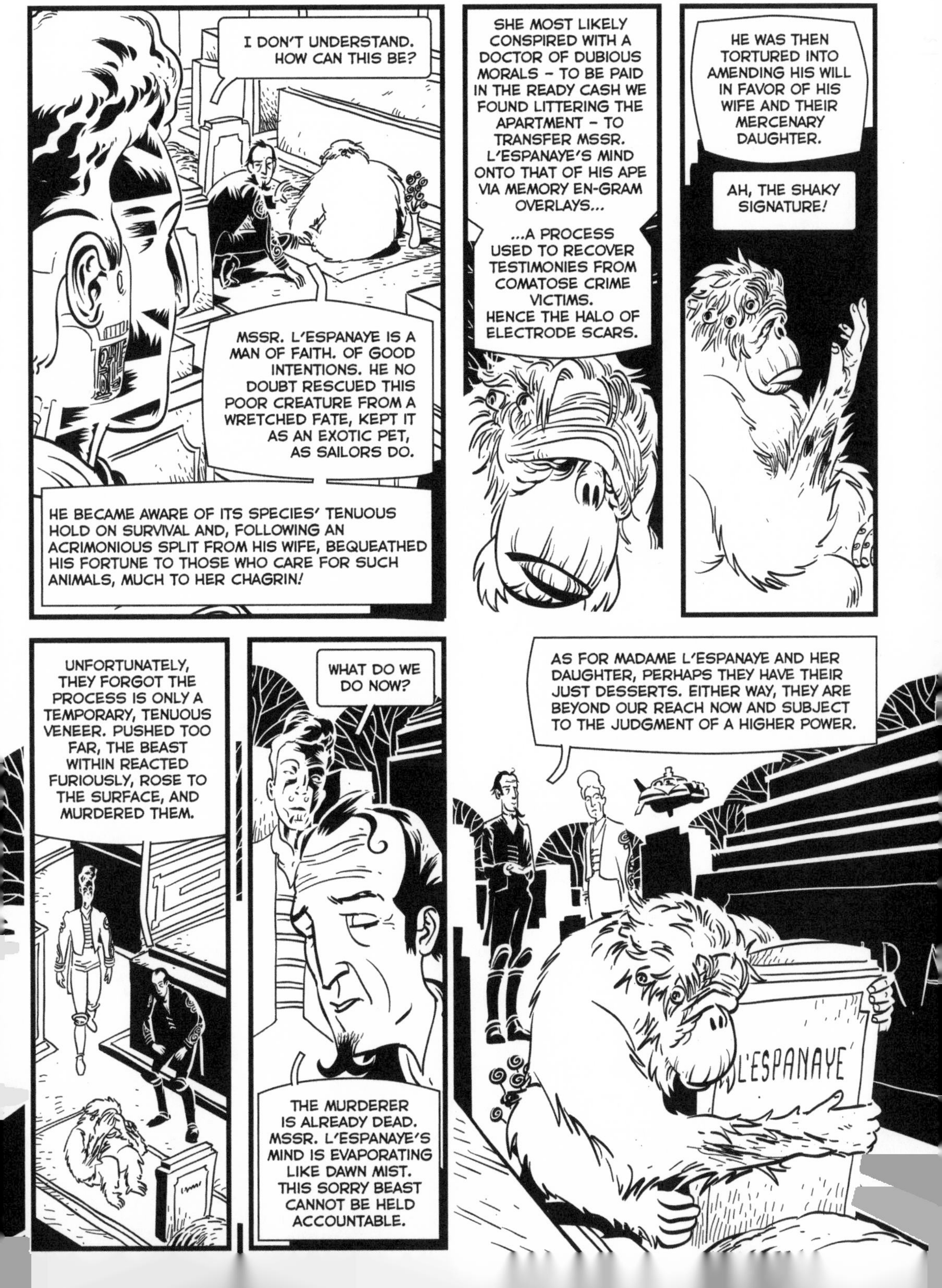
I DON'T UNDERSTAND. HOW CAN THIS BE?
MSSR. L'ESPANAYE IS A MAN OF FAITH. OF GOOD INTENTIONS. HE NO DOUBT RESCUED THIS POOR CREATURE FROM A WRETCHED FATE, KEPT IT AS AN EXOTIC PET, AS SAILORS DO.
HE BECAME AWARE OF ITS SPECIES' TENUOUS HOLD ON SURVIVAL AND, FOLLOWING AN ACRIMONIOUS SPLIT FROM HIS WIFE, BEQUEATHED HIS FORTUNE TO THOSE WHO CARE FOR SUCH ANIMALS, MUCH TO HER CHAGRIN!
SHE MOST LIKELY CONSPIRED WITH A DOCTOR OF DUBIOUS MORALS – TO BE PAID IN THE READY CASH WE FOUND LITTERING THE APARTMENT – TO TRANSFER MSSR. L'ESPANAYE'S MIND ONTO THAT OF HIS APE VIA MEMORY EN-GRAM OVERLAYS...
...A PROCESS USED TO RECOVER TESTIMONIES FROM COMATOSE CRIME VICTIMS. HENCE THE HALO OF ELECTRODE SCARS.
HE WAS THEN TORTURED INTO AMENDING HIS WILL IN FAVOR OF HIS WIFE AND THEIR MERCENARY DAUGHTER.
AH, THE SHAKY SIGNATURE!
UNFORTUNATELY, THEY FORGOT THE PROCESS IS ONLY A TEMPORARY, TENUOUS VENEER. PUSHED TOO FAR, THE BEAST WITHIN REACTED FURIOUSLY, ROSE TO THE SURFACE, AND MURDERED THEM.
WHAT DO WE DO NOW?
THE MURDERER IS ALREADY DEAD. MSSR. L'ESPANAYE'S MIND IS EVAPORATING LIKE DAWN MIST. THIS SORRY BEAST CANNOT BE HELD ACCOUNTABLE.
AS FOR MADAME L'ESPANAYE AND HER DAUGHTER, PERHAPS THEY HAVE THEIR JUST DESSERTS. EITHER WAY, THEY ARE BEYOND OUR REACH NOW AND SUBJECT TO THE JUDGMENT OF A HIGHER POWER.
L'ESPANAYE

THE FALL OF THE HOUSE OF USHER

Adapted by Dan Whitehead

Art by Shane Ivan Oakley

The terrible tragedy of Roderick Usher is one of Poe's most recognizable tales, having been adapted for the screen more than ten times, and features a range of his most common themes.

The sudden death of a beloved female relative is an especially common motif throughout Poe's writing, and some have suggested that losing both his birth mother and foster mother to tuberculosis before his twentieth birthday may have been the cause of this thematic obsession.

The story went through several revisions following its original publication in *Burton's Gentleman's Magazine* in 1839. The final version, as published in the 1840 volume *Tales of the Grotesque and Arabesque*, incorporates the text of the poem *The Haunted Palace*.

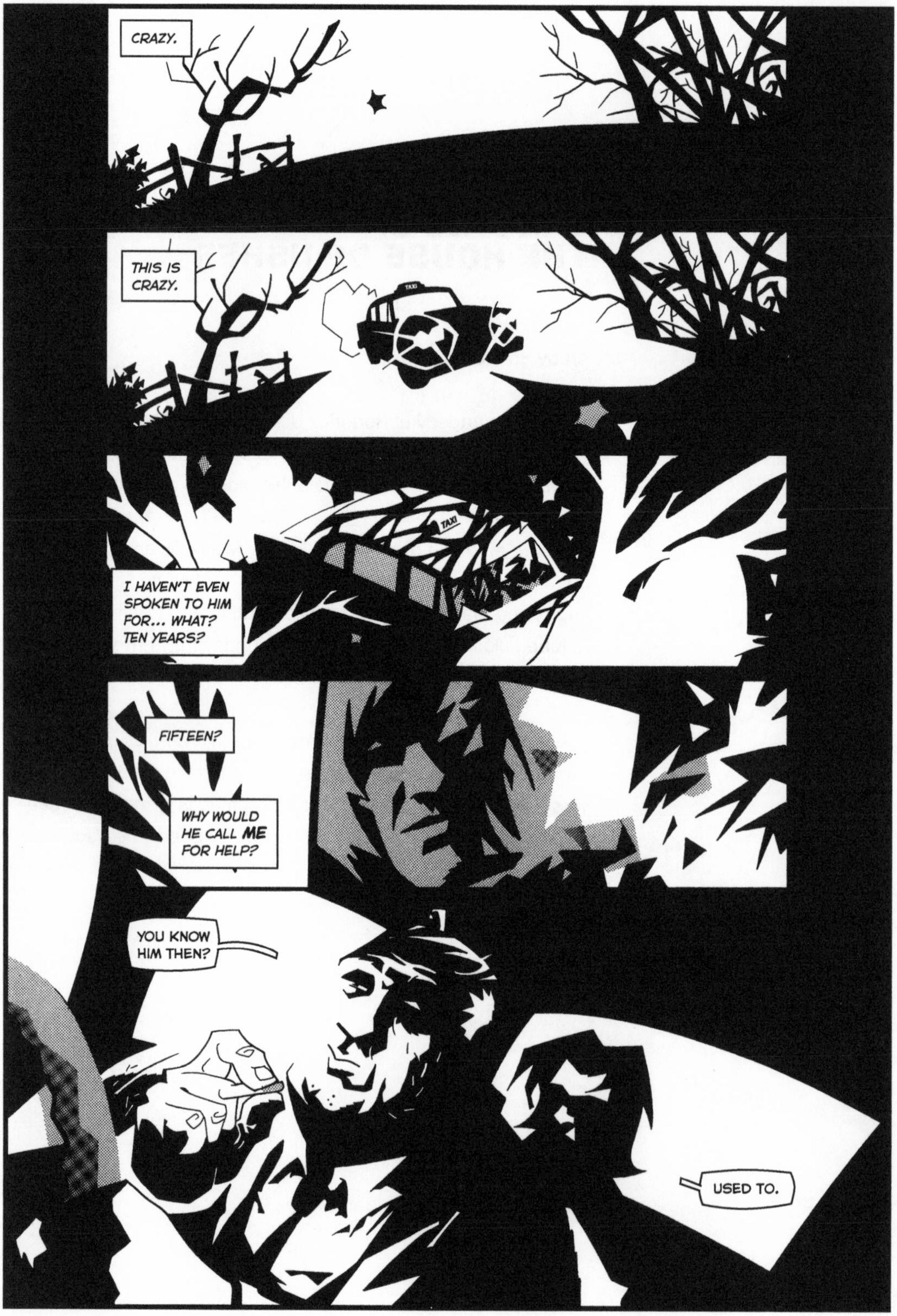
CRAZY.
THIS IS CRAZY.
TAXI
TAXI
I HAVEN'T EVEN SPOKEN TO HIM FOR... WHAT? TEN YEARS?
FIFTEEN?
WHY WOULD HE CALL ME FOR HELP?
YOU KNOW HIM THEN?
USED TO.

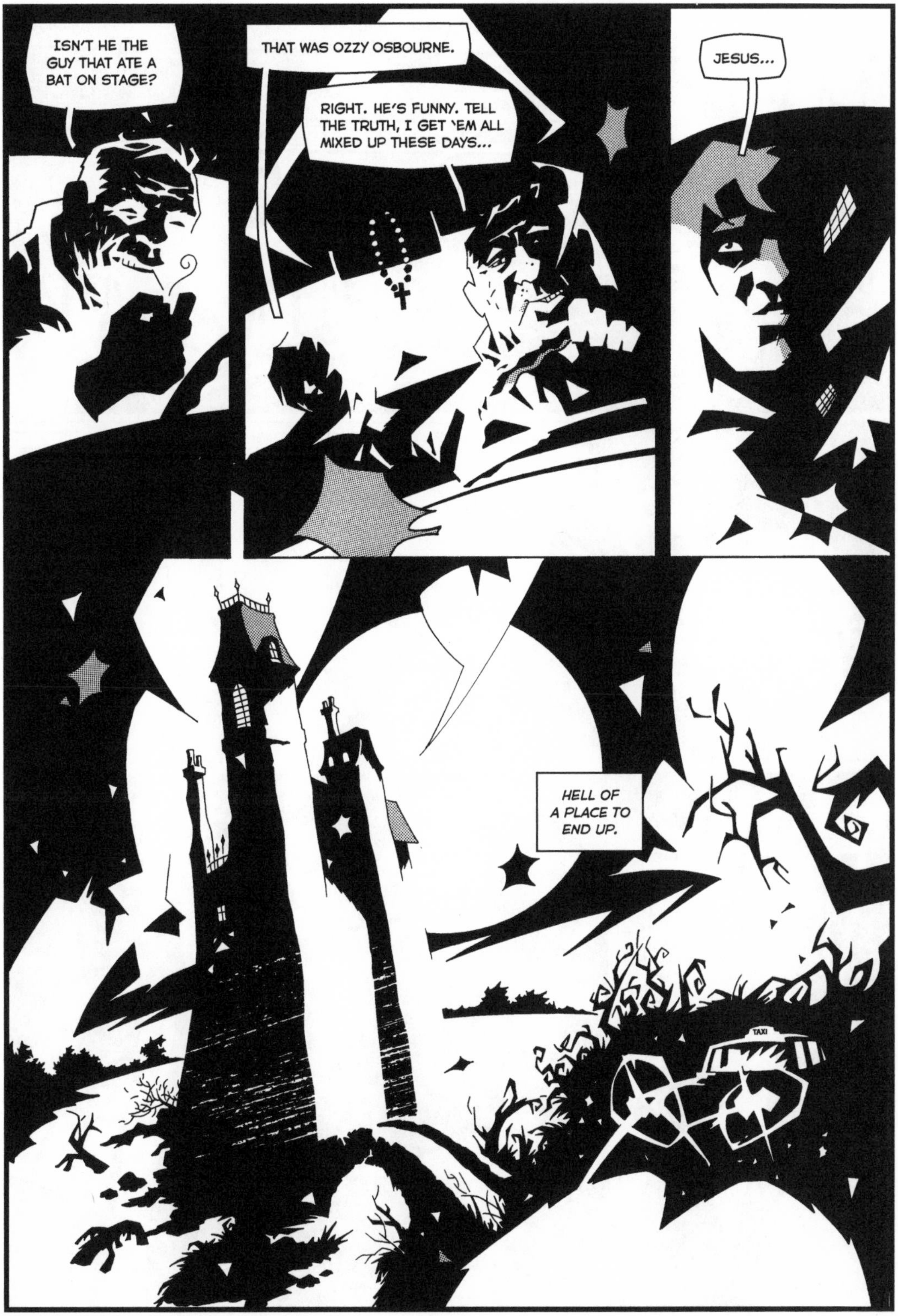
ISN'T HE THE GUY THAT ATE A BAT ON STAGE?
THAT WAS OZZY OSBOURNE.
RIGHT. HE'S FUNNY. TELL THE TRUTH, I GET 'EM ALL MIXED UP THESE DAYS...
JESUS...
HELL OF A PLACE TO END UP.
TAXI

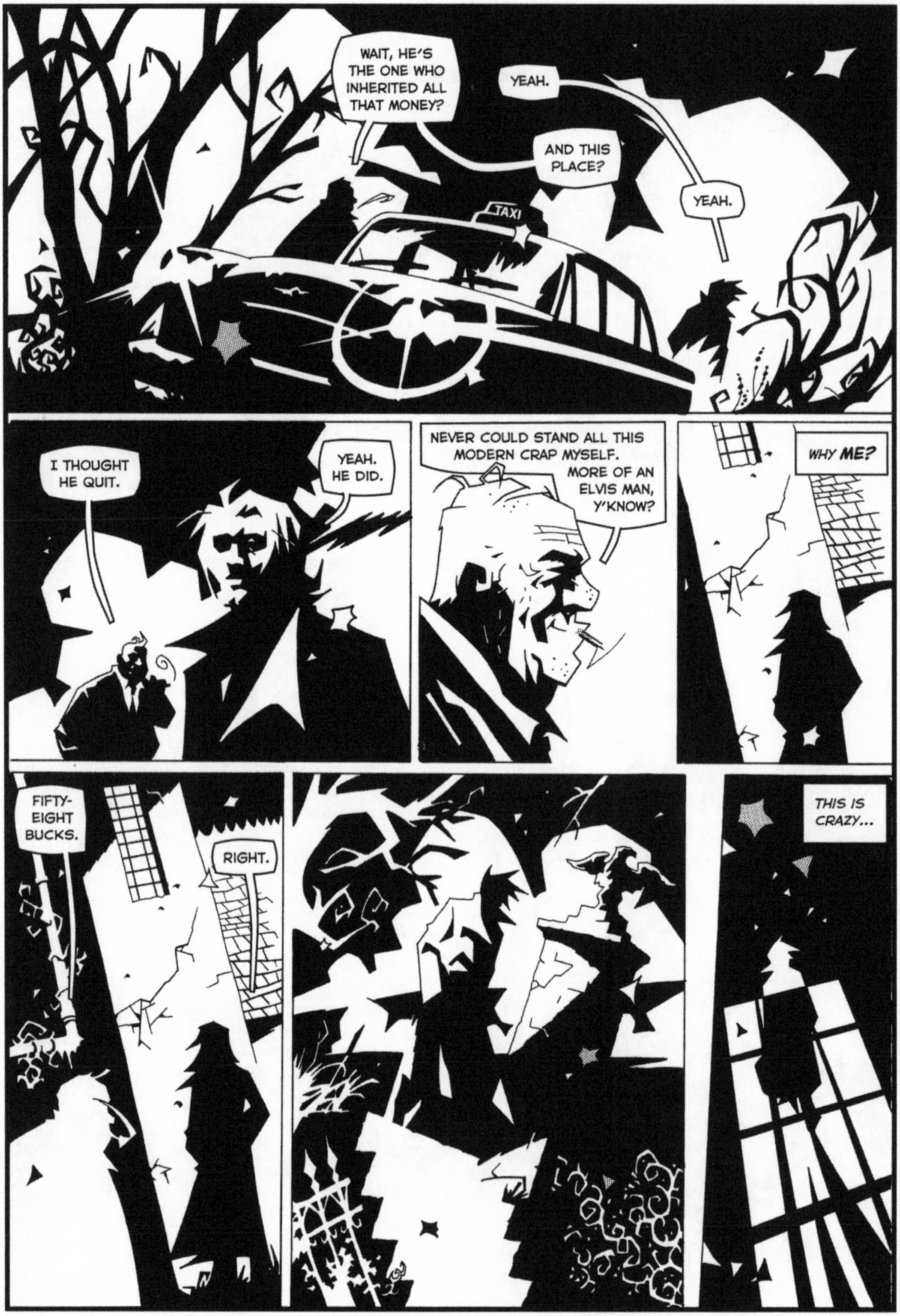
WAIT, HE'S THE ONE WHO INHERITED ALL THAT MONEY?
YEAH.
AND THIS PLACE?
YEAH.
TAXI
I THOUGHT HE QUIT.
YEAH. HE DID.
NEVER COULD STAND ALL THIS MODERN CRAP MYSELF.
MORE OF AN ELVIS MAN, Y'KNOW?
WHY ME?
FIFTY-EIGHT BUCKS.
RIGHT.
THIS IS CRAZY...

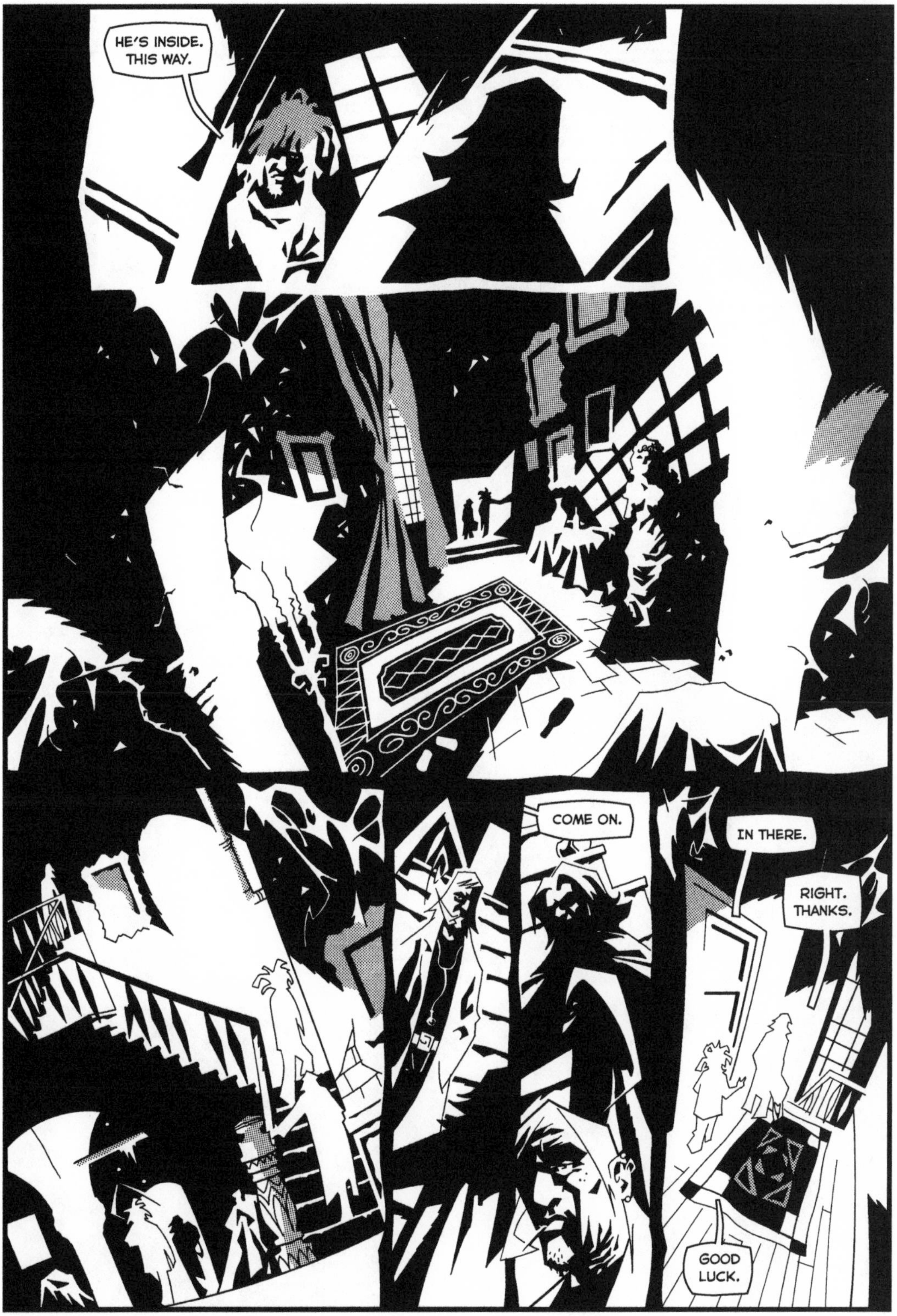
HE'S INSIDE. THIS WAY.
COME ON.
IN THERE.
RIGHT. THANKS.
GOOD LUCK.

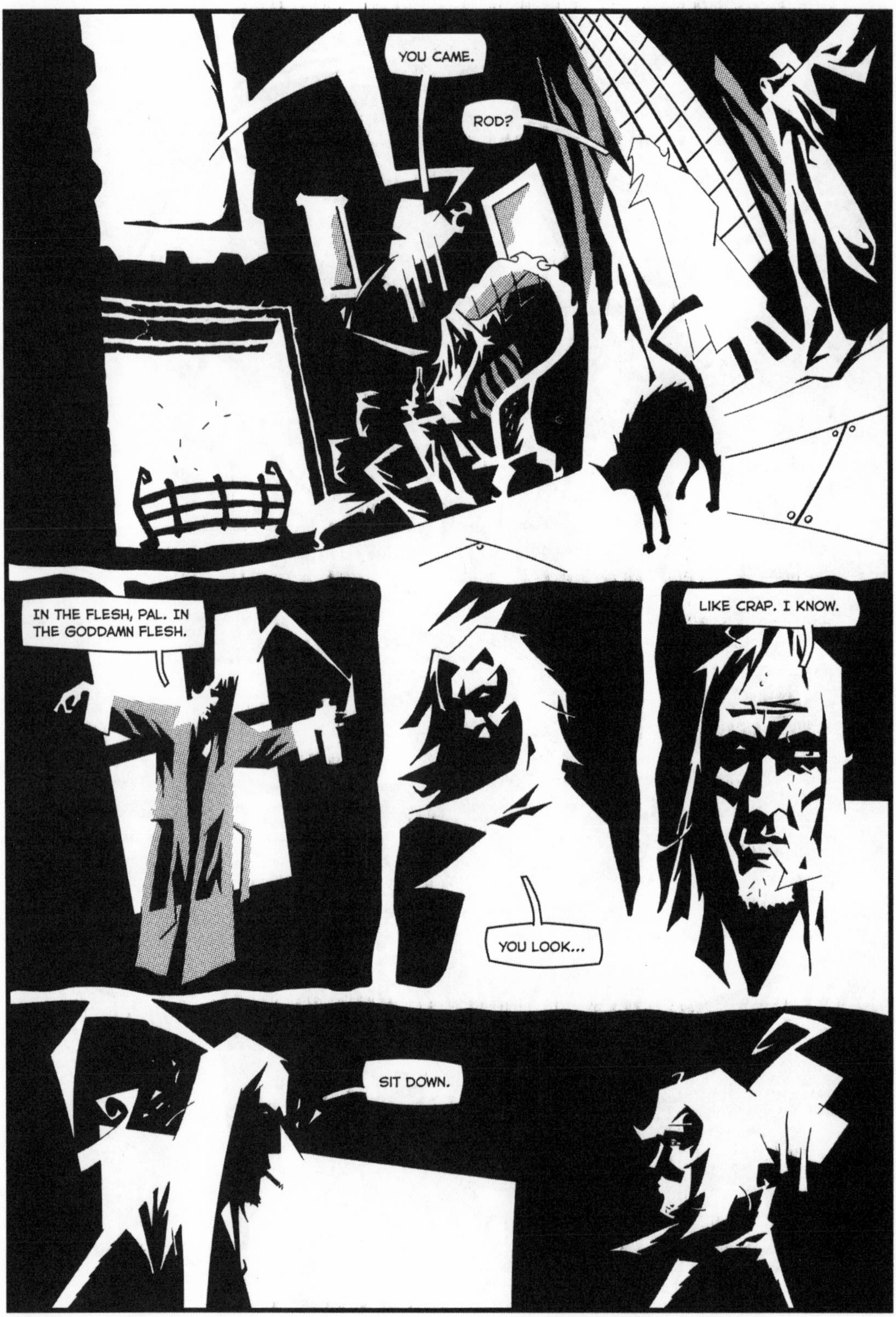
YOU CAME.
ROD?
IN THE FLESH, PAL. IN THE GODDAMN FLESH.
YOU LOOK...
LIKE CRAP. I KNOW.
SIT DOWN.

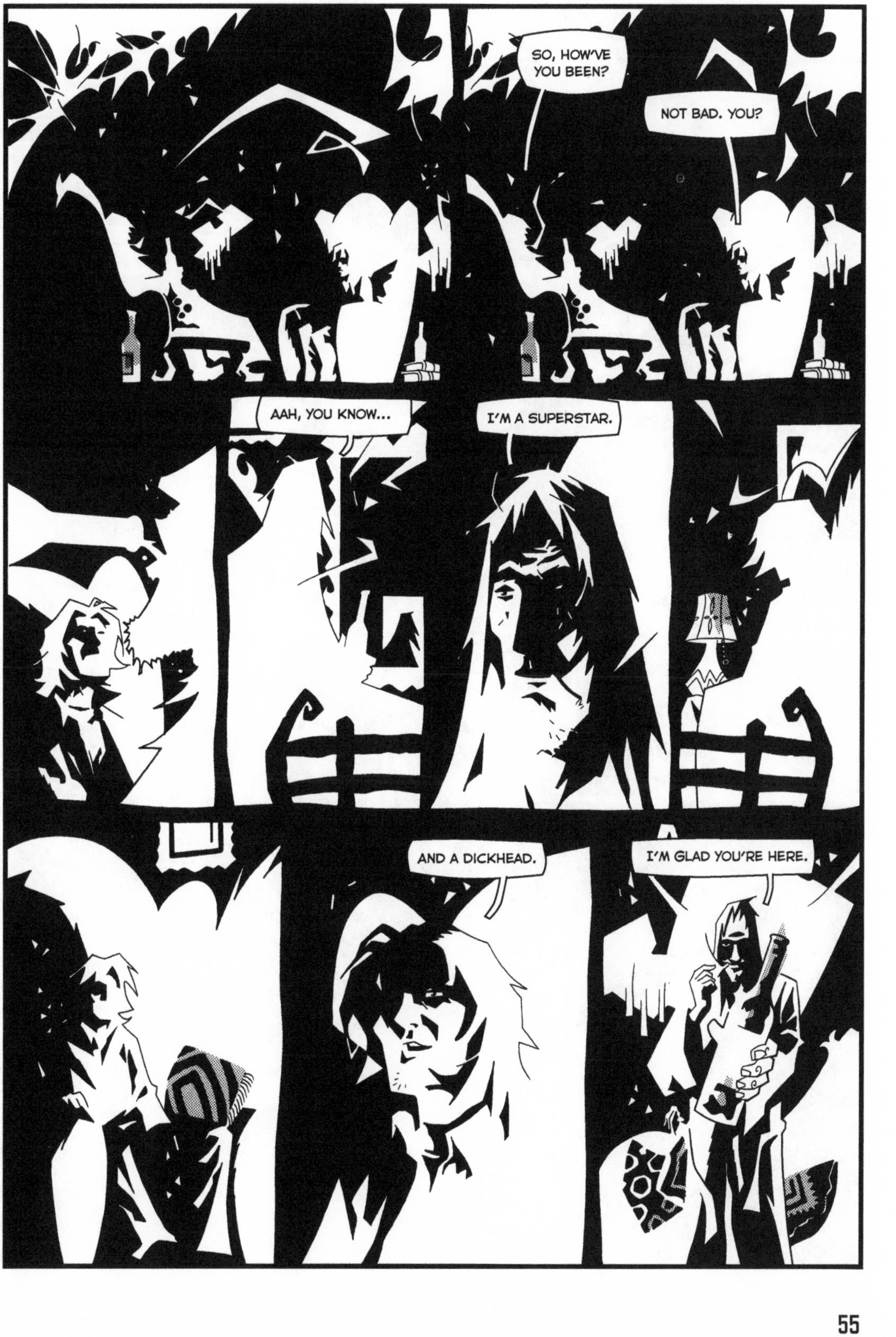
SO, HOW'VE YOU BEEN?
NOT BAD. YOU?
AAH, YOU KNOW...
I'M A SUPERSTAR.
AND A DICKHEAD.
I'M GLAD YOU'RE HERE.

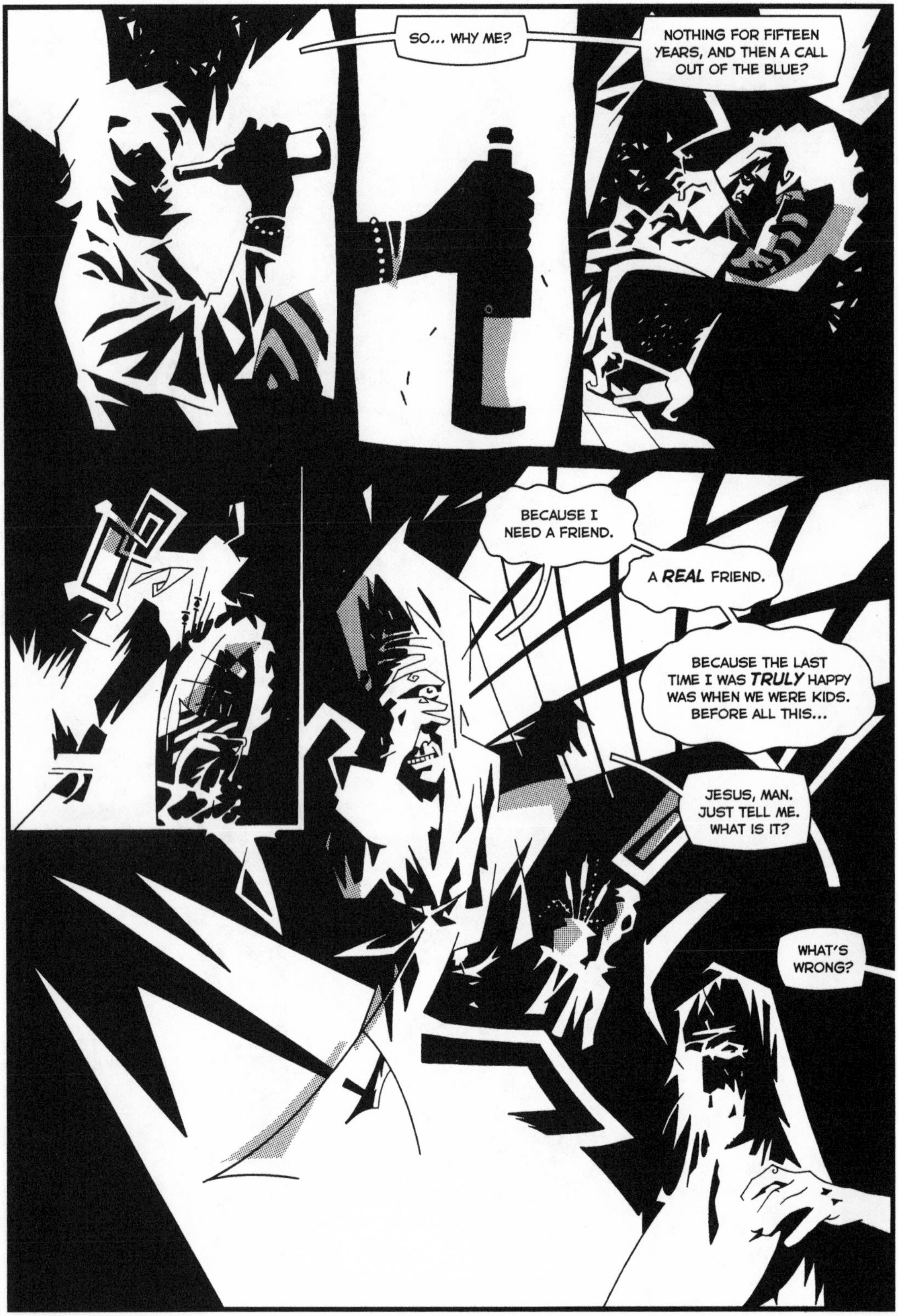
SO... WHY ME?
NOTHING FOR FIFTEEN YEARS, AND THEN A CALL OUT OF THE BLUE?
BECAUSE I NEED A FRIEND.
A *REAL* FRIEND.
BECAUSE THE LAST TIME I WAS *TRULY* HAPPY WAS WHEN WE WERE KIDS. BEFORE ALL THIS...
JESUS, MAN. JUST TELL ME. WHAT IS IT?
WHAT'S WRONG?

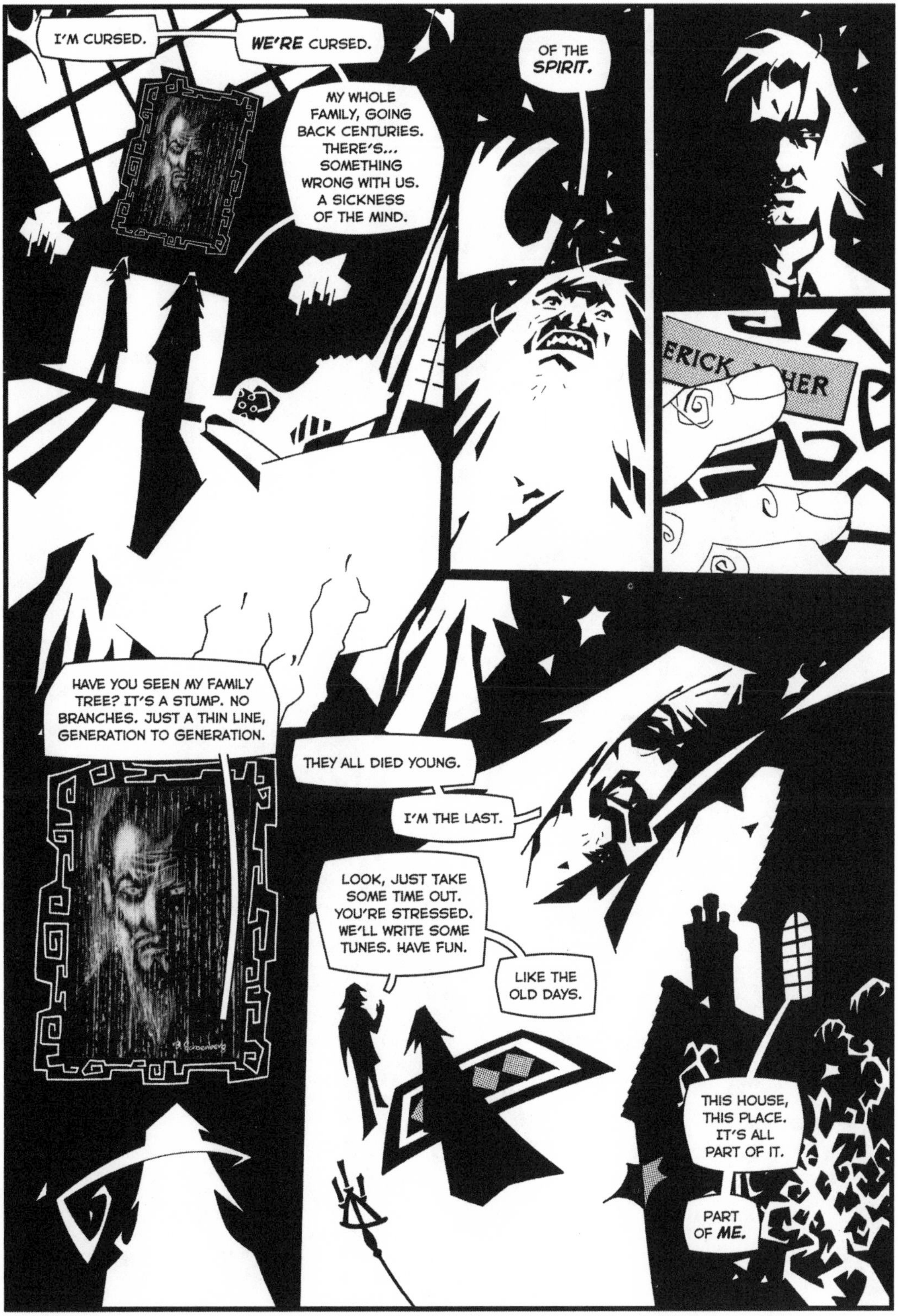
I'M CURSED.
WE'RE CURSED.
MY WHOLE FAMILY, GOING BACK CENTURIES. THERE'S... SOMETHING WRONG WITH US. A SICKNESS OF THE MIND.
OF THE SPIRIT.
ERICK USHER
HAVE YOU SEEN MY FAMILY TREE? IT'S A STUMP. NO BRANCHES. JUST A THIN LINE, GENERATION TO GENERATION.
THEY ALL DIED YOUNG.
I'M THE LAST.
LOOK, JUST TAKE SOME TIME OUT. YOU'RE STRESSED. WE'LL WRITE SOME TUNES. HAVE FUN.
LIKE THE OLD DAYS.
THIS HOUSE, THIS PLACE. IT'S ALL PART OF IT.
PART OF ME.

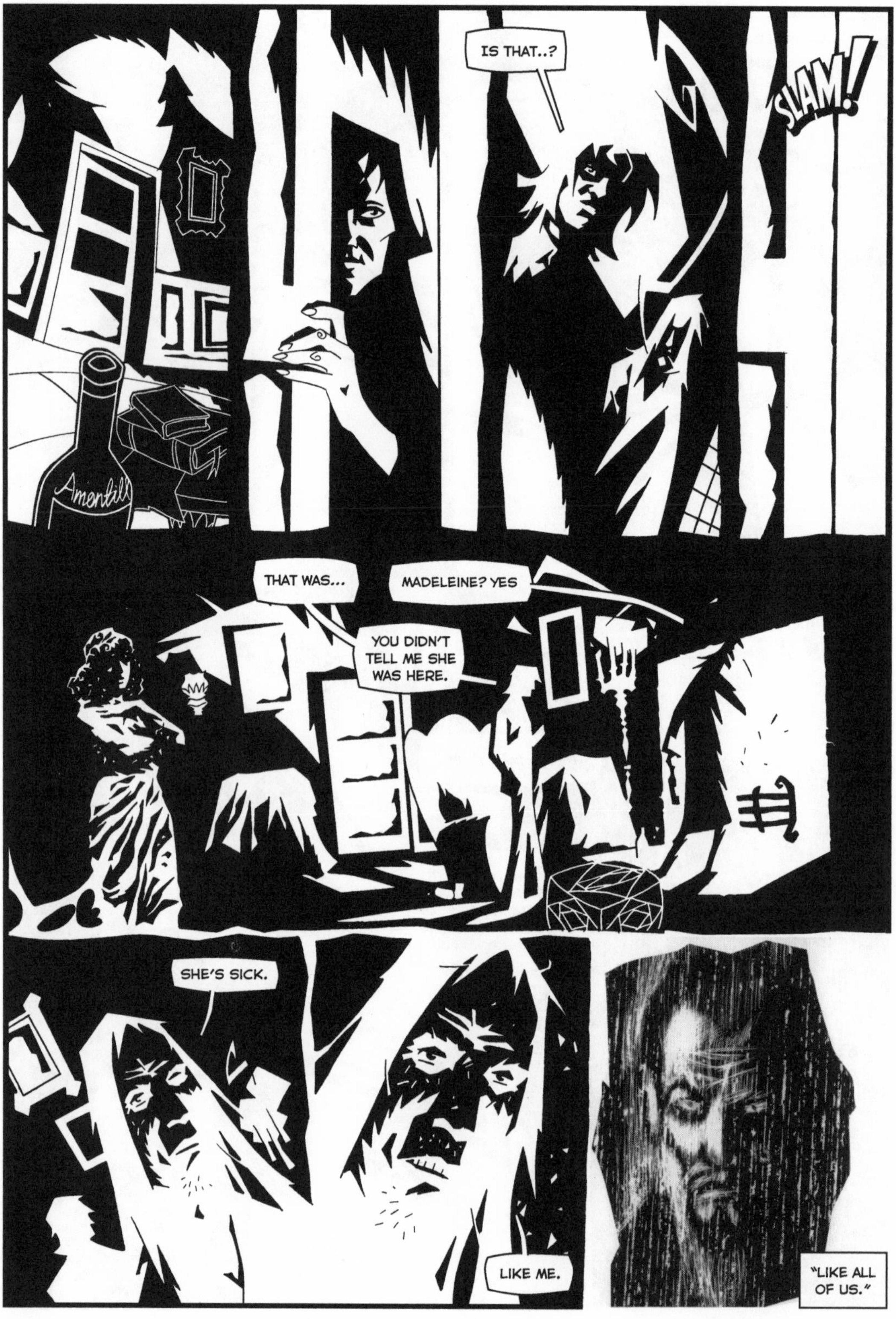
IS THAT..?
SLAM!
THAT WAS...
MADELEINE? YES
YOU DIDN'T TELL ME SHE WAS HERE.
SHE'S SICK.
LIKE ME.
"LIKE ALL OF US."

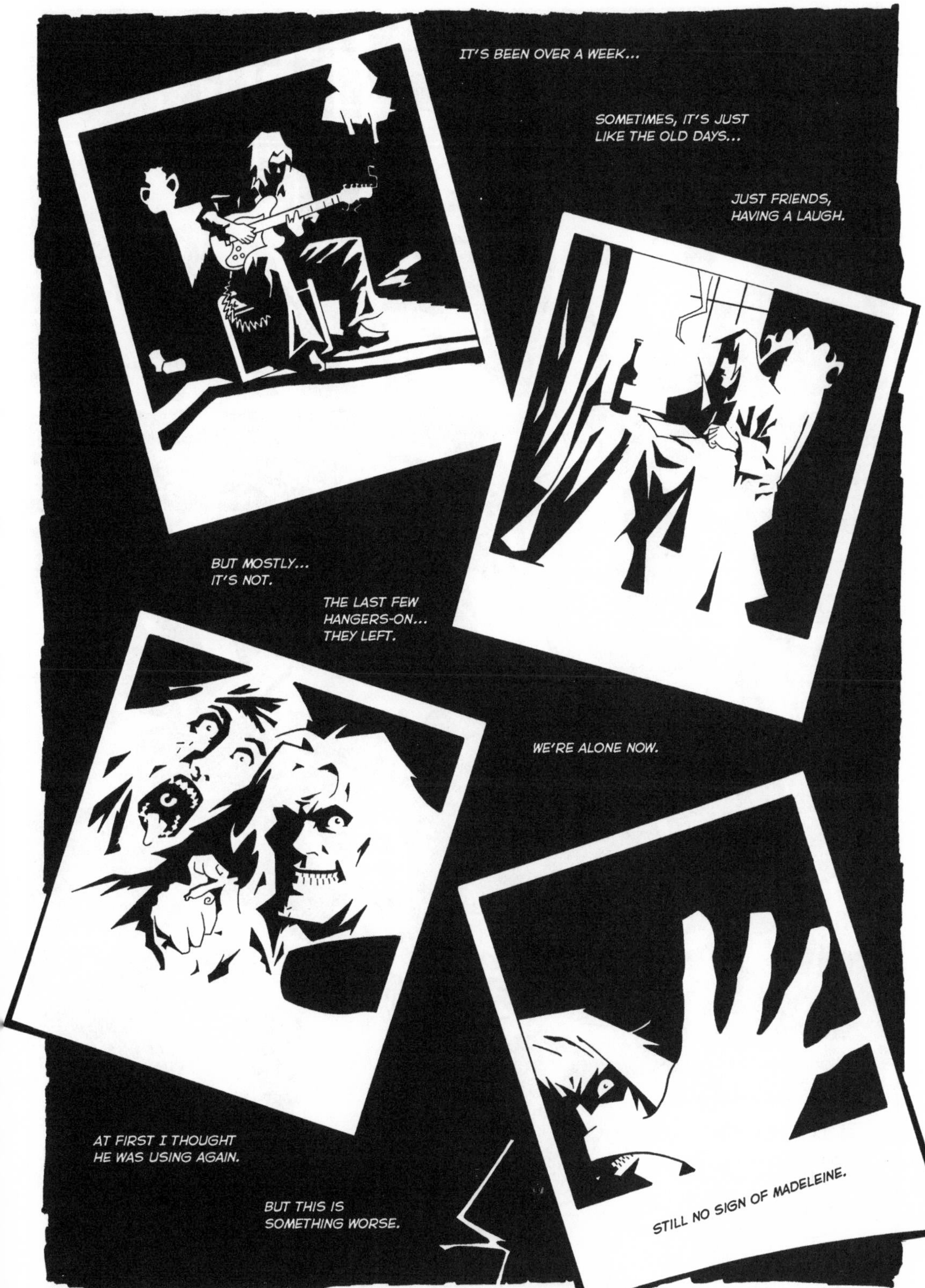
IT'S BEEN OVER A WEEK...
SOMETIMES, IT'S JUST LIKE THE OLD DAYS...
JUST FRIENDS, HAVING A LAUGH.
BUT MOSTLY... IT'S NOT.
THE LAST FEW HANGERS-ON... THEY LEFT.
WE'RE ALONE NOW.
AT FIRST I THOUGHT HE WAS USING AGAIN.
BUT THIS IS SOMETHING WORSE.
STILL NO SIGN OF MADELEINE.

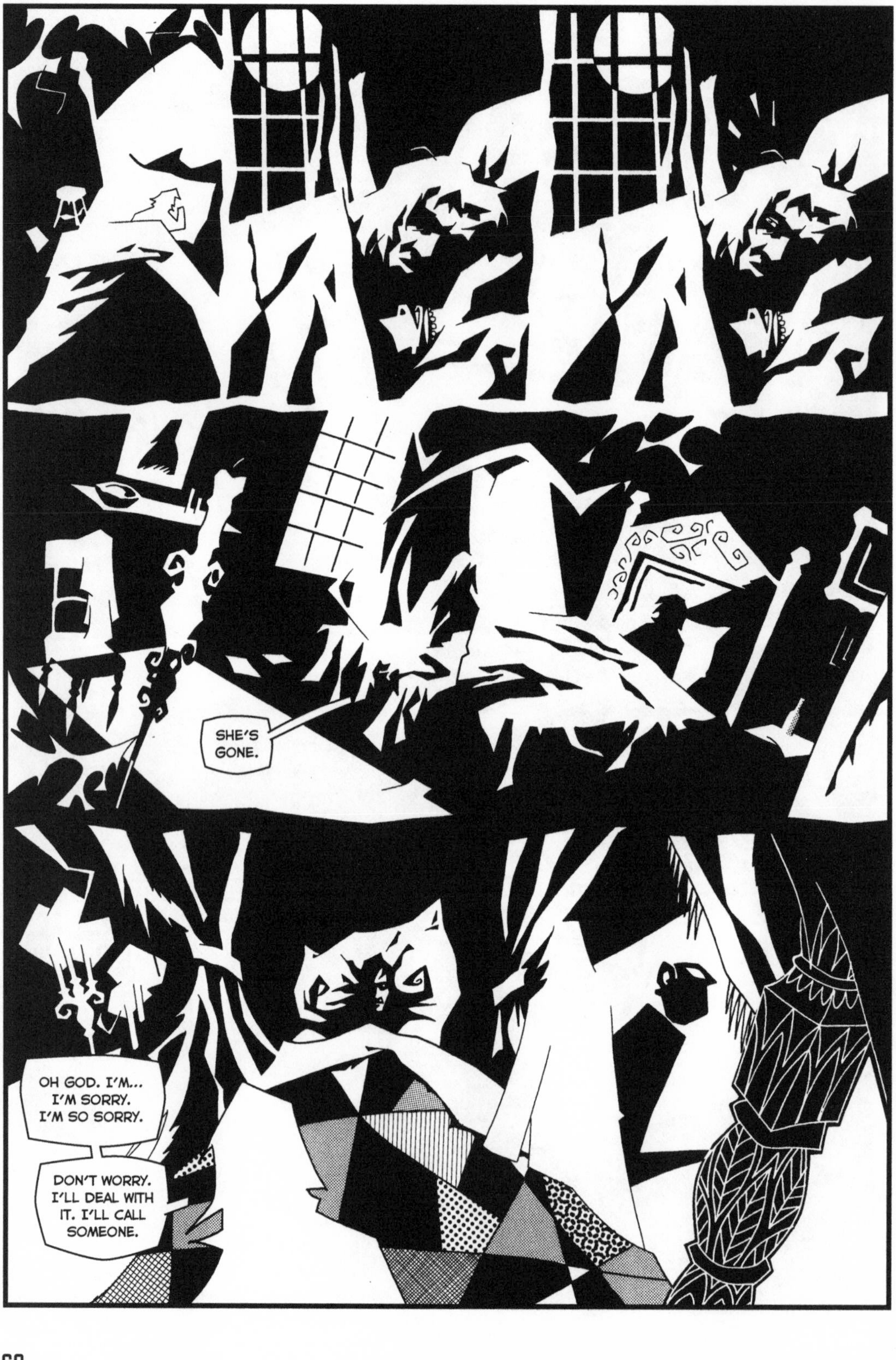
SHE'S GONE.
OH GOD. I'M... I'M SORRY. I'M SO SORRY.
DON'T WORRY. I'LL DEAL WITH IT. I'LL CALL SOMEONE.

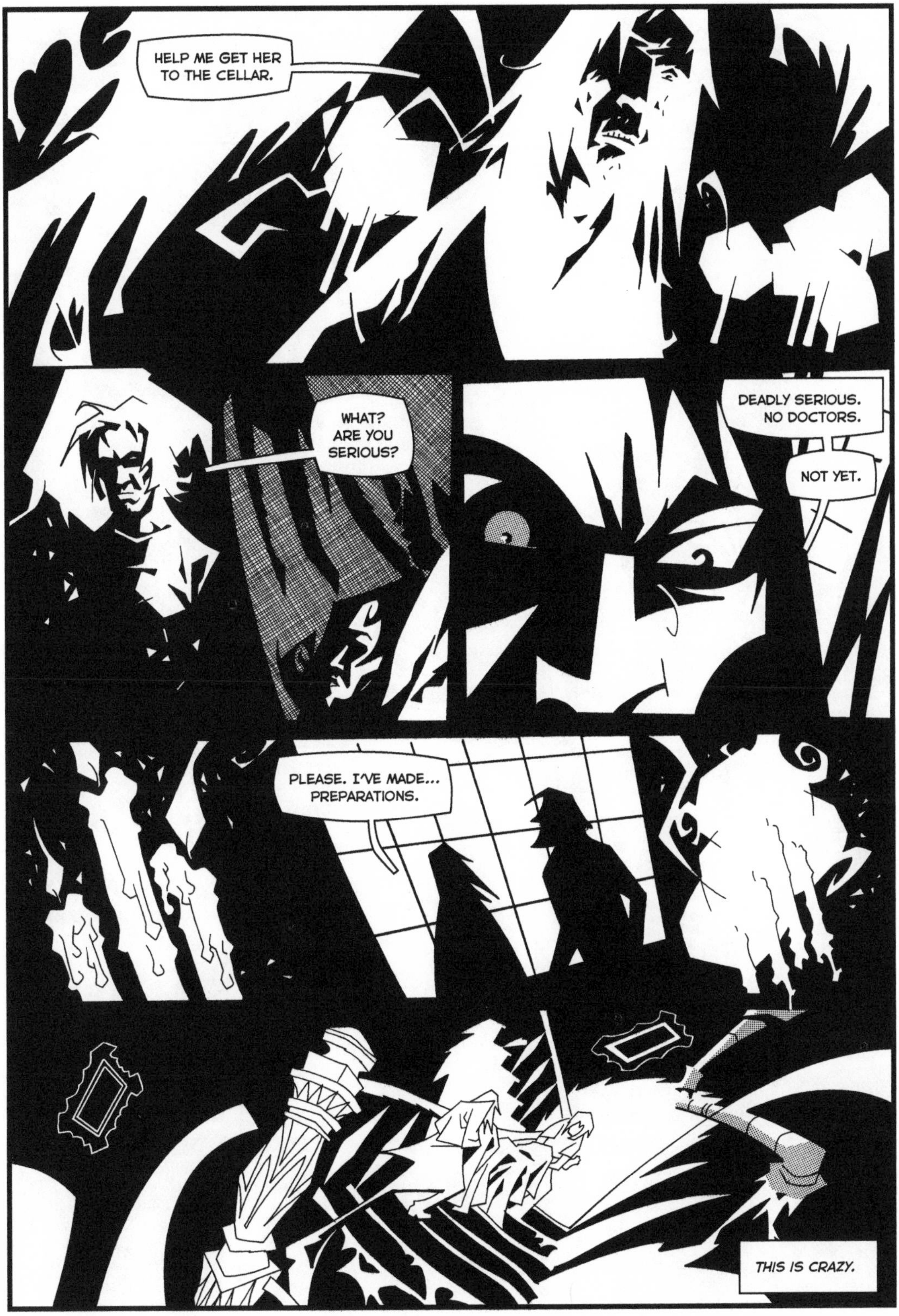
HELP ME GET HER TO THE CELLAR.
WHAT? ARE YOU SERIOUS?
DEADLY SERIOUS. NO DOCTORS.
NOT YET.
PLEASE. I'VE MADE... PREPARATIONS.
THIS IS CRAZY.

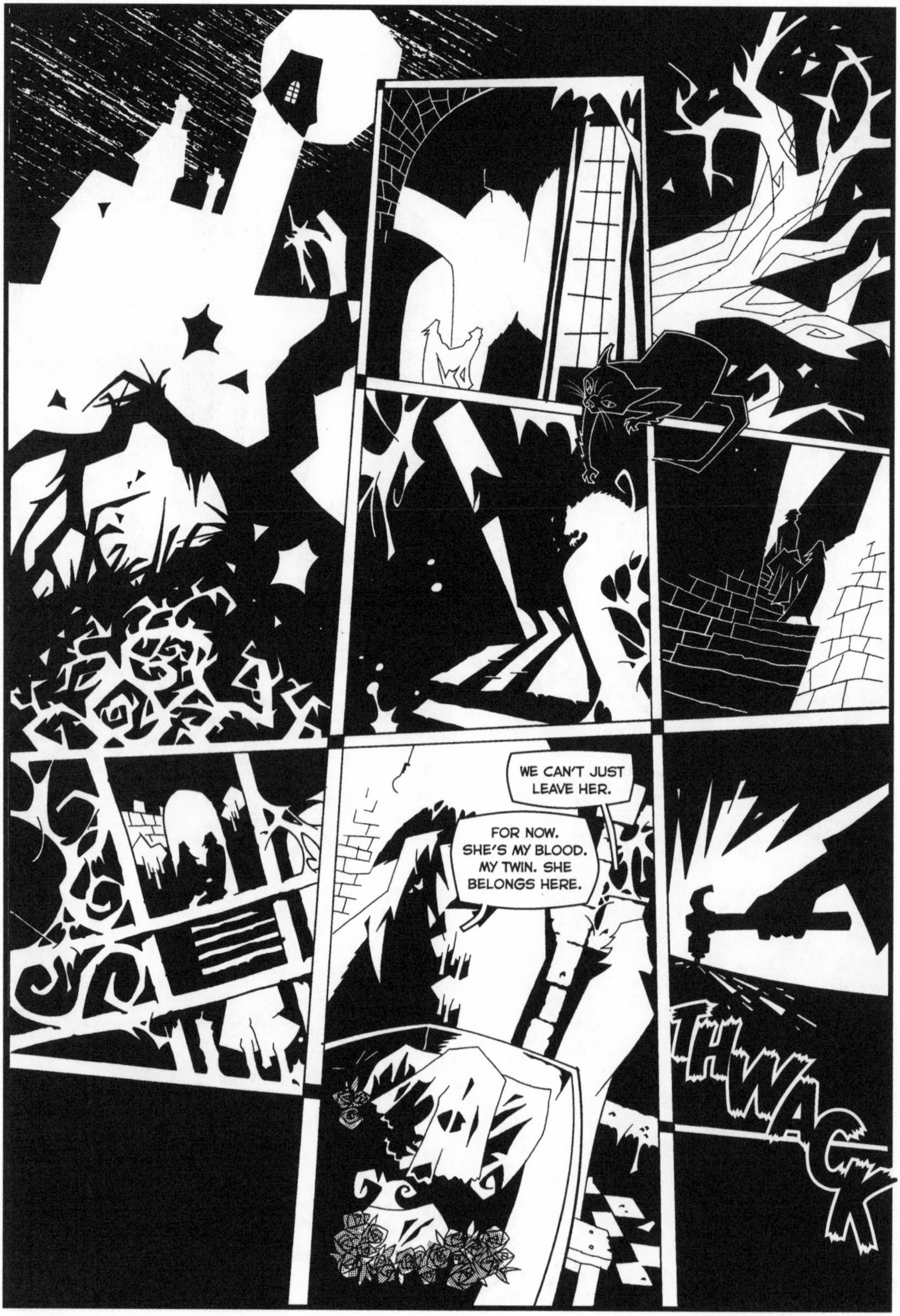
WE CAN'T JUST LEAVE HER.
FOR NOW. SHE'S MY BLOOD. MY TWIN. SHE BELONGS HERE.
THWACK

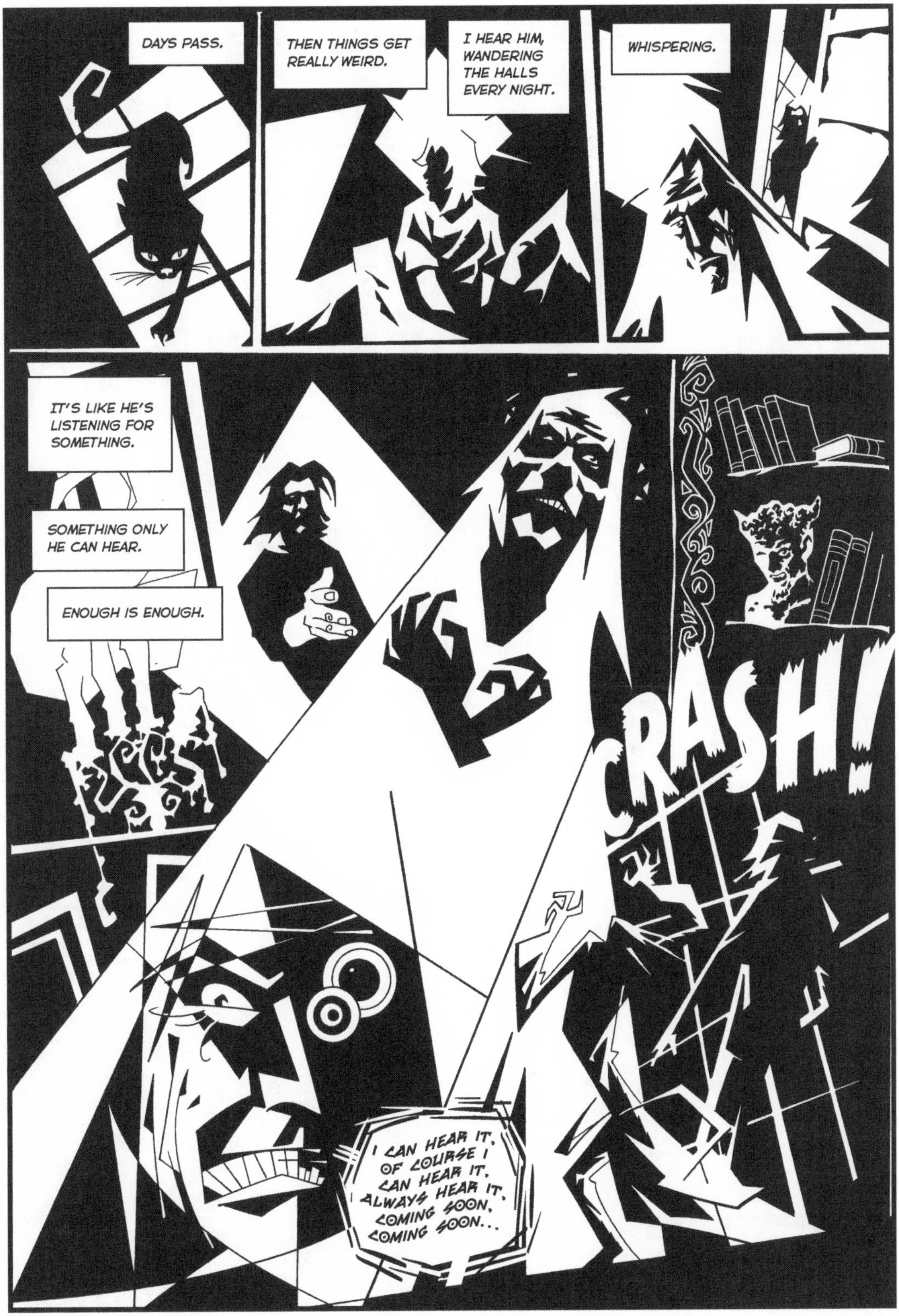
DAYS PASS.
THEN THINGS GET REALLY WEIRD.
I HEAR HIM, WANDERING THE HALLS EVERY NIGHT.
WHISPERING.
IT'S LIKE HE'S LISTENING FOR SOMETHING.
SOMETHING ONLY HE CAN HEAR.
ENOUGH IS ENOUGH.
CRASH!
I CAN HEAR IT. OF COURSE I CAN HEAR IT. ALWAYS HEAR IT. COMING SOON. COMING SOON...

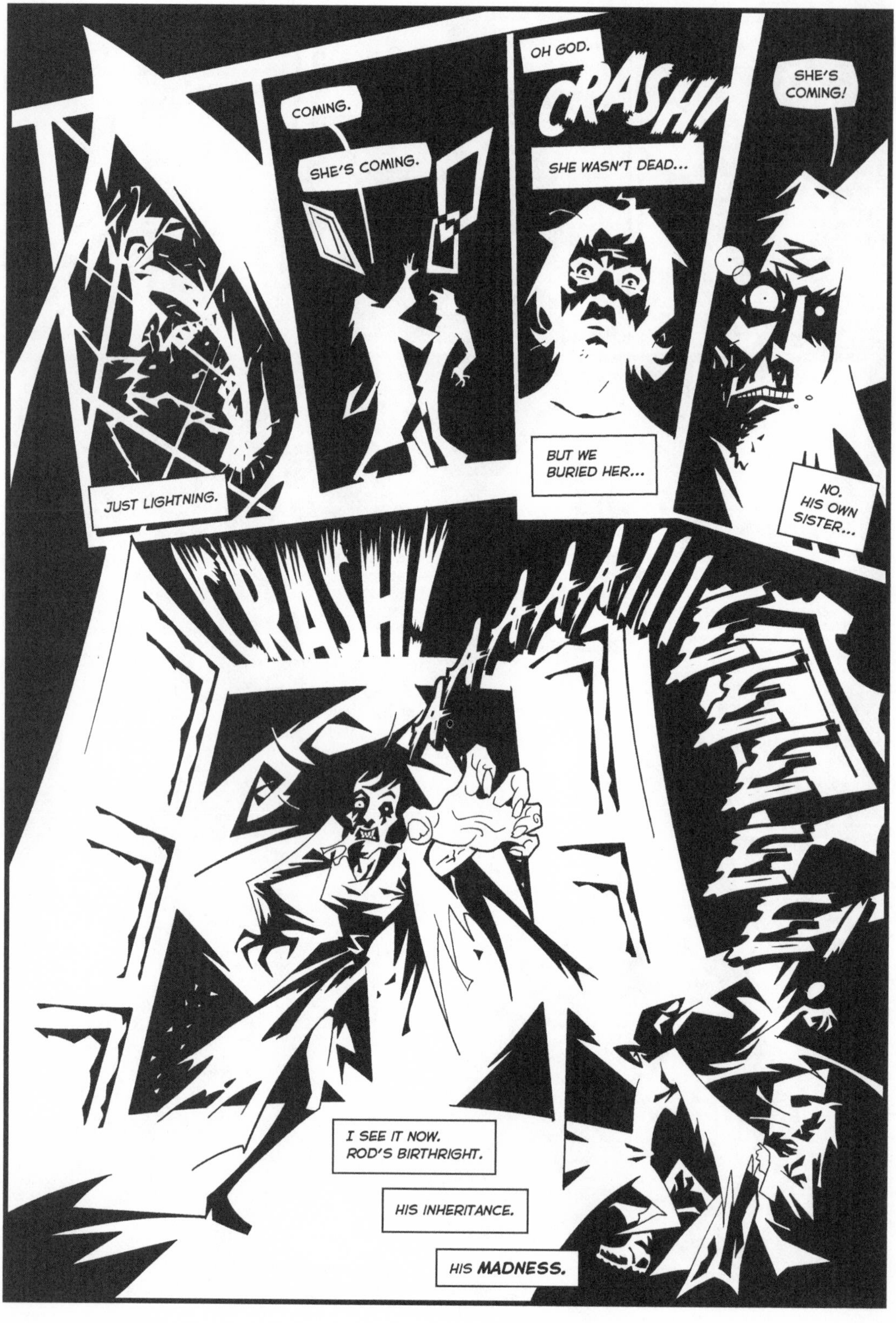
JUST LIGHTNING.
COMING.
SHE'S COMING.
OH GOD.
CRASH!
SHE WASN'T DEAD...
BUT WE BURIED HER...
SHE'S COMING!
NO. HIS OWN SISTER...
CRASH!
I SEE IT NOW. ROD'S BIRTHRIGHT.
HIS INHERITANCE.
HIS **MADNESS.**

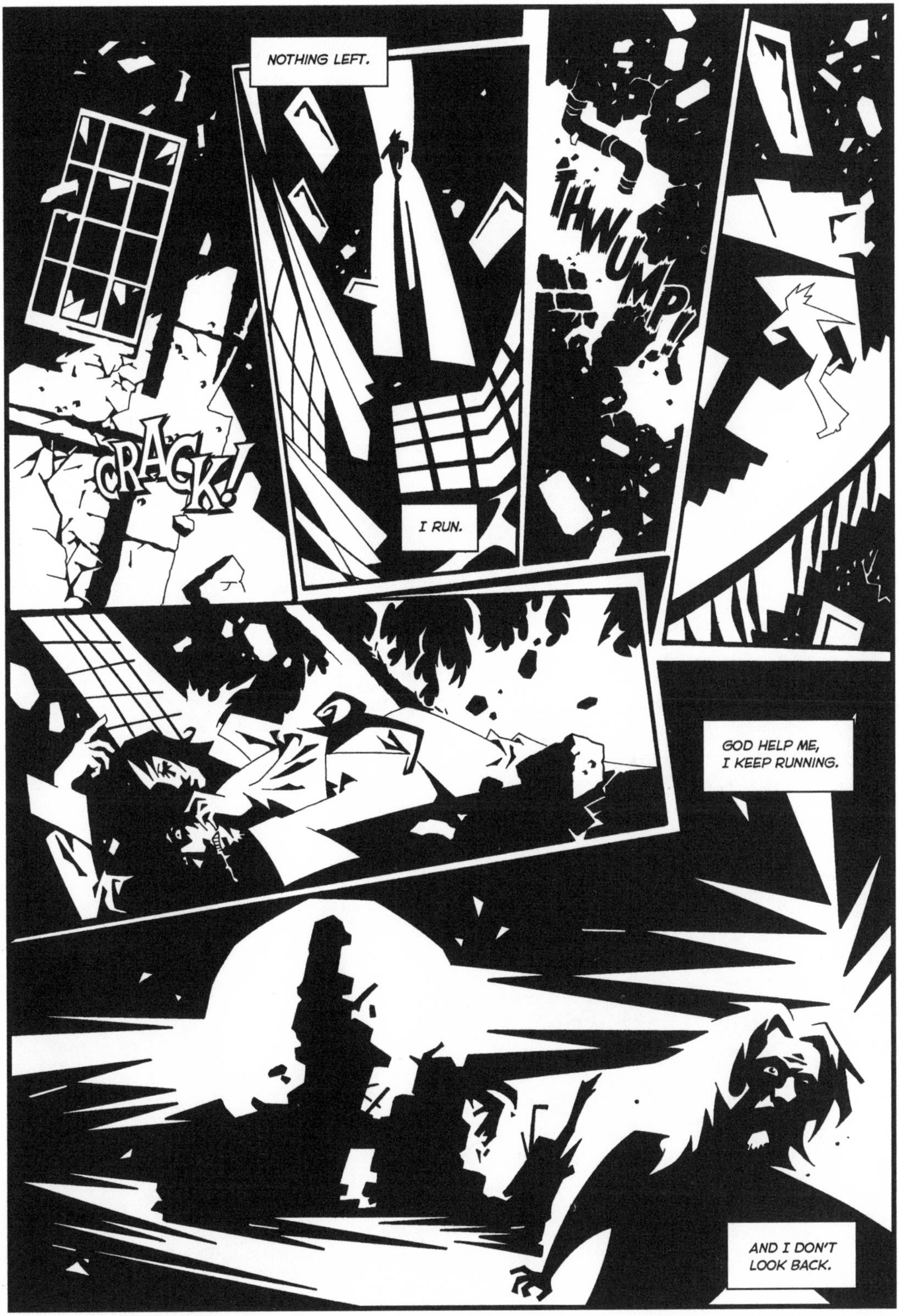
CRACK!
NOTHING LEFT.
I RUN.
THWUMP!!
GOD HELP ME,
I KEEP RUNNING.
AND I DON'T
LOOK BACK.

THE BLACK CAT

Adapted by Leah Moore and John Reppion
Art by James Fletcher

Often compared to *The Tell-Tale Heart*, this twisting tale of guilt and violence explores one of Poe's recurring themes—something he described as man's natural perverseness or "the human thirst for self-torture."

Poe's narrative device of a man committing what he believes to be the perfect crime, whether against human or animal, only to find himself unraveled by his own emotional breakdown and omens from beyond the grave, would provide the backbone for many classic horror comics of the 1950s, in particular EC Comics' *Tales from the Crypt*.

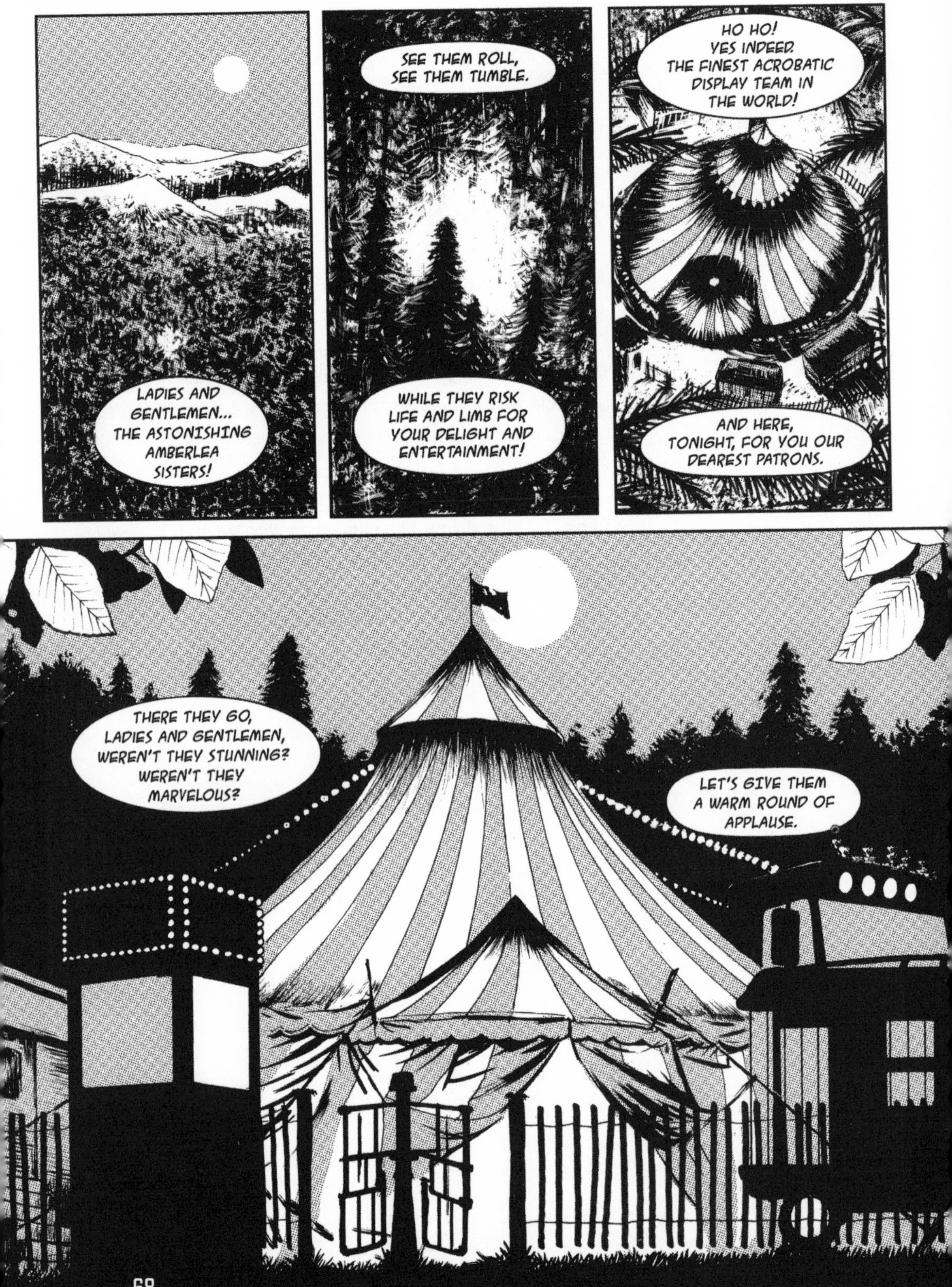
LADIES AND GENTLEMEN... THE ASTONISHING AMBERLEA SISTERS!
SEE THEM ROLL, SEE THEM TUMBLE.
WHILE THEY RISK LIFE AND LIMB FOR YOUR DELIGHT AND ENTERTAINMENT!
HO HO! YES INDEED. THE FINEST ACROBATIC DISPLAY TEAM IN THE WORLD!
AND HERE, TONIGHT, FOR YOU OUR DEAREST PATRONS.
THERE THEY GO, LADIES AND GENTLEMEN, WEREN'T THEY STUNNING? WEREN'T THEY MARVELOUS?
LET'S GIVE THEM A WARM ROUND OF APPLAUSE.

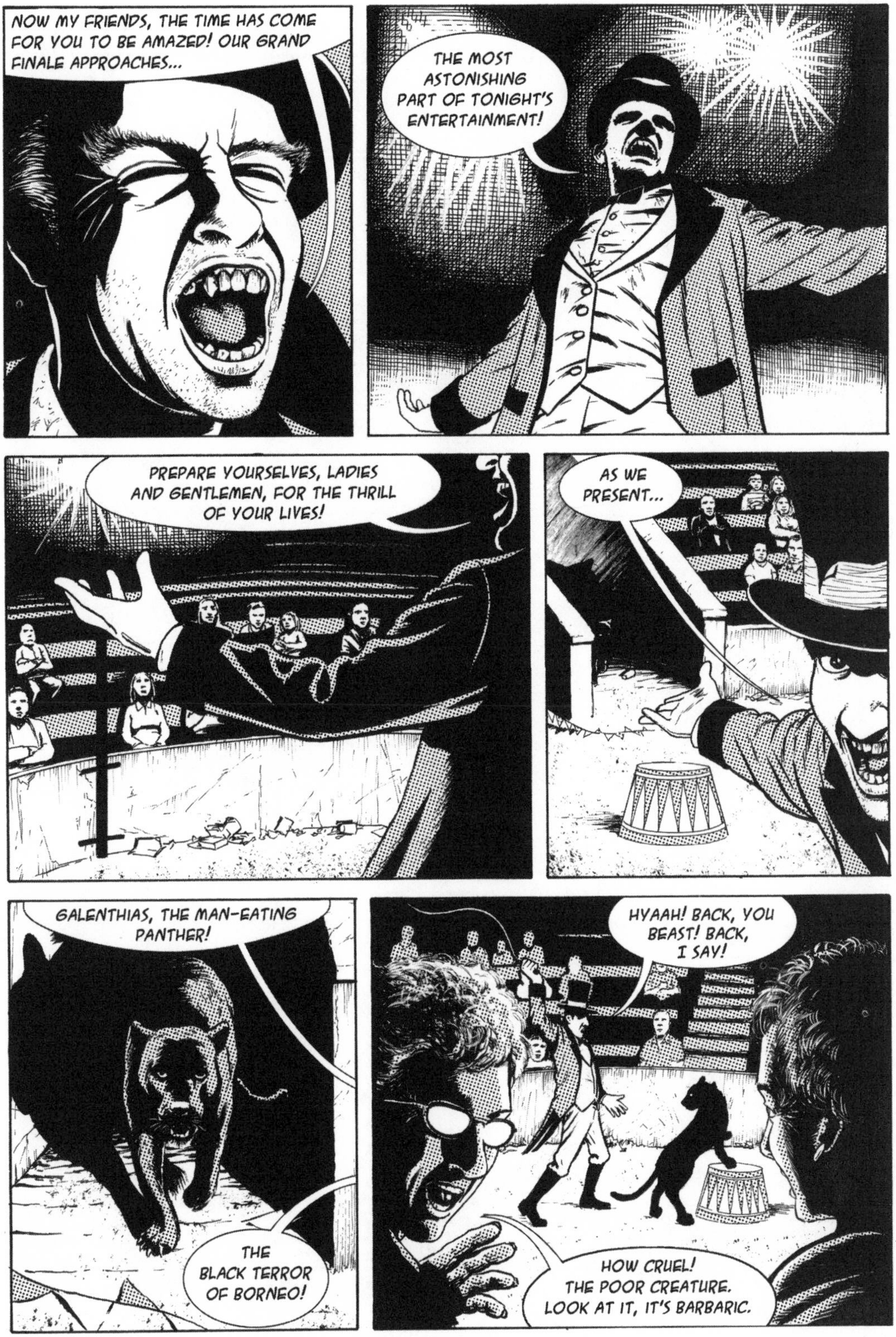
NOW MY FRIENDS, THE TIME HAS COME FOR YOU TO BE AMAZED! OUR GRAND FINALE APPROACHES...
THE MOST ASTONISHING PART OF TONIGHT'S ENTERTAINMENT!
PREPARE YOURSELVES, LADIES AND GENTLEMEN, FOR THE THRILL OF YOUR LIVES!
AS WE PRESENT...
GALENTHIAS, THE MAN-EATING PANTHER!
THE BLACK TERROR OF BORNEO!
HYAAH! BACK, YOU BEAST! BACK, I SAY!
HOW CRUEL! THE POOR CREATURE. LOOK AT IT, IT'S BARBARIC.

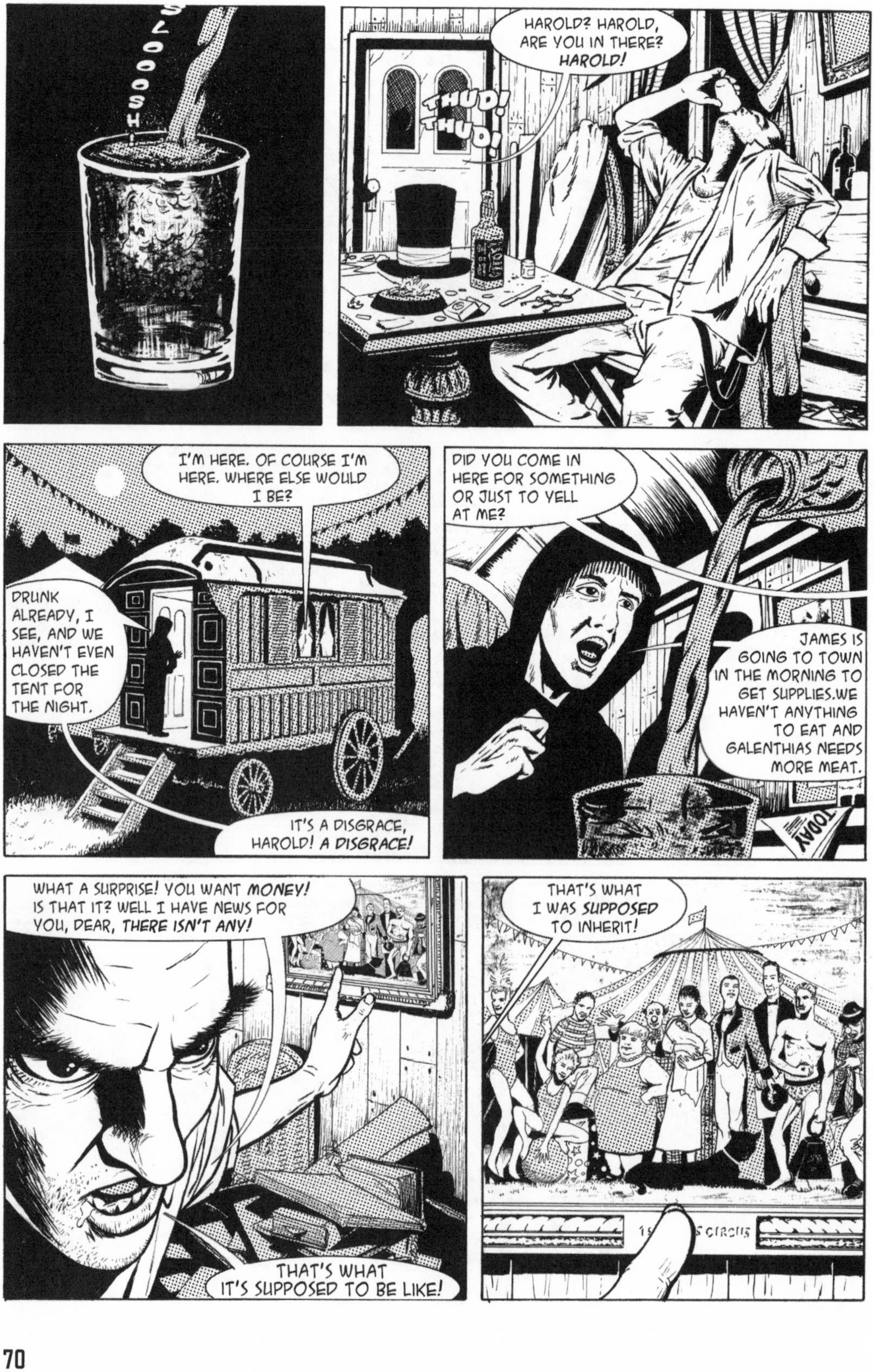
SLOOOOSH!
HAROLD? HAROLD, ARE YOU IN THERE? *HAROLD!*
THUD! THUD!
I'M HERE. OF COURSE I'M HERE. WHERE ELSE WOULD I BE?
DRUNK ALREADY, I SEE, AND WE HAVEN'T EVEN CLOSED THE TENT FOR THE NIGHT.
IT'S A DISGRACE, HAROLD! *A DISGRACE!*
DID YOU COME IN HERE FOR SOMETHING OR JUST TO YELL AT ME?
JAMES IS GOING TO TOWN IN THE MORNING TO GET SUPPLIES.WE HAVEN'T ANYTHING TO EAT AND GALENTHIAS NEEDS MORE MEAT.
TODAY
WHAT A SURPRISE! YOU WANT *MONEY!* IS THAT IT? WELL I HAVE NEWS FOR YOU, DEAR, *THERE ISN'T ANY!*
THAT'S WHAT IT'S SUPPOSED TO BE LIKE!
THAT'S WHAT I WAS *SUPPOSED* TO INHERIT!

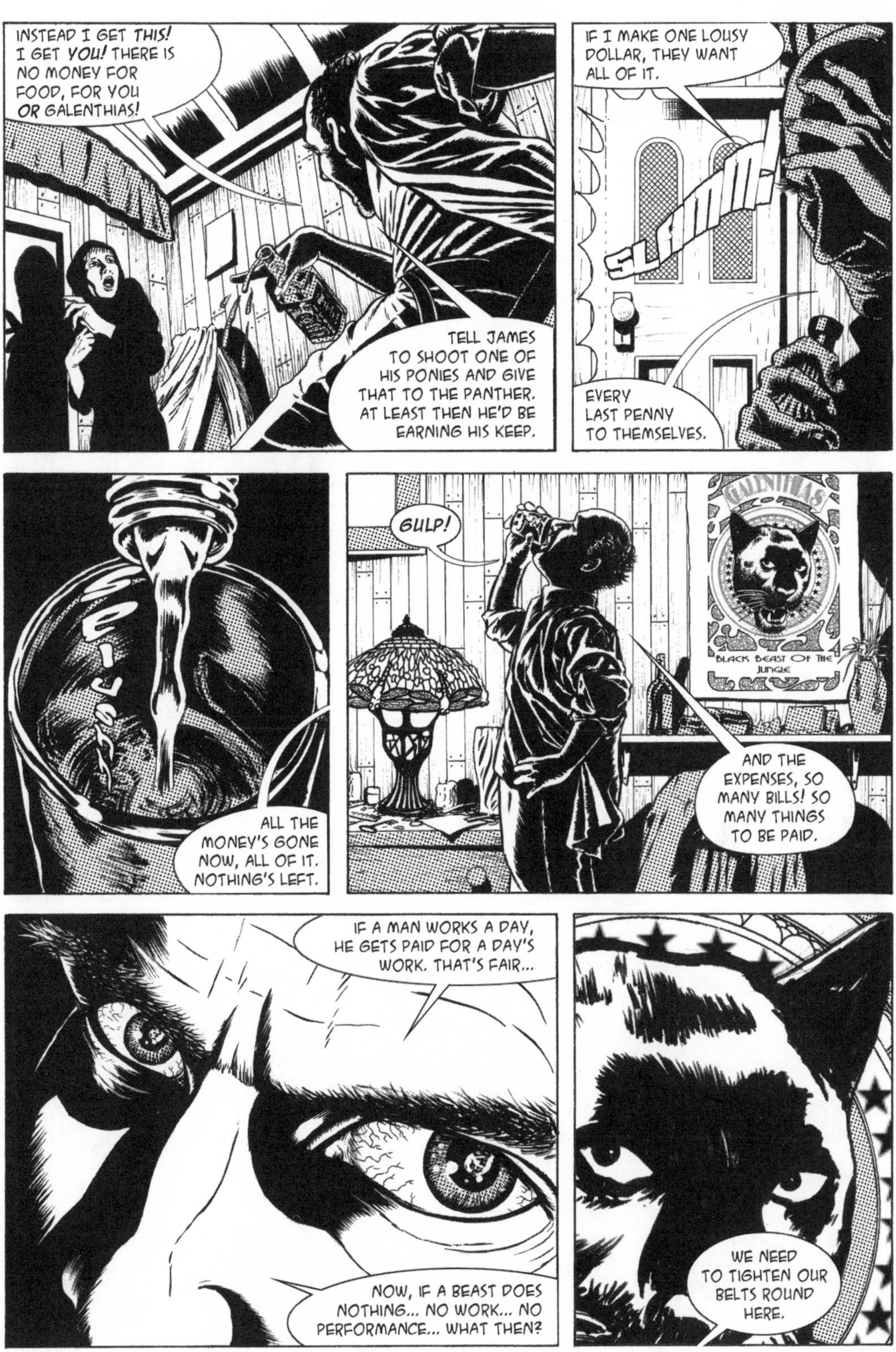
INSTEAD I GET THIS! I GET YOU! THERE IS NO MONEY FOR FOOD, FOR YOU OR GALENTHIAS!
TELL JAMES TO SHOOT ONE OF HIS PONIES AND GIVE THAT TO THE PANTHER. AT LEAST THEN HE'D BE EARNING HIS KEEP.
IF I MAKE ONE LOUSY DOLLAR, THEY WANT ALL OF IT.
SLAMM!
EVERY LAST PENNY TO THEMSELVES.
ALL THE MONEY'S GONE NOW, ALL OF IT. NOTHING'S LEFT.
GULP!
GALENTHIAS
BLACK BEAST OF THE JUNGLE
AND THE EXPENSES, SO MANY BILLS! SO MANY THINGS TO BE PAID.
IF A MAN WORKS A DAY, HE GETS PAID FOR A DAY'S WORK. THAT'S FAIR...
NOW, IF A BEAST DOES NOTHING... NO WORK... NO PERFORMANCE... WHAT THEN?
WE NEED TO TIGHTEN OUR BELTS ROUND HERE.

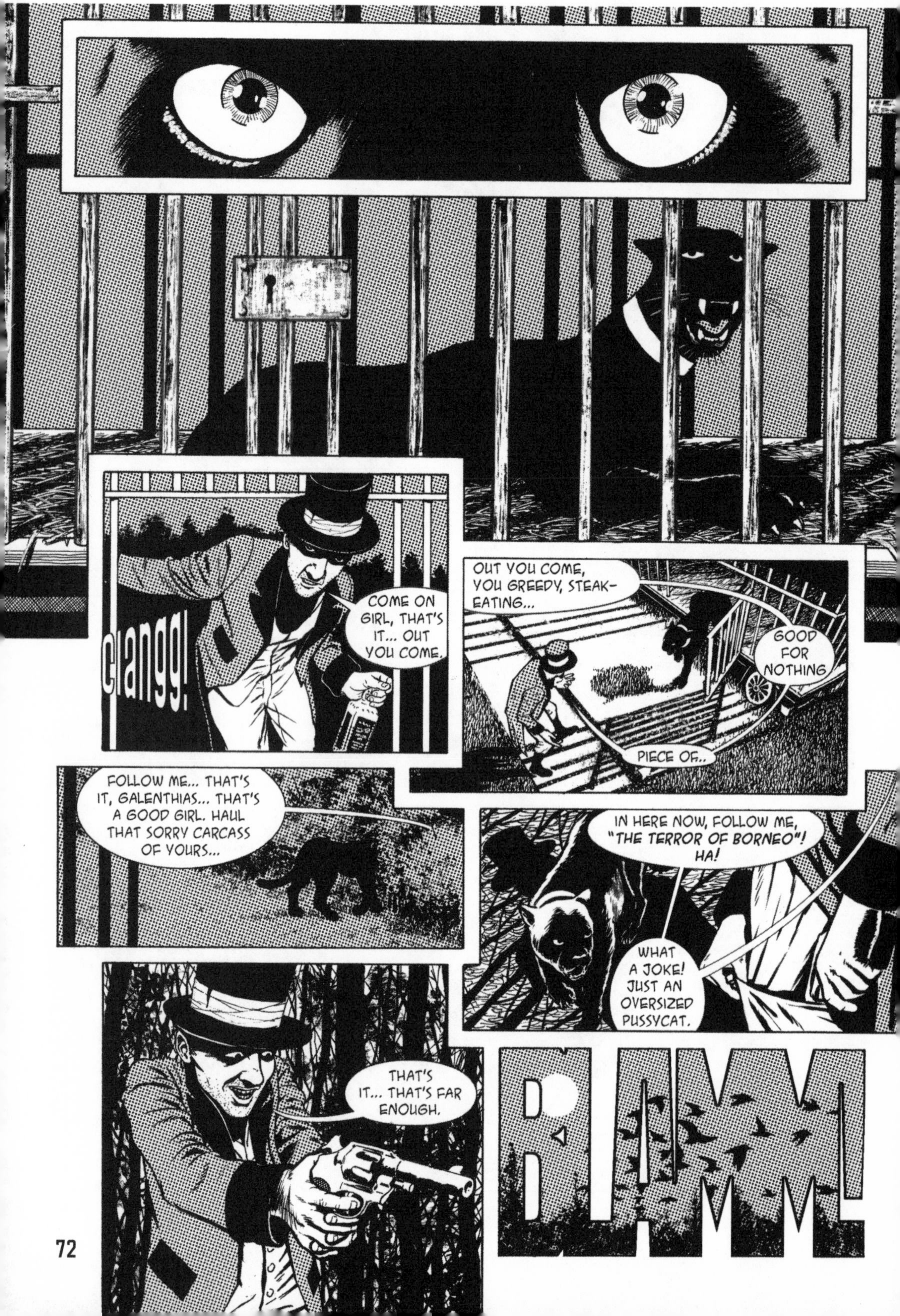
CLANGG!
COME ON GIRL, THAT'S IT... OUT YOU COME.
OUT YOU COME, YOU GREEDY, STEAK-EATING...
GOOD FOR NOTHING
PIECE OF..
FOLLOW ME... THAT'S IT, GALENTHIAS... THAT'S A GOOD GIRL. HAUL THAT SORRY CARCASS OF YOURS...
IN HERE NOW, FOLLOW ME, "THE TERROR OF BORNEO"! HA!
WHAT A JOKE! JUST AN OVERSIZED PUSSYCAT.
THAT'S IT... THAT'S FAR ENOUGH.
BLAMM!

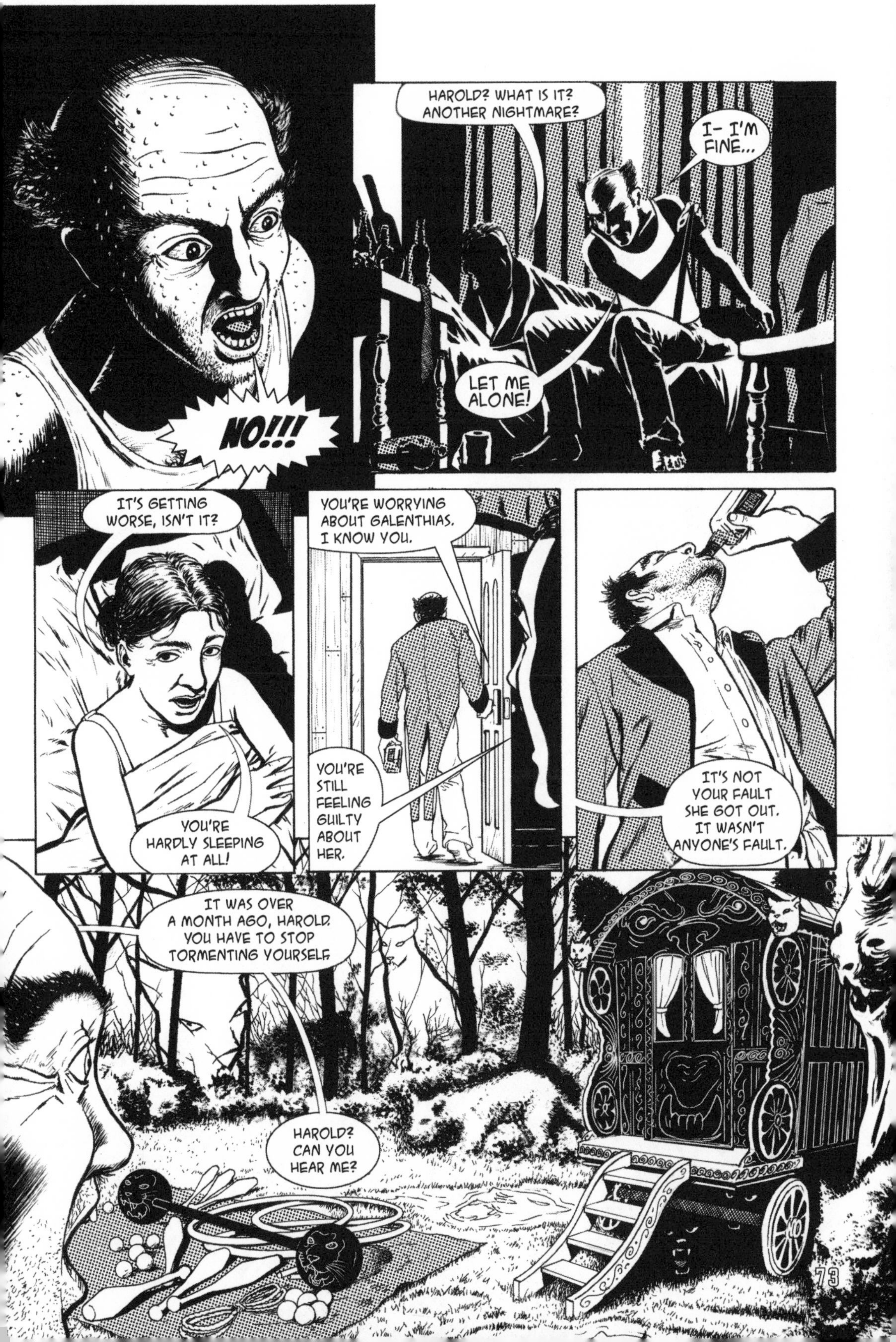
NO!!!
HAROLD? WHAT IS IT? ANOTHER NIGHTMARE?
I- I'M FINE...
LET ME ALONE!
IT'S GETTING WORSE, ISN'T IT?
YOU'RE HARDLY SLEEPING AT ALL!
YOU'RE WORRYING ABOUT GALENTHIAS. I KNOW YOU.
YOU'RE STILL FEELING GUILTY ABOUT HER.
IT'S NOT YOUR FAULT SHE GOT OUT. IT WASN'T ANYONE'S FAULT.
IT WAS OVER A MONTH AGO, HAROLD. YOU HAVE TO STOP TORMENTING YOURSELF.
HAROLD? CAN YOU HEAR ME?

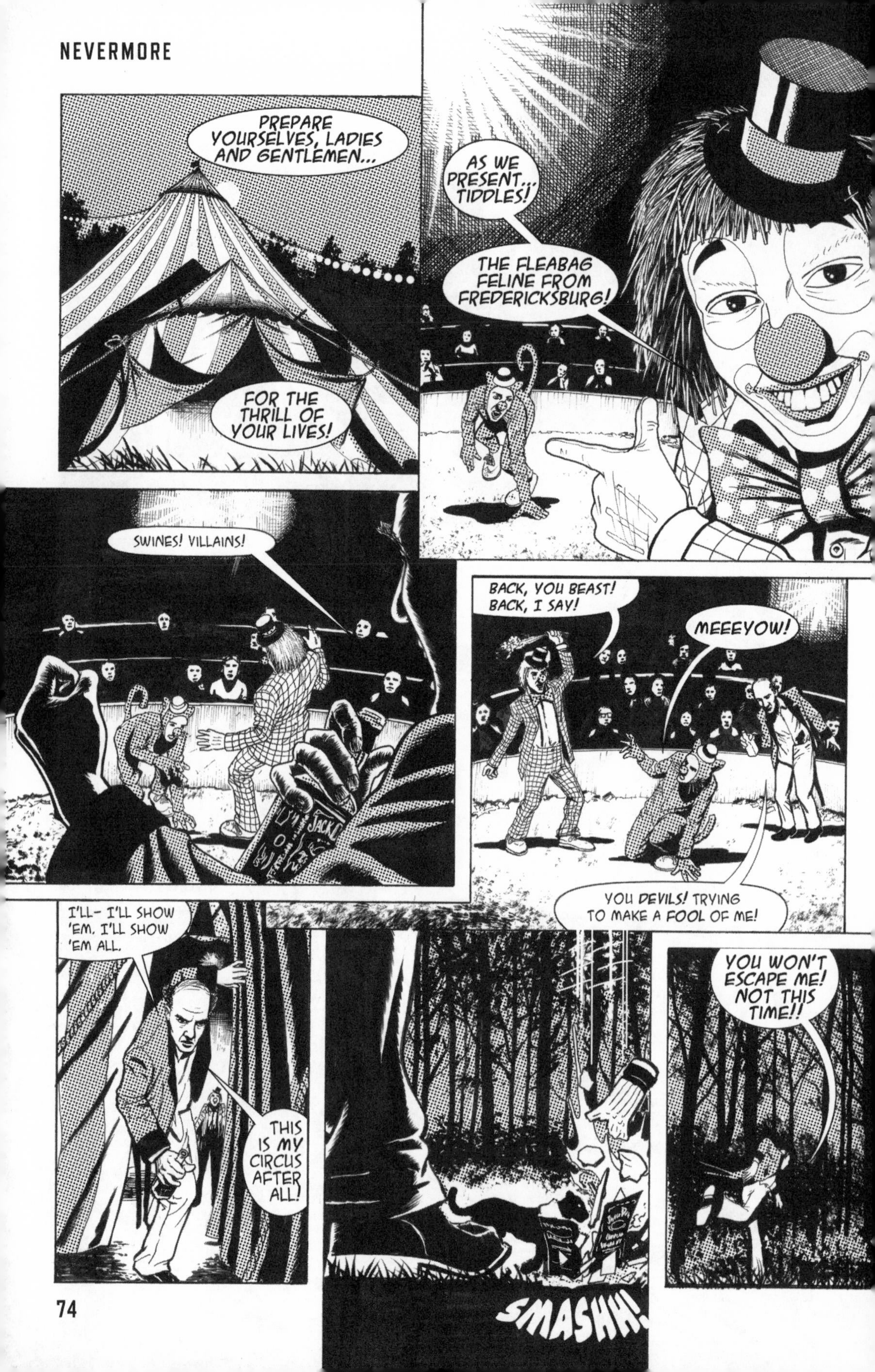
PREPARE YOURSELVES, LADIES AND GENTLEMEN...
FOR THE THRILL OF YOUR LIVES!
AS WE PRESENT... TIDDLES!
THE FLEABAG FELINE FROM FREDERICKSBURG!
SWINES! VILLAINS!
BACK, YOU BEAST! BACK, I SAY!
MEEEYOW!
YOU DEVILS! TRYING TO MAKE A FOOL OF ME!
I'LL- I'LL SHOW 'EM. I'LL SHOW 'EM ALL.
THIS IS MY CIRCUS AFTER ALL!
YOU WON'T ESCAPE ME! NOT THIS TIME!!
SMASHH!

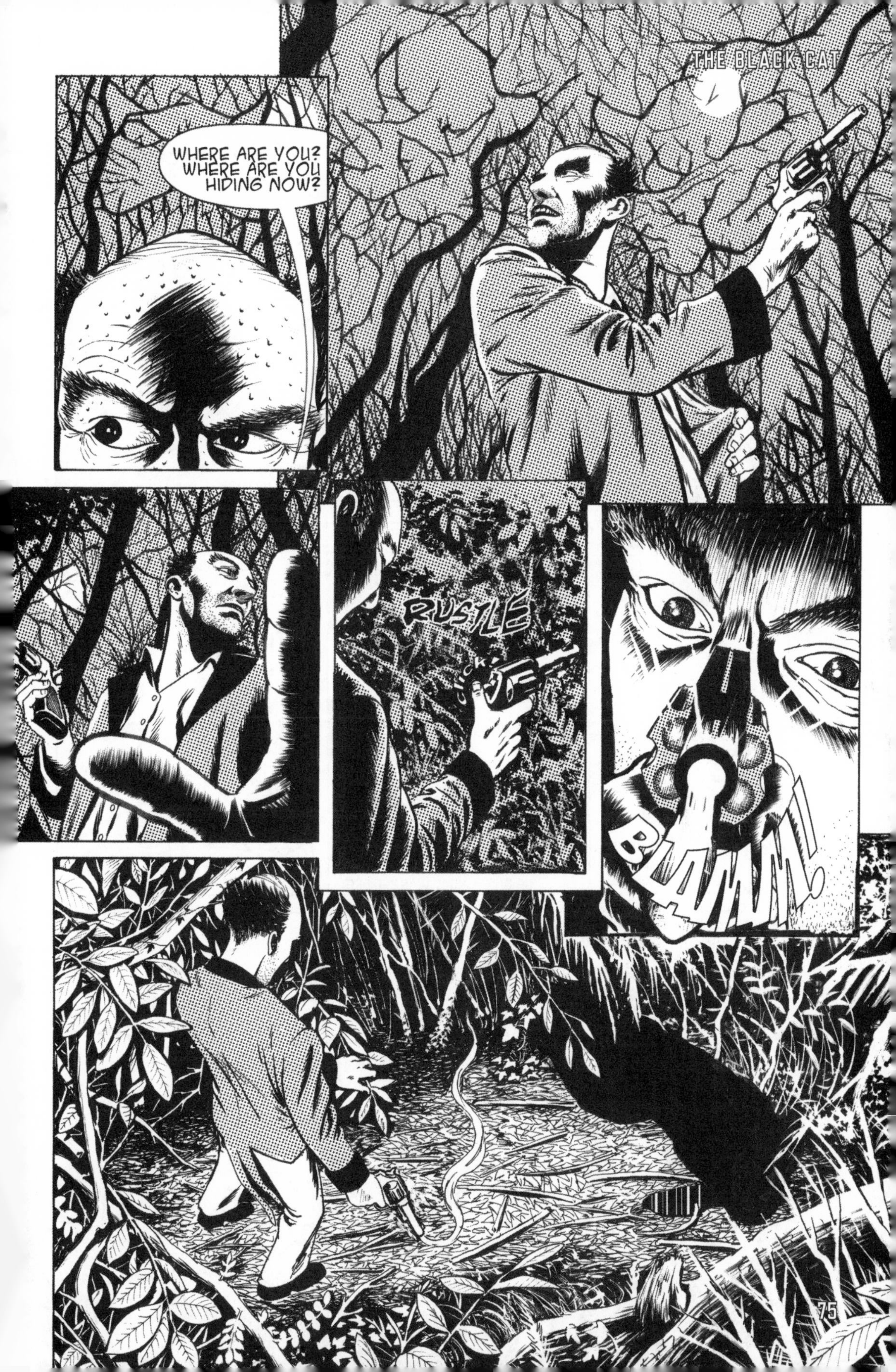
WHERE ARE YOU?
WHERE ARE YOU HIDING NOW?
RUSTLE
CLICK!
BLAMM!

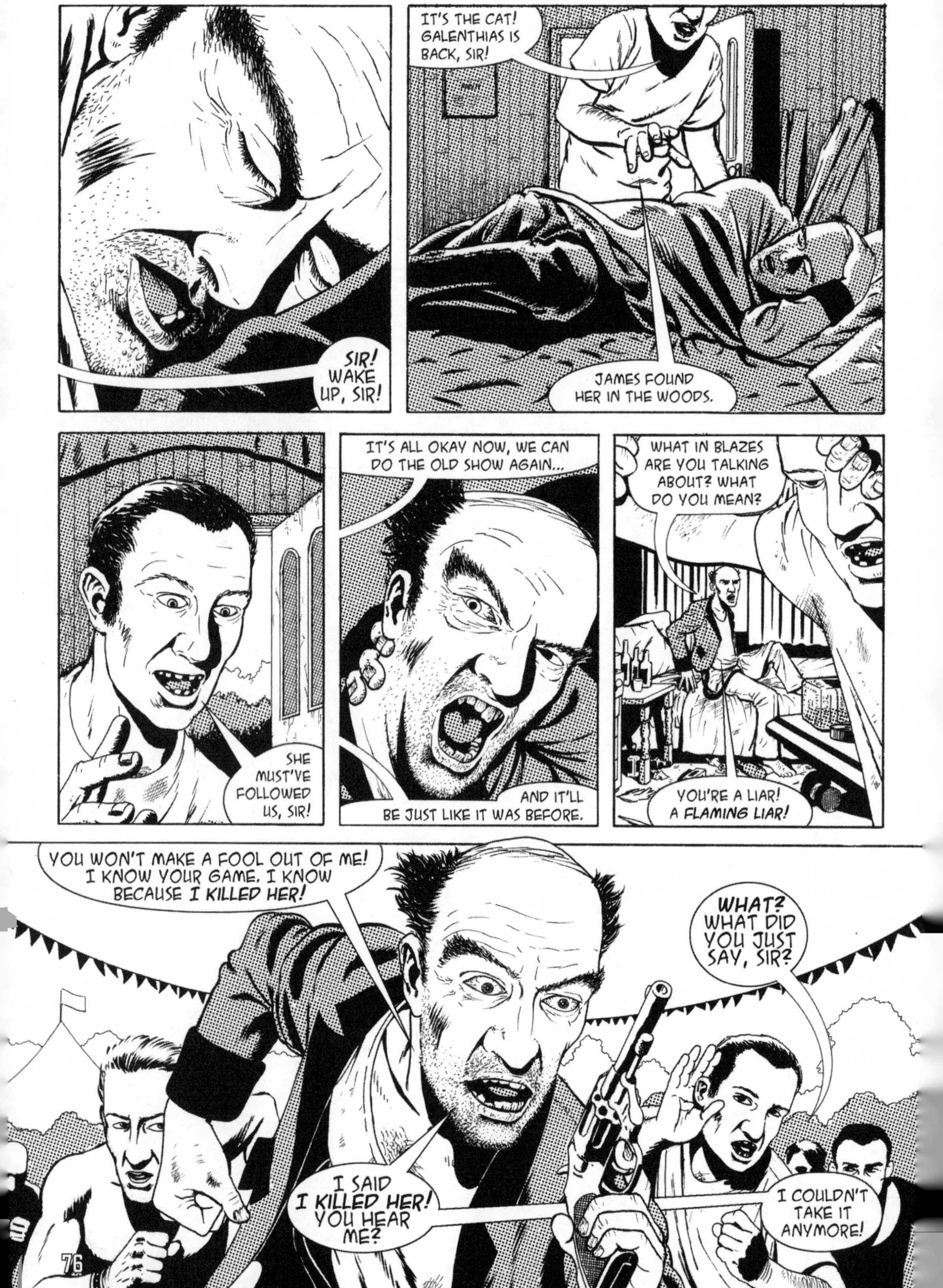
SIR! WAKE UP, SIR!
IT'S THE CAT! GALENTHIAS IS BACK, SIR!
JAMES FOUND HER IN THE WOODS.
SHE MUST'VE FOLLOWED US, SIR!
IT'S ALL OKAY NOW, WE CAN DO THE OLD SHOW AGAIN...
AND IT'LL BE JUST LIKE IT WAS BEFORE.
WHAT IN BLAZES ARE YOU TALKING ABOUT? WHAT DO YOU MEAN?
YOU'RE A LIAR! A FLAMING LIAR!
YOU WON'T MAKE A FOOL OUT OF ME! I KNOW YOUR GAME. I KNOW BECAUSE I KILLED HER!
WHAT? WHAT DID YOU JUST SAY, SIR?
I SAID I KILLED HER! YOU HEAR ME?
I COULDN'T TAKE IT ANYMORE!

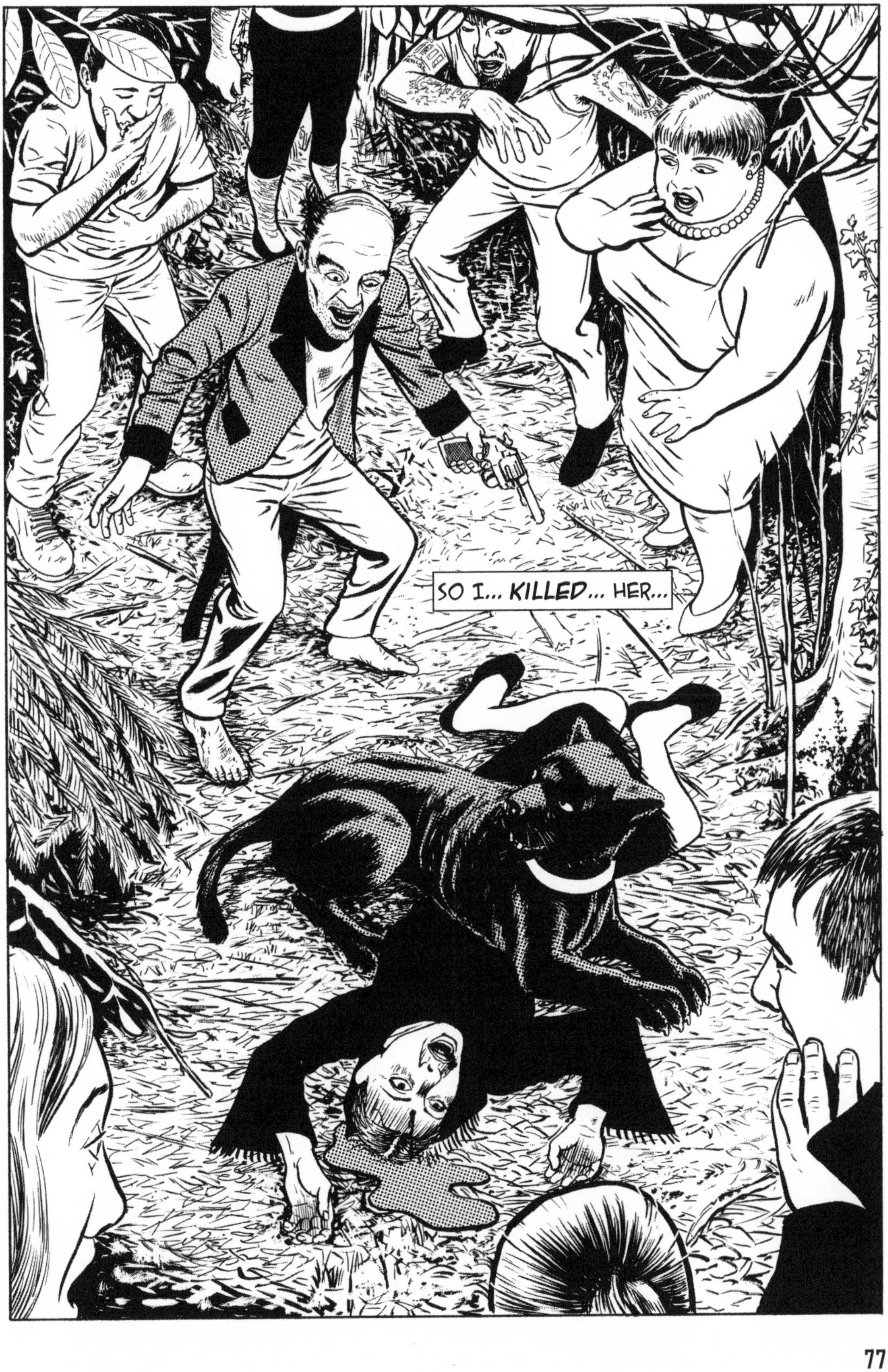
SO I... KILLED... HER...

THE OVAL PORTRAIT

Adapted by David Berner
Art by Natalie Sandells

The Oval Portrait is one of Poe's shortest stories.
With its story within a story and ruminations on reality
versus art, it could almost be described as an early example of
postmodernism.

Though the story was originally written as a much longer piece
entitled *Life in Death*, Poe excised a lengthy introduction that
explained that the narrator had been taking opium to relieve the
pain of a mysterious wound, presumably reasoning that such a
detail would lead readers to think the story was hallucinatory.

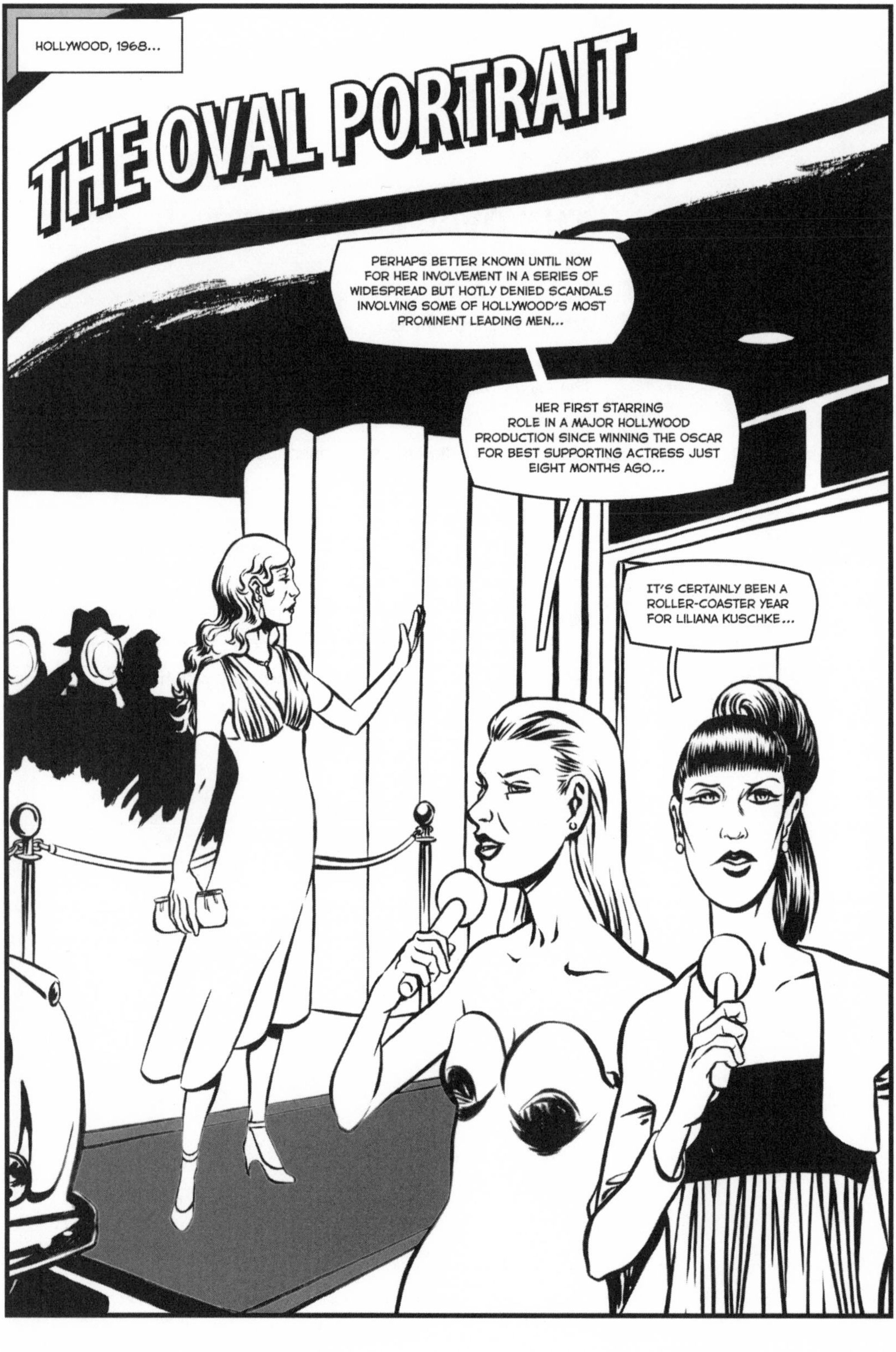
HOLLYWOOD, 1968...
THE OVAL PORTRAIT
PERHAPS BETTER KNOWN UNTIL NOW FOR HER INVOLVEMENT IN A SERIES OF WIDESPREAD BUT HOTLY DENIED SCANDALS INVOLVING SOME OF HOLLYWOOD'S MOST PROMINENT LEADING MEN...
HER FIRST STARRING ROLE IN A MAJOR HOLLYWOOD PRODUCTION SINCE WINNING THE OSCAR FOR BEST SUPPORTING ACTRESS JUST EIGHT MONTHS AGO...
IT'S CERTAINLY BEEN A ROLLER-COASTER YEAR FOR LILIANA KUSCHKE...

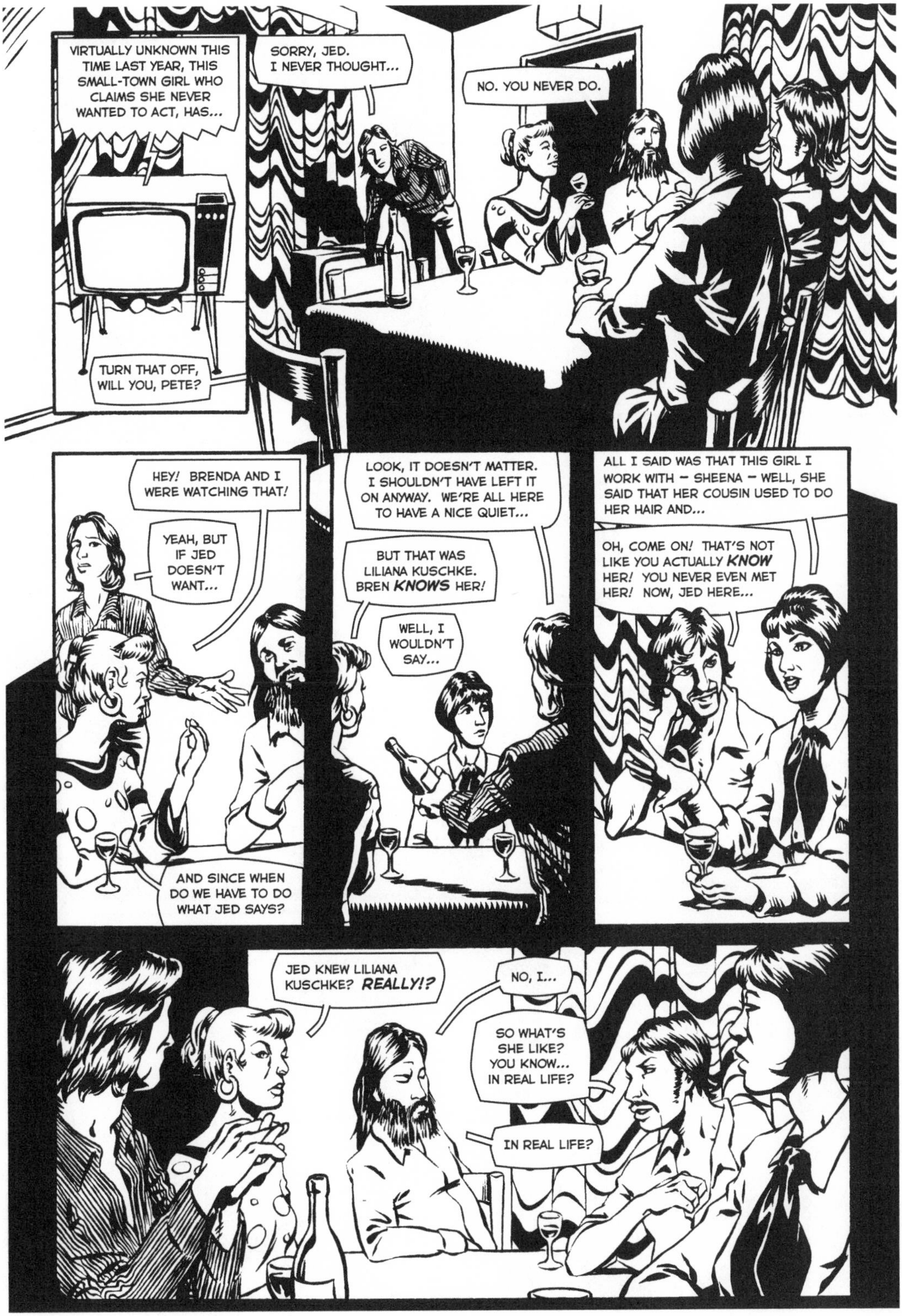
VIRTUALLY UNKNOWN THIS TIME LAST YEAR, THIS SMALL-TOWN GIRL WHO CLAIMS SHE NEVER WANTED TO ACT, HAS...
SORRY, JED. I NEVER THOUGHT...
NO. YOU NEVER DO.
TURN THAT OFF, WILL YOU, PETE?
HEY! BRENDA AND I WERE WATCHING THAT!
YEAH, BUT IF JED DOESN'T WANT...
AND SINCE WHEN DO WE HAVE TO DO WHAT JED SAYS?
LOOK, IT DOESN'T MATTER. I SHOULDN'T HAVE LEFT IT ON ANYWAY. WE'RE ALL HERE TO HAVE A NICE QUIET...
BUT THAT WAS LILIANA KUSCHKE. BREN ***KNOWS*** HER!
WELL, I WOULDN'T SAY...
ALL I SAID WAS THAT THIS GIRL I WORK WITH – SHEENA – WELL, SHE SAID THAT HER COUSIN USED TO DO HER HAIR AND...
OH, COME ON! THAT'S NOT LIKE YOU ACTUALLY ***KNOW*** HER! YOU NEVER EVEN MET HER! NOW, JED HERE...
JED KNEW LILIANA KUSCHKE? ***REALLY!?***
NO, I...
SO WHAT'S SHE LIKE? YOU KNOW... IN REAL LIFE?
IN REAL LIFE?

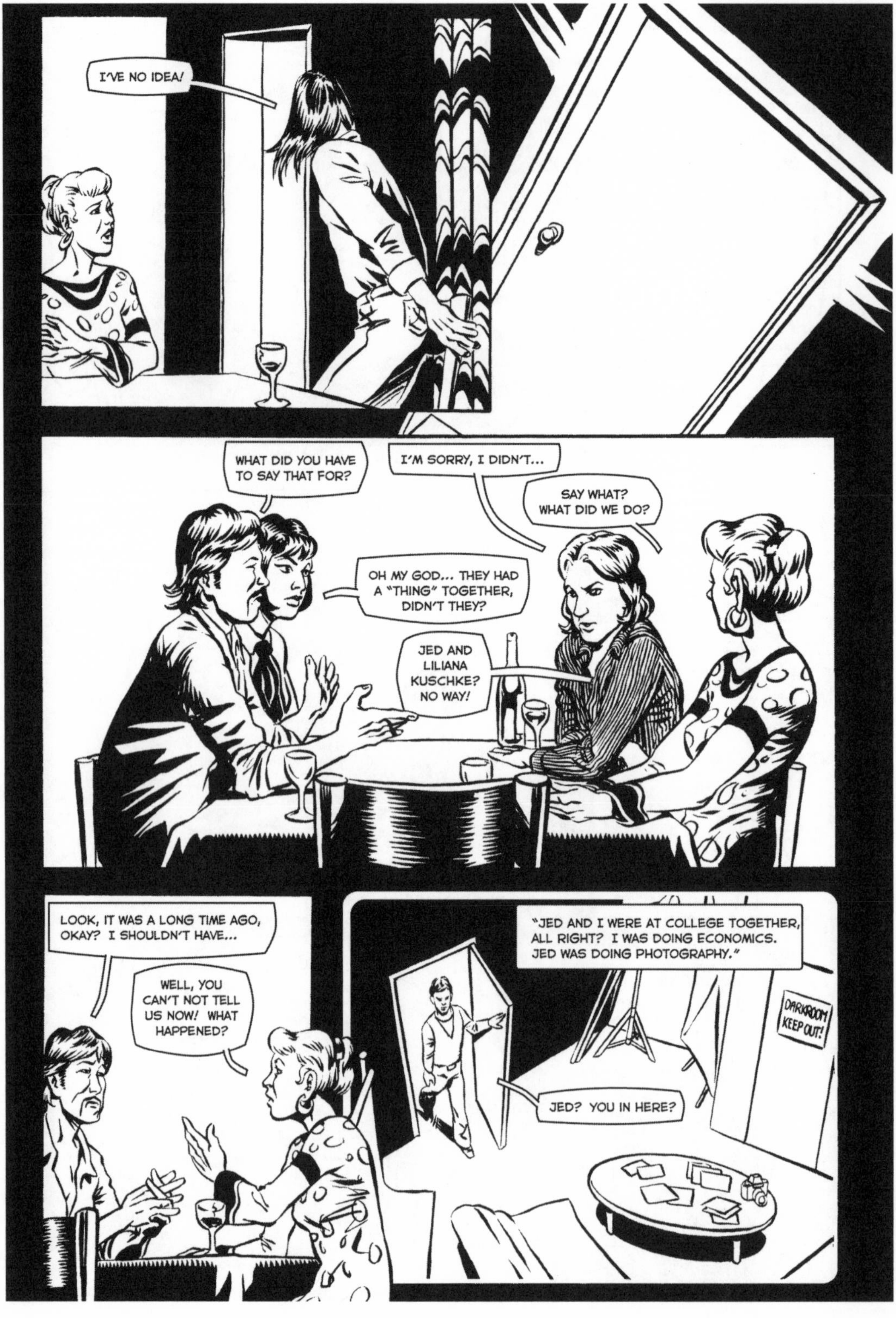
I'VE NO IDEA!
WHAT DID YOU HAVE TO SAY THAT FOR?
I'M SORRY, I DIDN'T...
SAY WHAT? WHAT DID WE DO?
OH MY GOD... THEY HAD A "THING" TOGETHER, DIDN'T THEY?
JED AND LILIANA KUSCHKE? NO WAY!
LOOK, IT WAS A LONG TIME AGO, OKAY? I SHOULDN'T HAVE...
WELL, YOU CAN'T NOT TELL US NOW! WHAT HAPPENED?
"JED AND I WERE AT COLLEGE TOGETHER, ALL RIGHT? I WAS DOING ECONOMICS. JED WAS DOING PHOTOGRAPHY."
DARKROOM KEEP OUT!
JED? YOU IN HERE?

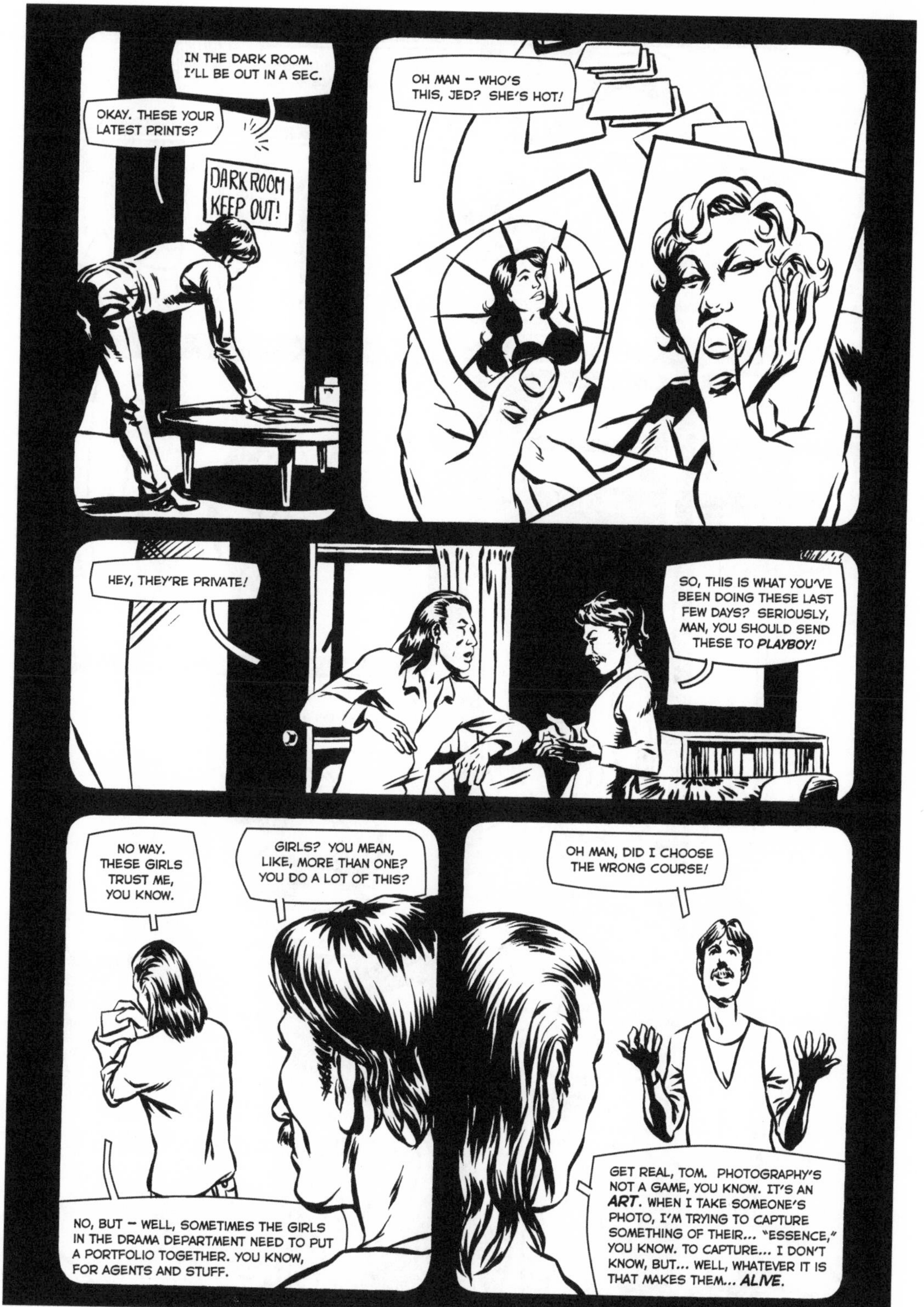
IN THE DARK ROOM. I'LL BE OUT IN A SEC.
OKAY. THESE YOUR LATEST PRINTS?
DARK ROOM KEEP OUT!
OH MAN – WHO'S THIS, JED? SHE'S HOT!
HEY, THEY'RE PRIVATE!
SO, THIS IS WHAT YOU'VE BEEN DOING THESE LAST FEW DAYS? SERIOUSLY, MAN, YOU SHOULD SEND THESE TO *PLAYBOY*!
NO WAY. THESE GIRLS TRUST ME, YOU KNOW.
GIRLS? YOU MEAN, LIKE, MORE THAN ONE? YOU DO A LOT OF THIS?
NO, BUT – WELL, SOMETIMES THE GIRLS IN THE DRAMA DEPARTMENT NEED TO PUT A PORTFOLIO TOGETHER. YOU KNOW, FOR AGENTS AND STUFF.
OH MAN, DID I CHOOSE THE WRONG COURSE!
GET REAL, TOM. PHOTOGRAPHY'S NOT A GAME, YOU KNOW. IT'S AN **ART**. WHEN I TAKE SOMEONE'S PHOTO, I'M TRYING TO CAPTURE SOMETHING OF THEIR... "ESSENCE," YOU KNOW. TO CAPTURE... I DON'T KNOW, BUT... WELL, WHATEVER IT IS THAT MAKES THEM... ***ALIVE***.

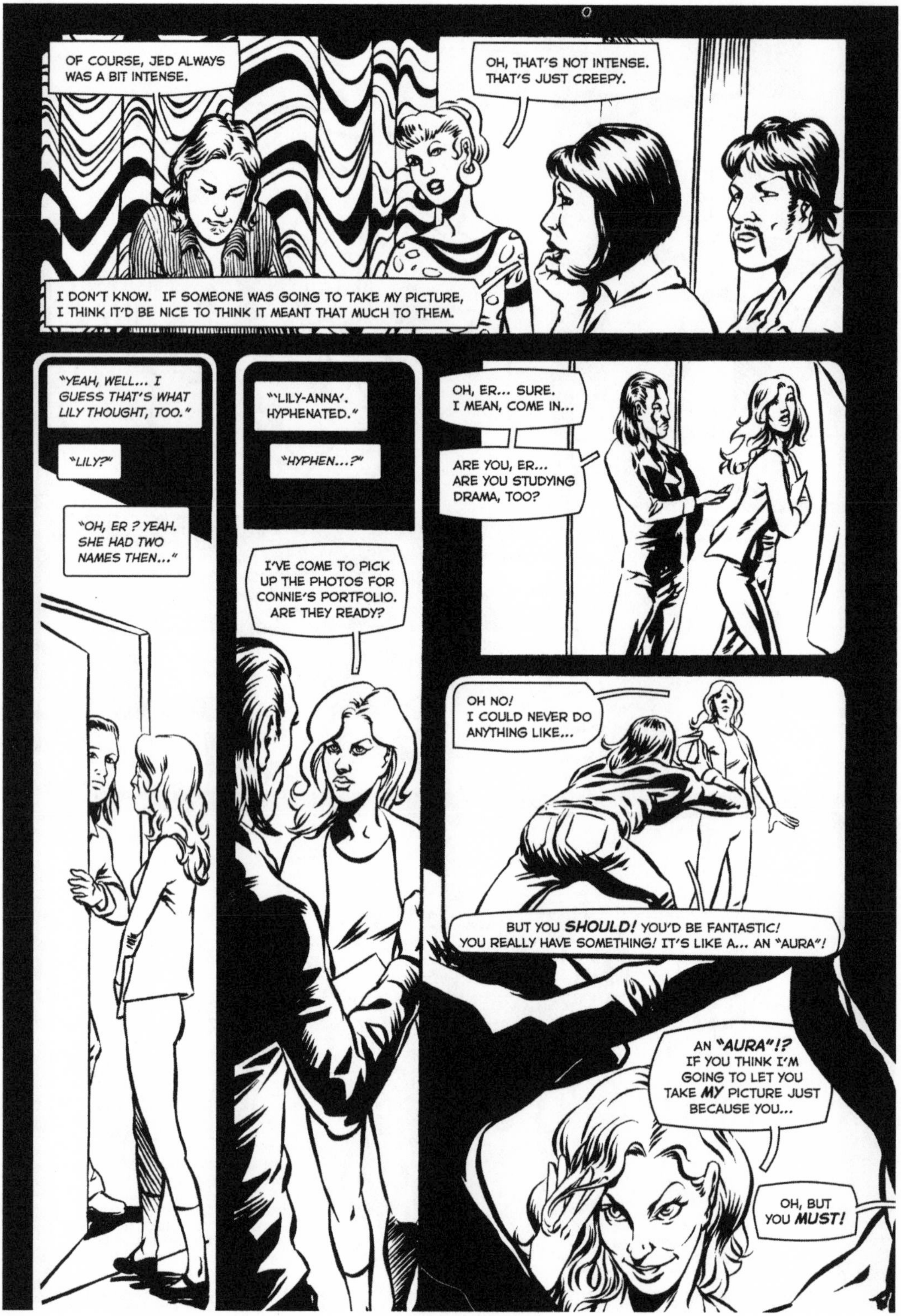
OF COURSE, JED ALWAYS WAS A BIT INTENSE.
OH, THAT'S NOT INTENSE. THAT'S JUST CREEPY.
I DON'T KNOW. IF SOMEONE WAS GOING TO TAKE MY PICTURE, I THINK IT'D BE NICE TO THINK IT MEANT THAT MUCH TO THEM.
"YEAH, WELL... I GUESS THAT'S WHAT LILY THOUGHT, TOO."
"LILY?"
"OH, ER ? YEAH. SHE HAD TWO NAMES THEN..."
"'LILY-ANNA'. HYPHENATED."
"HYPHEN...?"
I'VE COME TO PICK UP THE PHOTOS FOR CONNIE'S PORTFOLIO. ARE THEY READY?
OH, ER... SURE. I MEAN, COME IN...
ARE YOU, ER... ARE YOU STUDYING DRAMA, TOO?
OH NO! I COULD NEVER DO ANYTHING LIKE...
BUT YOU SHOULD! YOU'D BE FANTASTIC! YOU REALLY HAVE SOMETHING! IT'S LIKE A... AN "AURA"!
AN "AURA"!? IF YOU THINK I'M GOING TO LET YOU TAKE MY PICTURE JUST BECAUSE YOU...
OH, BUT YOU MUST!

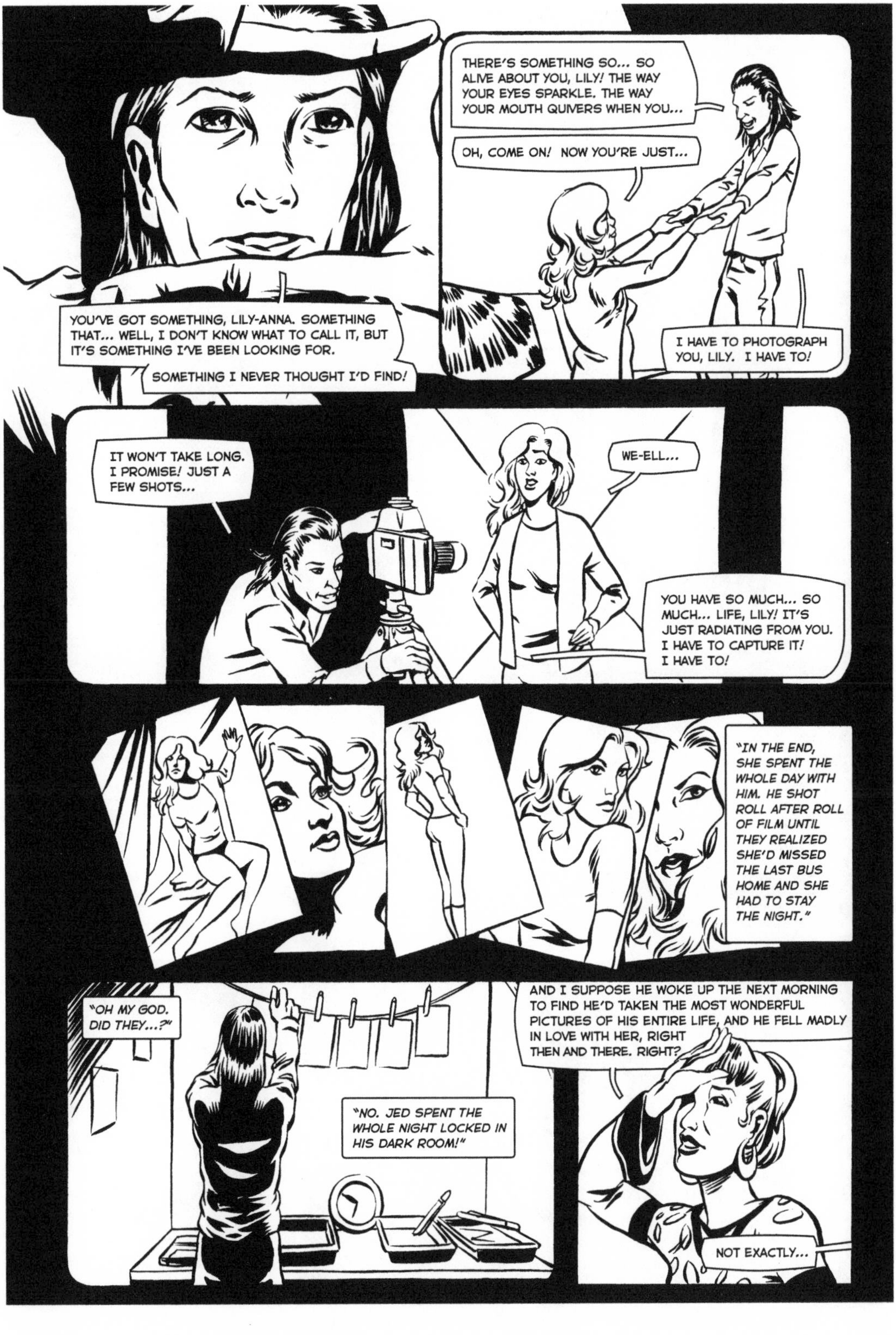
YOU'VE GOT SOMETHING, LILY-ANNA. SOMETHING THAT... WELL, I DON'T KNOW WHAT TO CALL IT, BUT IT'S SOMETHING I'VE BEEN LOOKING FOR.
SOMETHING I NEVER THOUGHT I'D FIND!
THERE'S SOMETHING SO... SO ALIVE ABOUT YOU, LILY! THE WAY YOUR EYES SPARKLE. THE WAY YOUR MOUTH QUIVERS WHEN YOU...
OH, COME ON! NOW YOU'RE JUST...
I HAVE TO PHOTOGRAPH YOU, LILY. I HAVE TO!
IT WON'T TAKE LONG. I PROMISE! JUST A FEW SHOTS...
WE-ELL...
YOU HAVE SO MUCH... SO MUCH... LIFE, LILY! IT'S JUST RADIATING FROM YOU. I HAVE TO CAPTURE IT! I HAVE TO!
"IN THE END, SHE SPENT THE WHOLE DAY WITH HIM. HE SHOT ROLL AFTER ROLL OF FILM UNTIL THEY REALIZED SHE'D MISSED THE LAST BUS HOME AND SHE HAD TO STAY THE NIGHT."
"OH MY GOD. DID THEY...?"
"NO. JED SPENT THE WHOLE NIGHT LOCKED IN HIS DARK ROOM!"
AND I SUPPOSE HE WOKE UP THE NEXT MORNING TO FIND HE'D TAKEN THE MOST WONDERFUL PICTURES OF HIS ENTIRE LIFE, AND HE FELL MADLY IN LOVE WITH HER, RIGHT THEN AND THERE. RIGHT?
NOT EXACTLY...

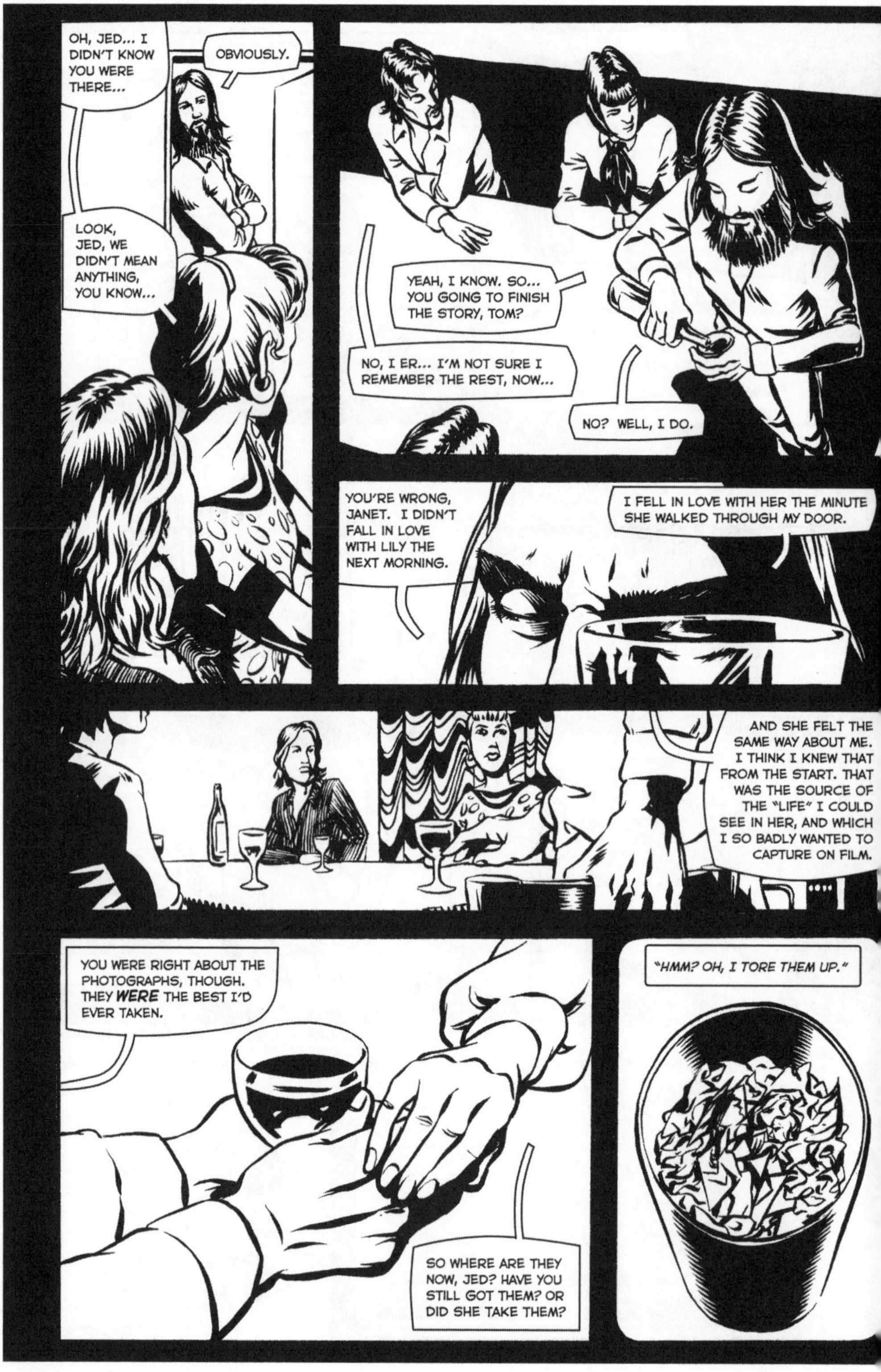
OH, JED... I DIDN'T KNOW YOU WERE THERE...
OBVIOUSLY.
LOOK, JED, WE DIDN'T MEAN ANYTHING, YOU KNOW...
YEAH, I KNOW. SO... YOU GOING TO FINISH THE STORY, TOM?
NO, I ER... I'M NOT SURE I REMEMBER THE REST, NOW...
NO? WELL, I DO.
YOU'RE WRONG, JANET. I DIDN'T FALL IN LOVE WITH LILY THE NEXT MORNING.
I FELL IN LOVE WITH HER THE MINUTE SHE WALKED THROUGH MY DOOR.
AND SHE FELT THE SAME WAY ABOUT ME. I THINK I KNEW THAT FROM THE START. THAT WAS THE SOURCE OF THE "LIFE" I COULD SEE IN HER, AND WHICH I SO BADLY WANTED TO CAPTURE ON FILM.
YOU WERE RIGHT ABOUT THE PHOTOGRAPHS, THOUGH. THEY ***WERE*** THE BEST I'D EVER TAKEN.
SO WHERE ARE THEY NOW, JED? HAVE YOU STILL GOT THEM? OR DID SHE TAKE THEM?
"HMM? OH, I TORE THEM UP."

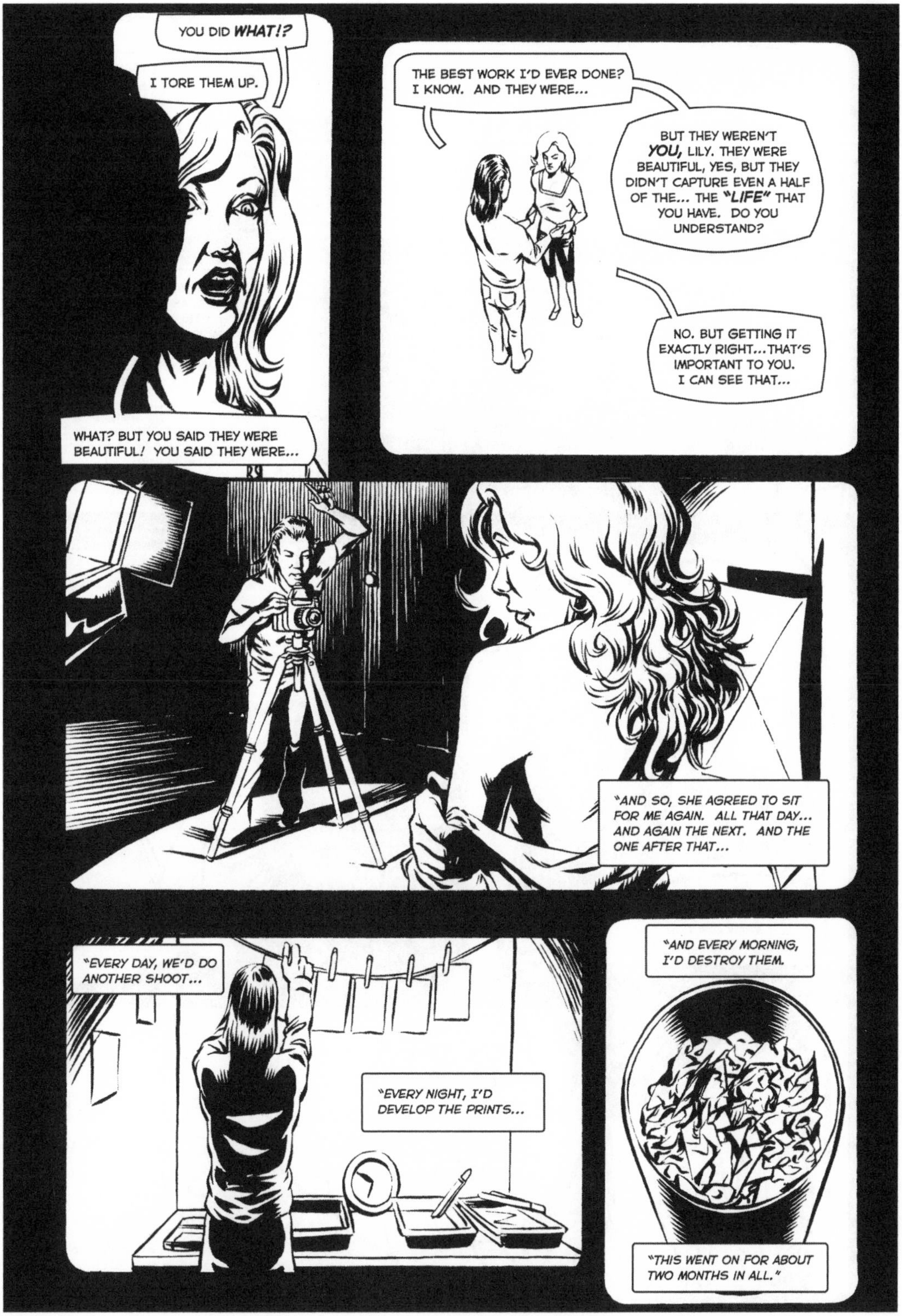
YOU DID WHAT!?
I TORE THEM UP.
WHAT? BUT YOU SAID THEY WERE BEAUTIFUL! YOU SAID THEY WERE...
THE BEST WORK I'D EVER DONE? I KNOW. AND THEY WERE...
BUT THEY WEREN'T YOU, LILY. THEY WERE BEAUTIFUL, YES, BUT THEY DIDN'T CAPTURE EVEN A HALF OF THE... THE "LIFE" THAT YOU HAVE. DO YOU UNDERSTAND?
NO. BUT GETTING IT EXACTLY RIGHT...THAT'S IMPORTANT TO YOU. I CAN SEE THAT...
"AND SO, SHE AGREED TO SIT FOR ME AGAIN. ALL THAT DAY... AND AGAIN THE NEXT. AND THE ONE AFTER THAT...
"EVERY DAY, WE'D DO ANOTHER SHOOT...
"EVERY NIGHT, I'D DEVELOP THE PRINTS...
"AND EVERY MORNING, I'D DESTROY THEM.
"THIS WENT ON FOR ABOUT TWO MONTHS IN ALL."

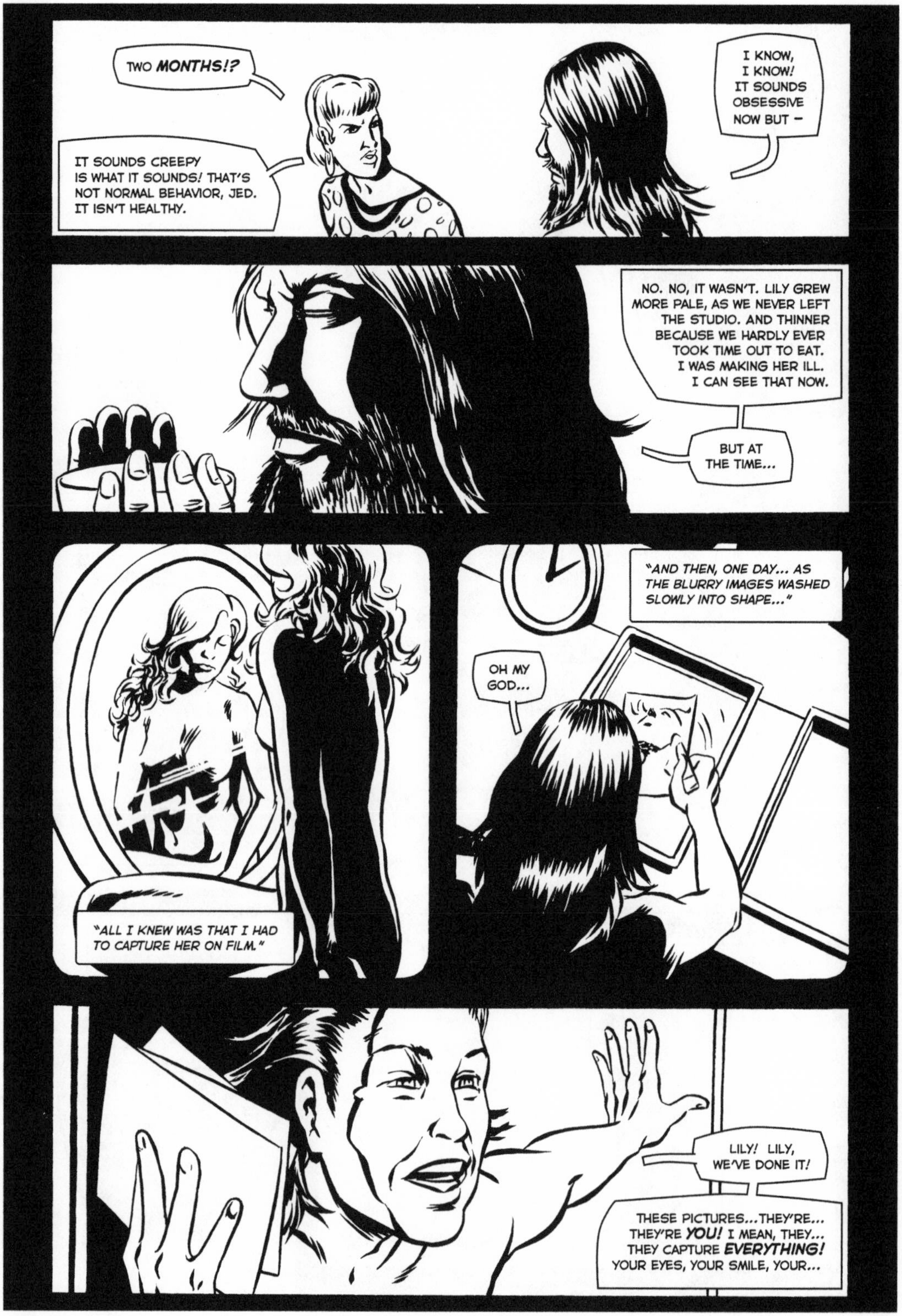
TWO MONTHS!?
IT SOUNDS CREEPY IS WHAT IT SOUNDS! THAT'S NOT NORMAL BEHAVIOR, JED. IT ISN'T HEALTHY.
I KNOW, I KNOW! IT SOUNDS OBSESSIVE NOW BUT –
NO. NO, IT WASN'T. LILY GREW MORE PALE, AS WE NEVER LEFT THE STUDIO. AND THINNER BECAUSE WE HARDLY EVER TOOK TIME OUT TO EAT. I WAS MAKING HER ILL. I CAN SEE THAT NOW.
BUT AT THE TIME...
"ALL I KNEW WAS THAT I HAD TO CAPTURE HER ON FILM."
"AND THEN, ONE DAY... AS THE BLURRY IMAGES WASHED SLOWLY INTO SHAPE..."
OH MY GOD...
LILY! LILY, WE'VE DONE IT!
THESE PICTURES...THEY'RE... THEY'RE YOU! I MEAN, THEY... THEY CAPTURE EVERYTHING! YOUR EYES, YOUR SMILE, YOUR...

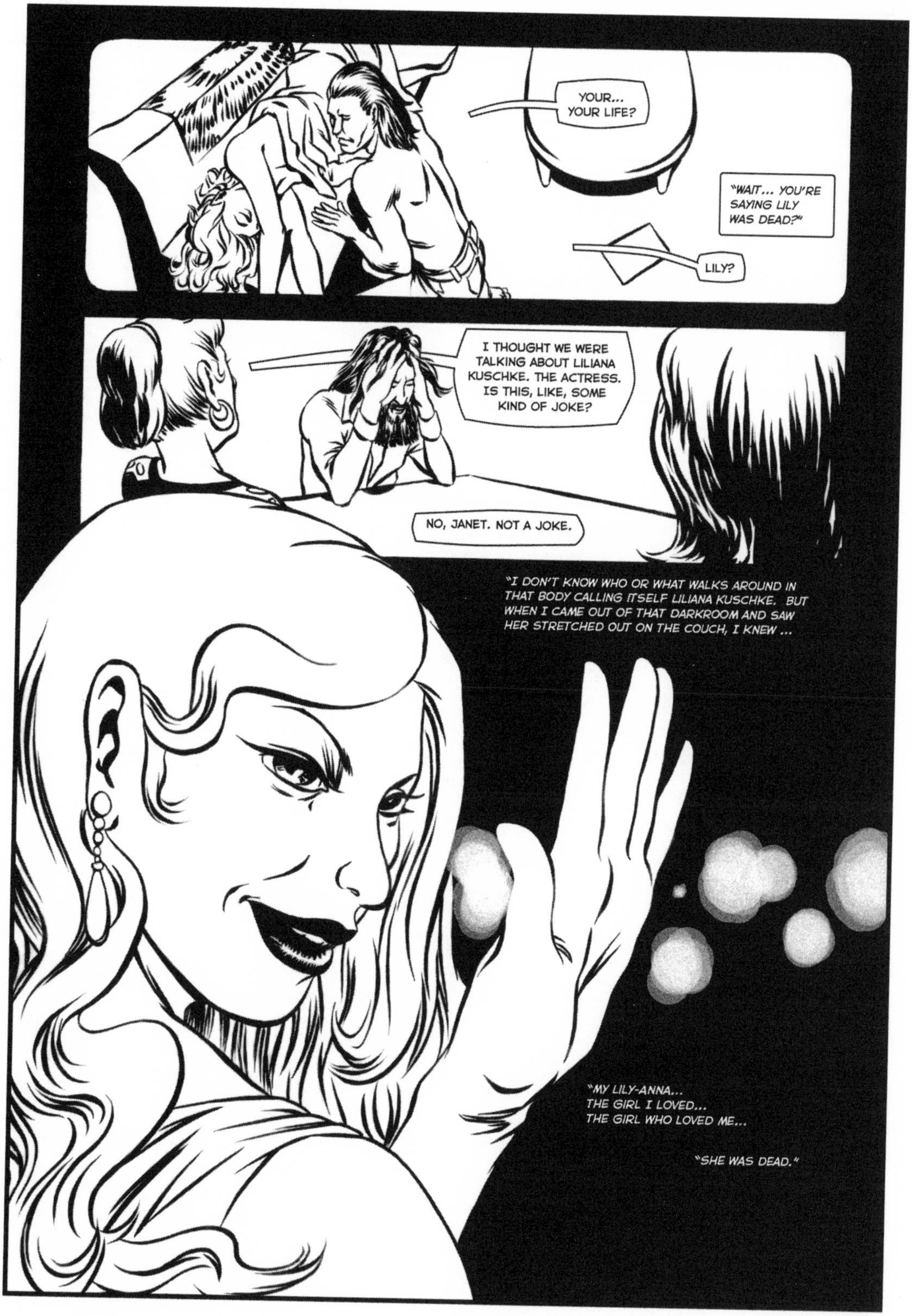
YOUR... YOUR LIFE?
"WAIT... YOU'RE SAYING LILY WAS DEAD?"
LILY?
I THOUGHT WE WERE TALKING ABOUT LILIANA KUSCHKE. THE ACTRESS. IS THIS, LIKE, SOME KIND OF JOKE?
NO, JANET. NOT A JOKE.
"I DON'T KNOW WHO OR WHAT WALKS AROUND IN THAT BODY CALLING ITSELF LILIANA KUSCHKE. BUT WHEN I CAME OUT OF THAT DARKROOM AND SAW HER STRETCHED OUT ON THE COUCH, I KNEW ...
"MY LILY-ANNA... THE GIRL I LOVED... THE GIRL WHO LOVED ME...
"SHE WAS DEAD."

THE TELL-TALE HEART

Adapted by Jeremy Slater
Art by Alice Duke

A classic narrative of murder and madness, *The Tell-Tale Heart* is one of Poe's best known and most enduring stories. Its visceral realization of the emotional price of a guilty conscience, as depicted by the ceaseless beating of a disembodied heart, would go on to influence generations of horror and mystery writers.

The image of the human eye also looms large in Poe's tale, from the victim's milky gaze that so obsesses the frantic narrator to the underlying theme of reality and perception.

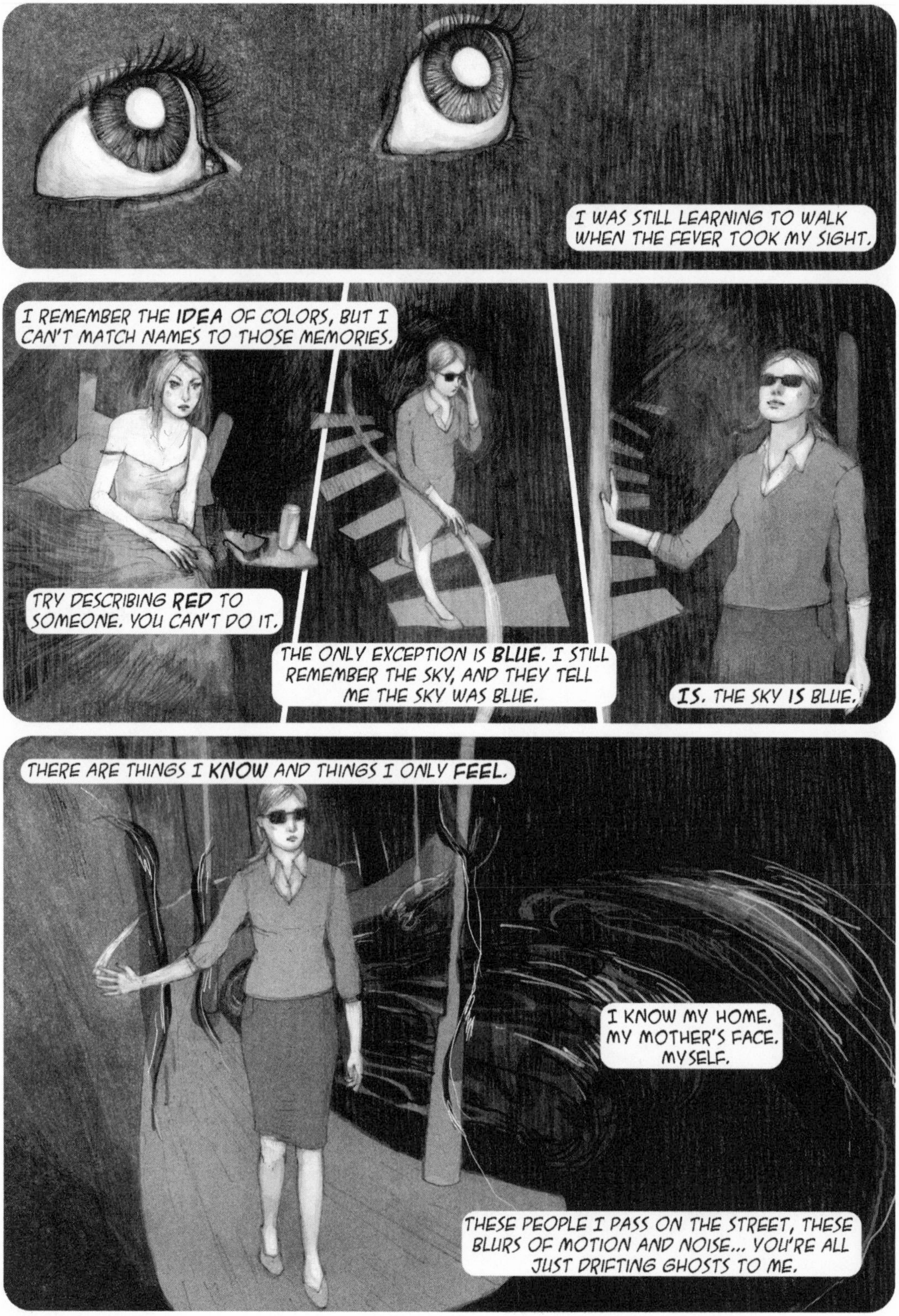
I WAS STILL LEARNING TO WALK WHEN THE FEVER TOOK MY SIGHT.
I REMEMBER THE **IDEA** OF COLORS, BUT I CAN'T MATCH NAMES TO THOSE MEMORIES.
TRY DESCRIBING **RED** TO SOMEONE. YOU CAN'T DO IT.
THE ONLY EXCEPTION IS **BLUE**. I STILL REMEMBER THE SKY, AND THEY TELL ME THE SKY WAS BLUE.
IS. THE SKY **IS** BLUE.
THERE ARE THINGS I **KNOW** AND THINGS I ONLY **FEEL**.
I KNOW MY HOME. MY MOTHER'S FACE. MYSELF.
THESE PEOPLE I PASS ON THE STREET, THESE BLURS OF MOTION AND NOISE... YOU'RE ALL JUST DRIFTING GHOSTS TO ME.

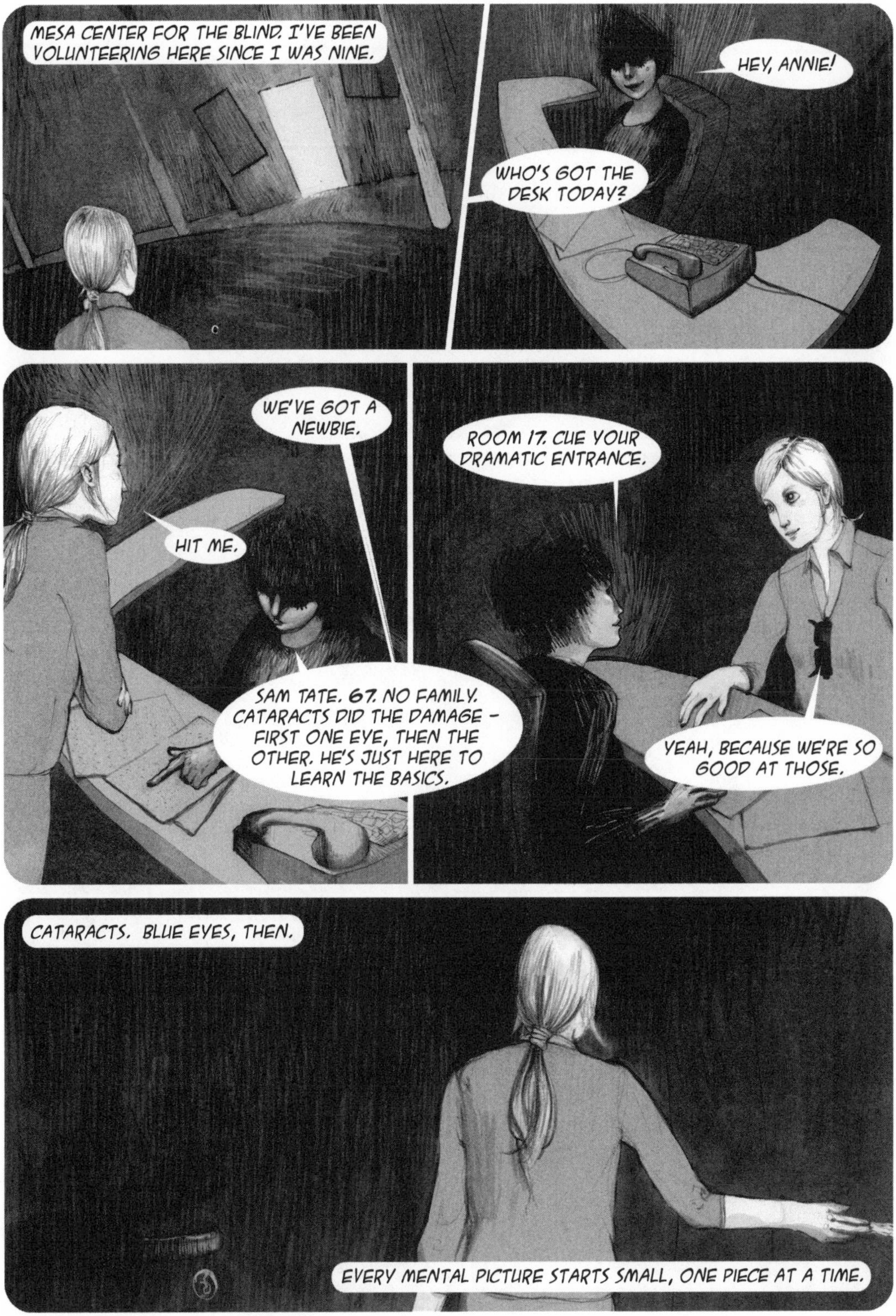
MESA CENTER FOR THE BLIND. I'VE BEEN VOLUNTEERING HERE SINCE I WAS NINE.
HEY, ANNIE!
WHO'S GOT THE DESK TODAY?
WE'VE GOT A NEWBIE.
HIT ME.
SAM TATE. 67. NO FAMILY. CATARACTS DID THE DAMAGE - FIRST ONE EYE, THEN THE OTHER. HE'S JUST HERE TO LEARN THE BASICS.
ROOM 17. CUE YOUR DRAMATIC ENTRANCE.
YEAH, BECAUSE WE'RE SO GOOD AT THOSE.
CATARACTS. BLUE EYES, THEN.
EVERY MENTAL PICTURE STARTS SMALL, ONE PIECE AT A TIME.

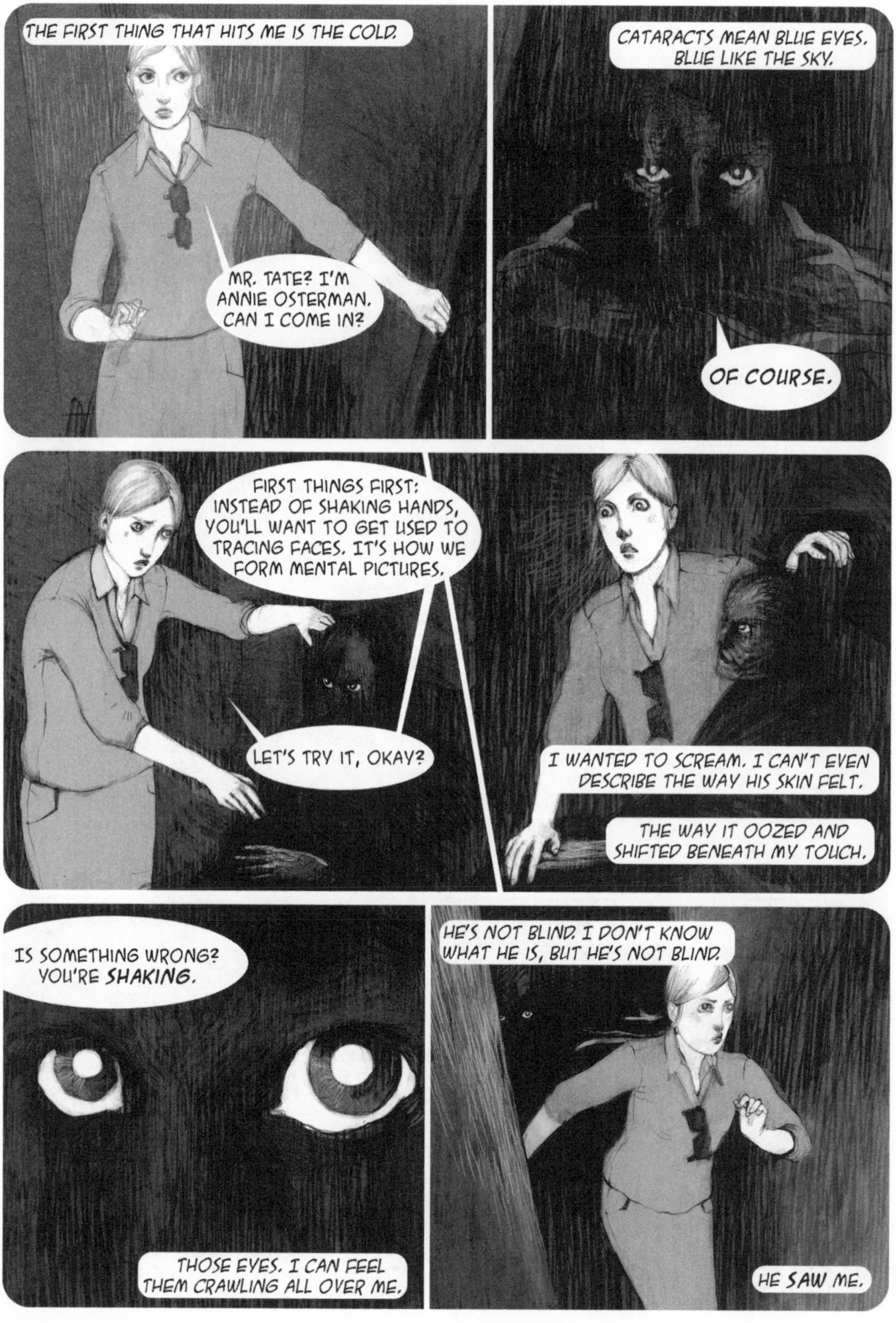
THE FIRST THING THAT HITS ME IS THE COLD.
MR. TATE? I'M ANNIE OSTERMAN. CAN I COME IN?
CATARACTS MEAN BLUE EYES. BLUE LIKE THE SKY.
OF COURSE.
FIRST THINGS FIRST: INSTEAD OF SHAKING HANDS, YOU'LL WANT TO GET USED TO TRACING FACES. IT'S HOW WE FORM MENTAL PICTURES.
LET'S TRY IT, OKAY?
I WANTED TO SCREAM. I CAN'T EVEN DESCRIBE THE WAY HIS SKIN FELT.
THE WAY IT OOZED AND SHIFTED BENEATH MY TOUCH.
IS SOMETHING WRONG? YOU'RE SHAKING.
THOSE EYES. I CAN FEEL THEM CRAWLING ALL OVER ME.
HE'S NOT BLIND. I DON'T KNOW WHAT HE IS, BUT HE'S NOT BLIND.
HE SAW ME.

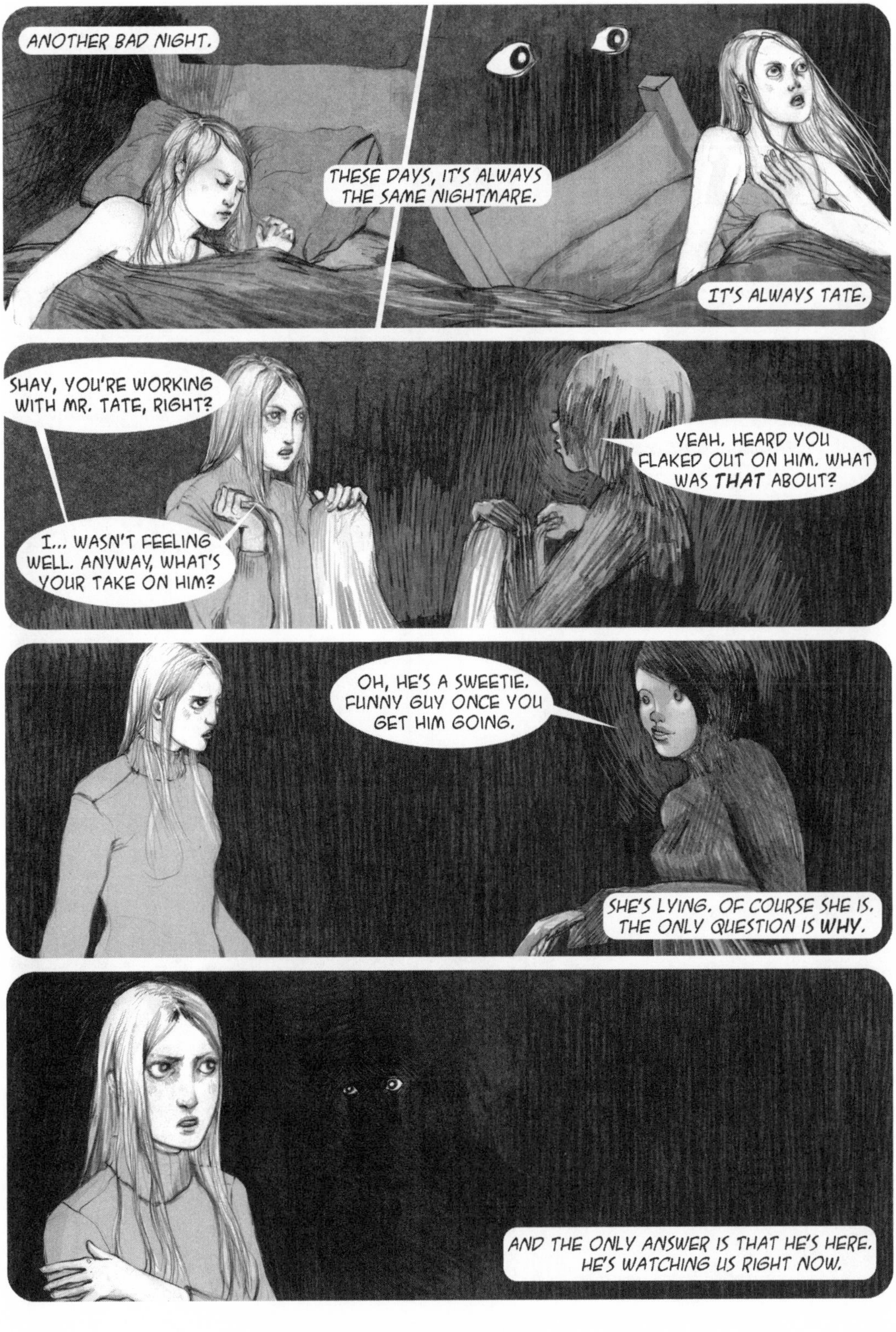
ANOTHER BAD NIGHT.
THESE DAYS, IT'S ALWAYS THE SAME NIGHTMARE.
IT'S ALWAYS TATE.
SHAY, YOU'RE WORKING WITH MR. TATE, RIGHT?
YEAH. HEARD YOU FLAKED OUT ON HIM. WHAT WAS THAT ABOUT?
I... WASN'T FEELING WELL. ANYWAY, WHAT'S YOUR TAKE ON HIM?
OH, HE'S A SWEETIE. FUNNY GUY ONCE YOU GET HIM GOING.
SHE'S LYING. OF COURSE SHE IS. THE ONLY QUESTION IS WHY.
AND THE ONLY ANSWER IS THAT HE'S HERE. HE'S WATCHING US RIGHT NOW.

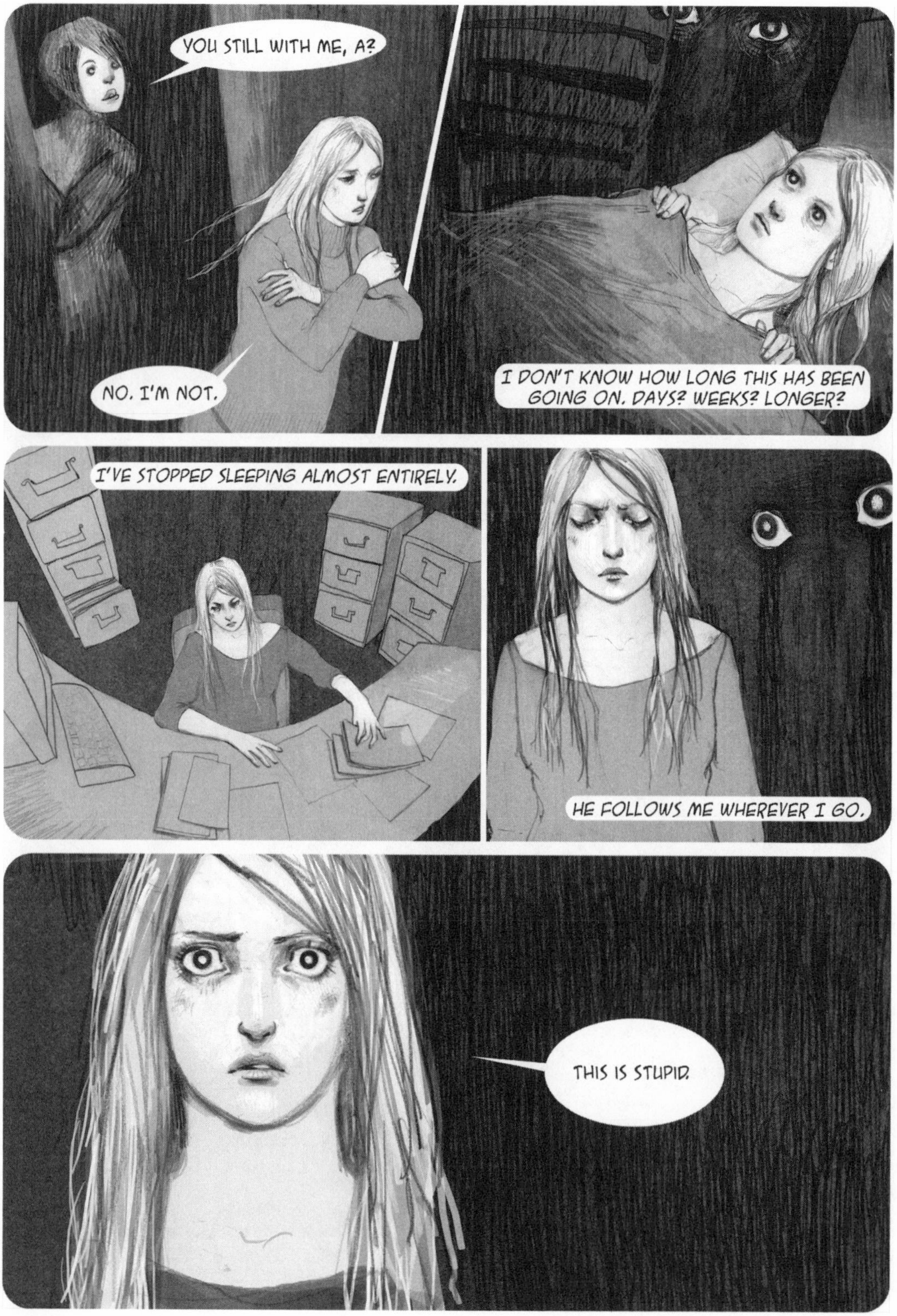
YOU STILL WITH ME, A?
NO. I'M NOT.
I DON'T KNOW HOW LONG THIS HAS BEEN GOING ON. DAYS? WEEKS? LONGER?
I'VE STOPPED SLEEPING ALMOST ENTIRELY.
HE FOLLOWS ME WHEREVER I GO.
THIS IS STUPID.

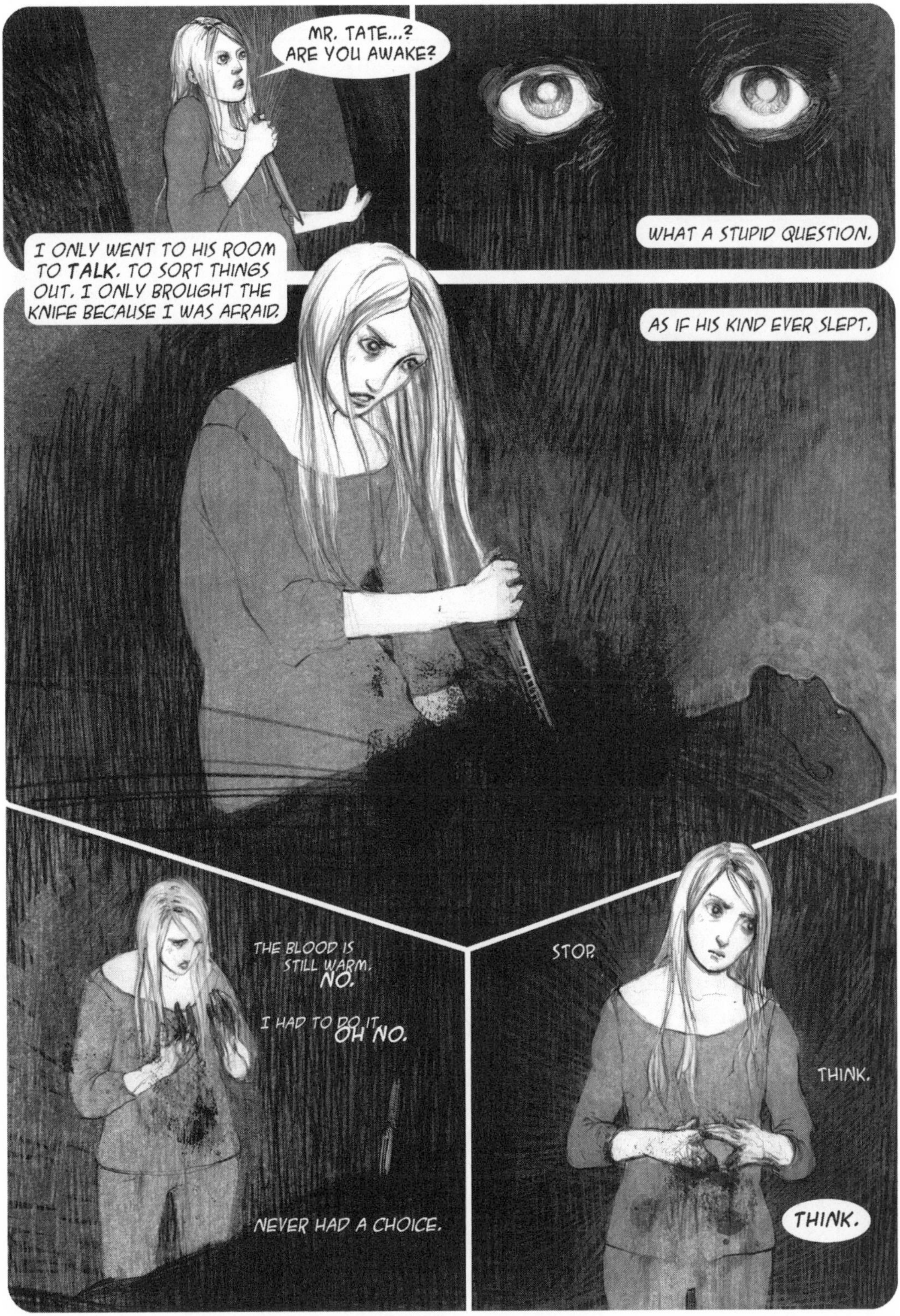
MR. TATE...?
ARE YOU AWAKE?
WHAT A STUPID QUESTION.
I ONLY WENT TO HIS ROOM TO TALK. TO SORT THINGS OUT. I ONLY BROUGHT THE KNIFE BECAUSE I WAS AFRAID.
AS IF HIS KIND EVER SLEPT.
THE BLOOD IS STILL WARM.
NO.
I HAD TO DO IT.
OH NO.
NEVER HAD A CHOICE.
STOP.
THINK.
THINK.

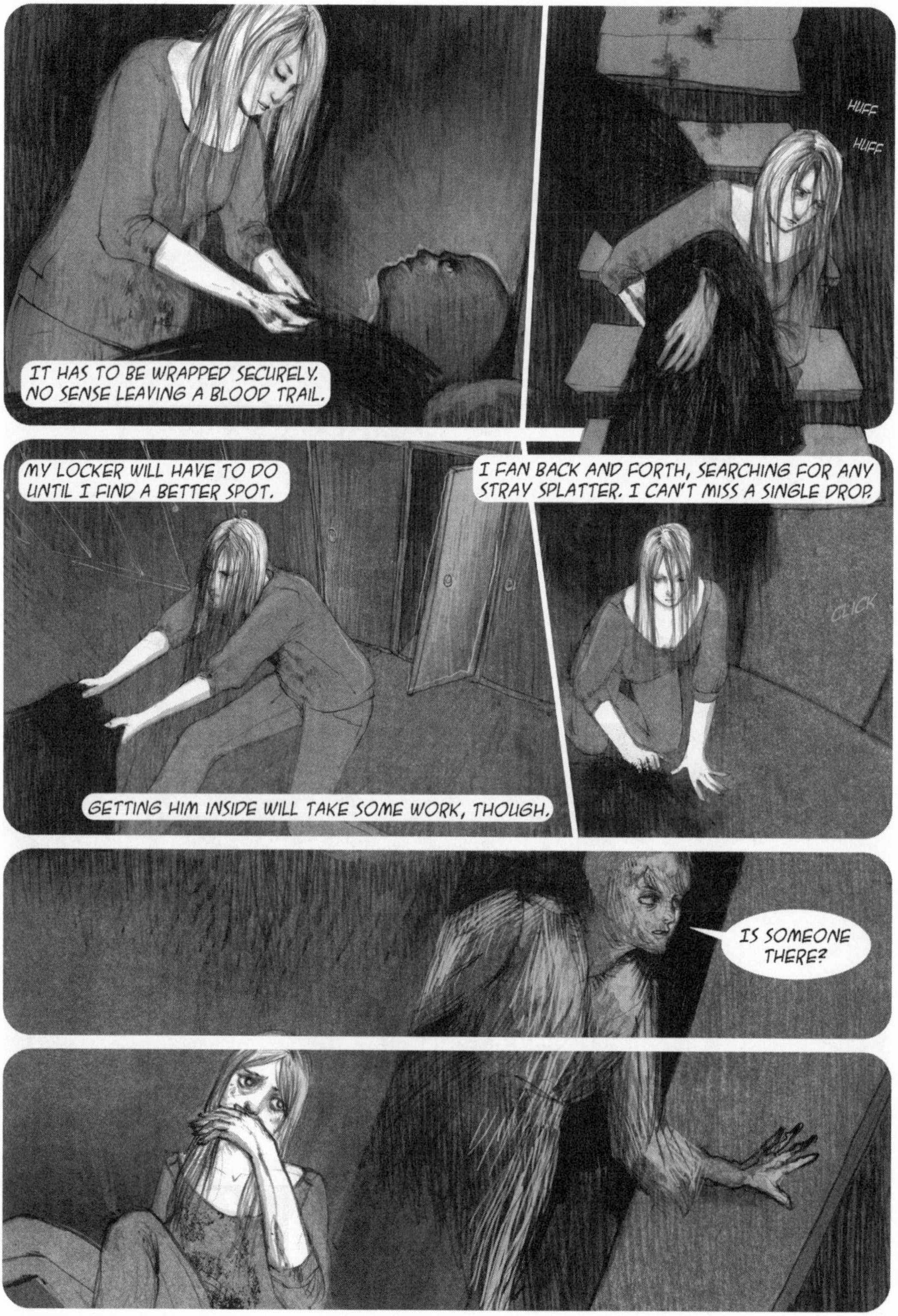
IT HAS TO BE WRAPPED SECURELY. NO SENSE LEAVING A BLOOD TRAIL.
HUFF
HUFF
MY LOCKER WILL HAVE TO DO UNTIL I FIND A BETTER SPOT.
GETTING HIM INSIDE WILL TAKE SOME WORK, THOUGH.
I FAN BACK AND FORTH, SEARCHING FOR ANY STRAY SPLATTER. I CAN'T MISS A SINGLE DROP.
CLICK
IS SOMEONE THERE?

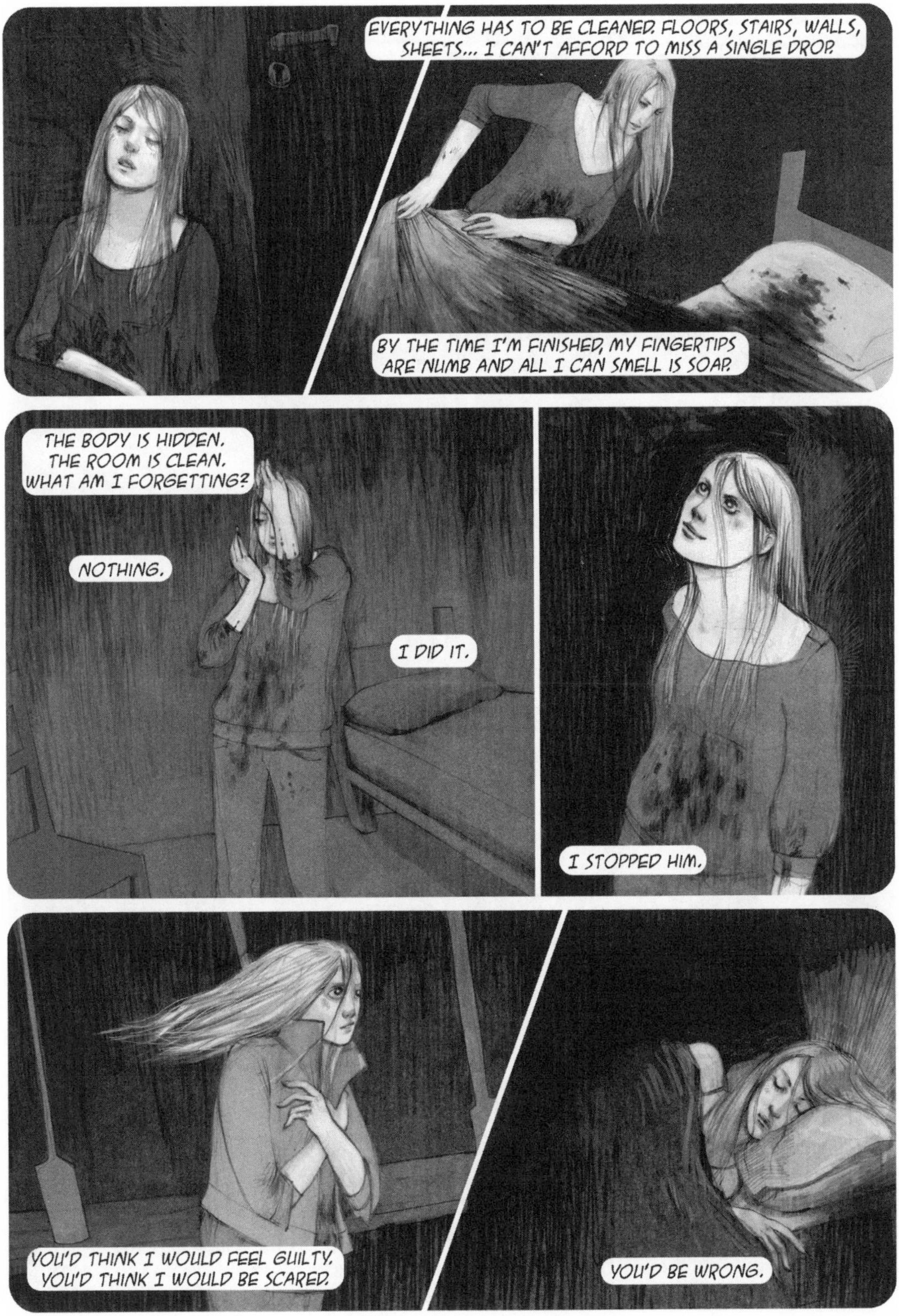
EVERYTHING HAS TO BE CLEANED. FLOORS, STAIRS, WALLS, SHEETS... I CAN'T AFFORD TO MISS A SINGLE DROP.
BY THE TIME I'M FINISHED, MY FINGERTIPS ARE NUMB AND ALL I CAN SMELL IS SOAP.
THE BODY IS HIDDEN. THE ROOM IS CLEAN. WHAT AM I FORGETTING?
NOTHING.
I DID IT.
I STOPPED HIM.
YOU'D THINK I WOULD FEEL GUILTY. YOU'D THINK I WOULD BE SCARED.
YOU'D BE WRONG.

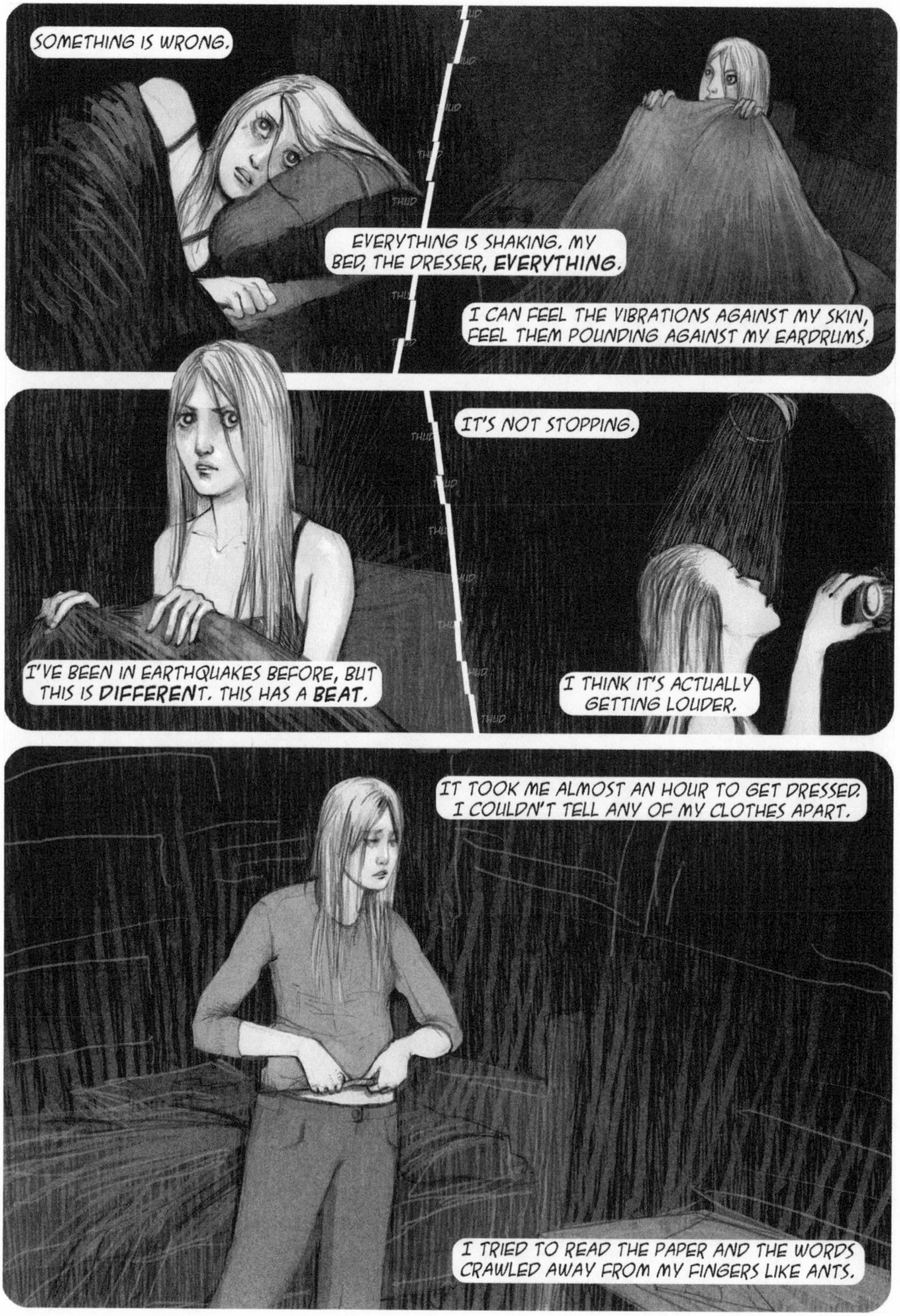
SOMETHING IS WRONG.
EVERYTHING IS SHAKING. MY BED, THE DRESSER, **EVERYTHING**.
I CAN FEEL THE VIBRATIONS AGAINST MY SKIN, FEEL THEM POUNDING AGAINST MY EARDRUMS.
I'VE BEEN IN EARTHQUAKES BEFORE, BUT THIS IS **DIFFERENT**. THIS HAS A **BEAT**.
IT'S NOT STOPPING.
I THINK IT'S ACTUALLY GETTING LOUDER.
IT TOOK ME ALMOST AN HOUR TO GET DRESSED. I COULDN'T TELL ANY OF MY CLOTHES APART.
I TRIED TO READ THE PAPER AND THE WORDS CRAWLED AWAY FROM MY FINGERS LIKE ANTS.

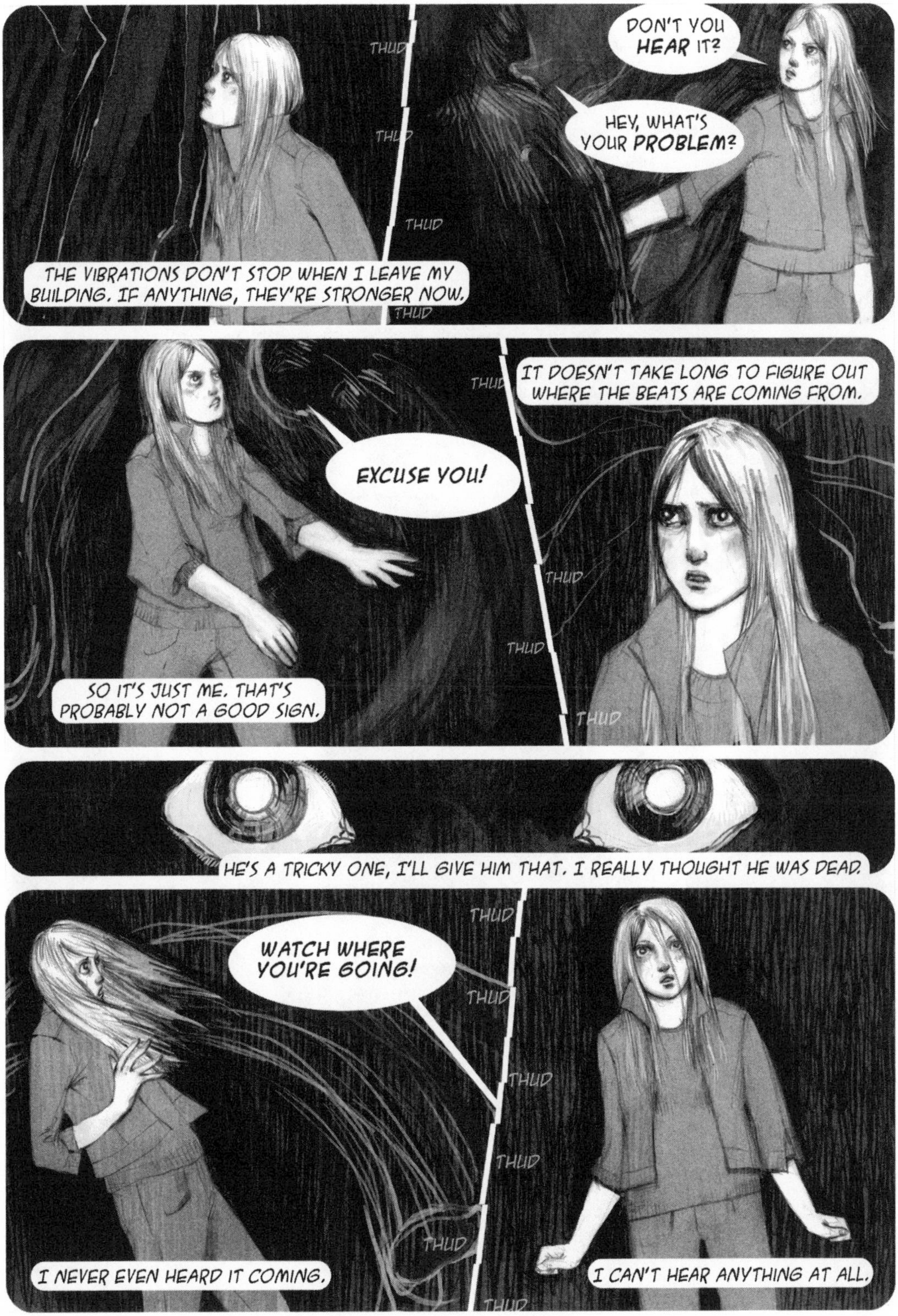
THUD
THUD
THUD
THE VIBRATIONS DON'T STOP WHEN I LEAVE MY BUILDING. IF ANYTHING, THEY'RE STRONGER NOW.
THUD
DON'T YOU HEAR IT?
HEY, WHAT'S YOUR PROBLEM?
THUD
EXCUSE YOU!
SO IT'S JUST ME. THAT'S PROBABLY NOT A GOOD SIGN.
IT DOESN'T TAKE LONG TO FIGURE OUT WHERE THE BEATS ARE COMING FROM.
THUD
THUD
THUD
HE'S A TRICKY ONE, I'LL GIVE HIM THAT. I REALLY THOUGHT HE WAS DEAD.
THUD
WATCH WHERE YOU'RE GOING!
THUD
THUD
THUD
THUD
I NEVER EVEN HEARD IT COMING.
I CAN'T HEAR ANYTHING AT ALL.
THUD

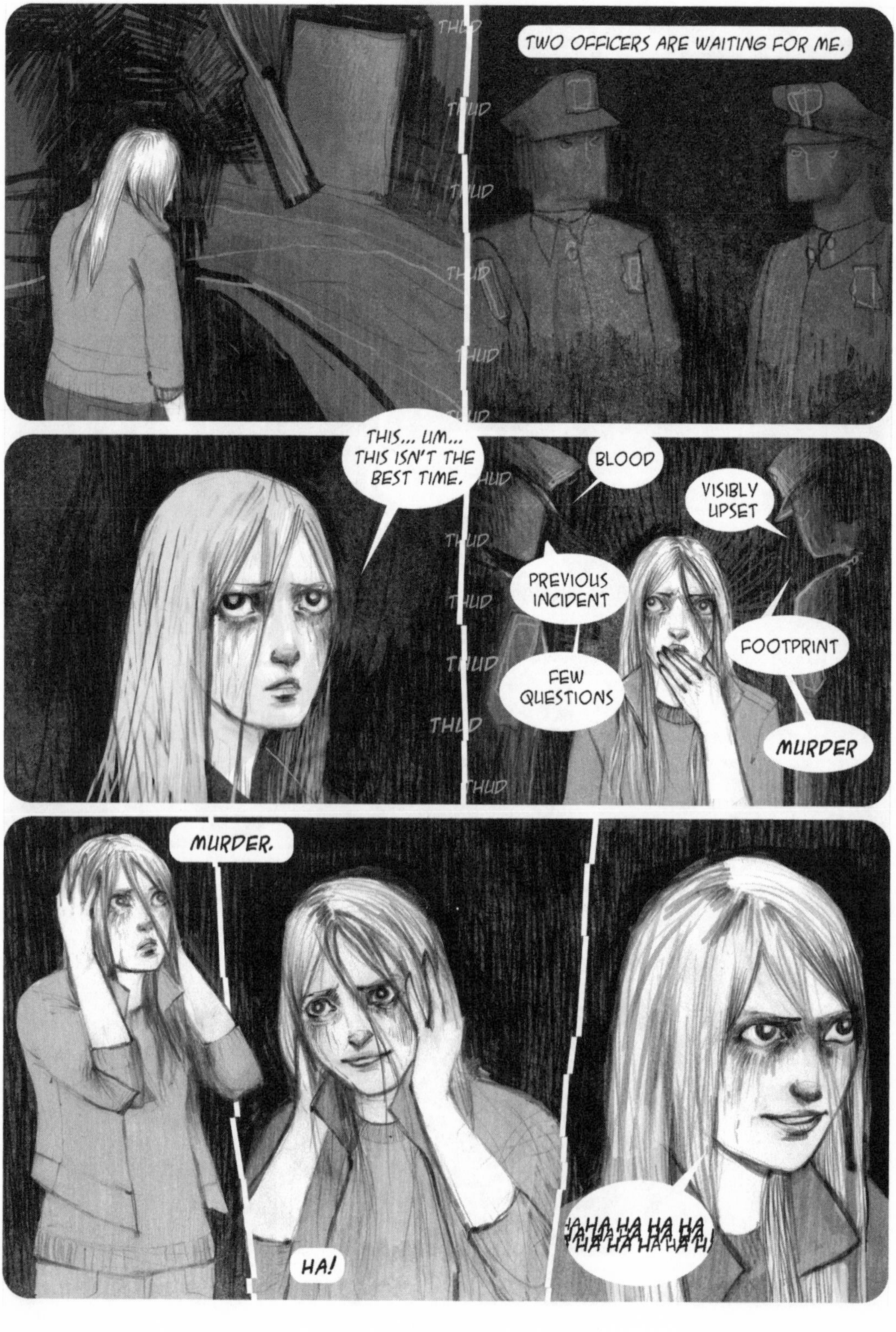
THUD
THUD
THUD
THUD
THUD
THUD
TWO OFFICERS ARE WAITING FOR ME.
THIS... UM... THIS ISN'T THE BEST TIME.
THUD
THUD
THUD
THUD
THUD
THUD
BLOOD
VISIBLY UPSET
PREVIOUS INCIDENT
FOOTPRINT
FEW QUESTIONS
MURDER
MURDER.
HA!
HA HA HA HA HA
HA HA HA HA HA

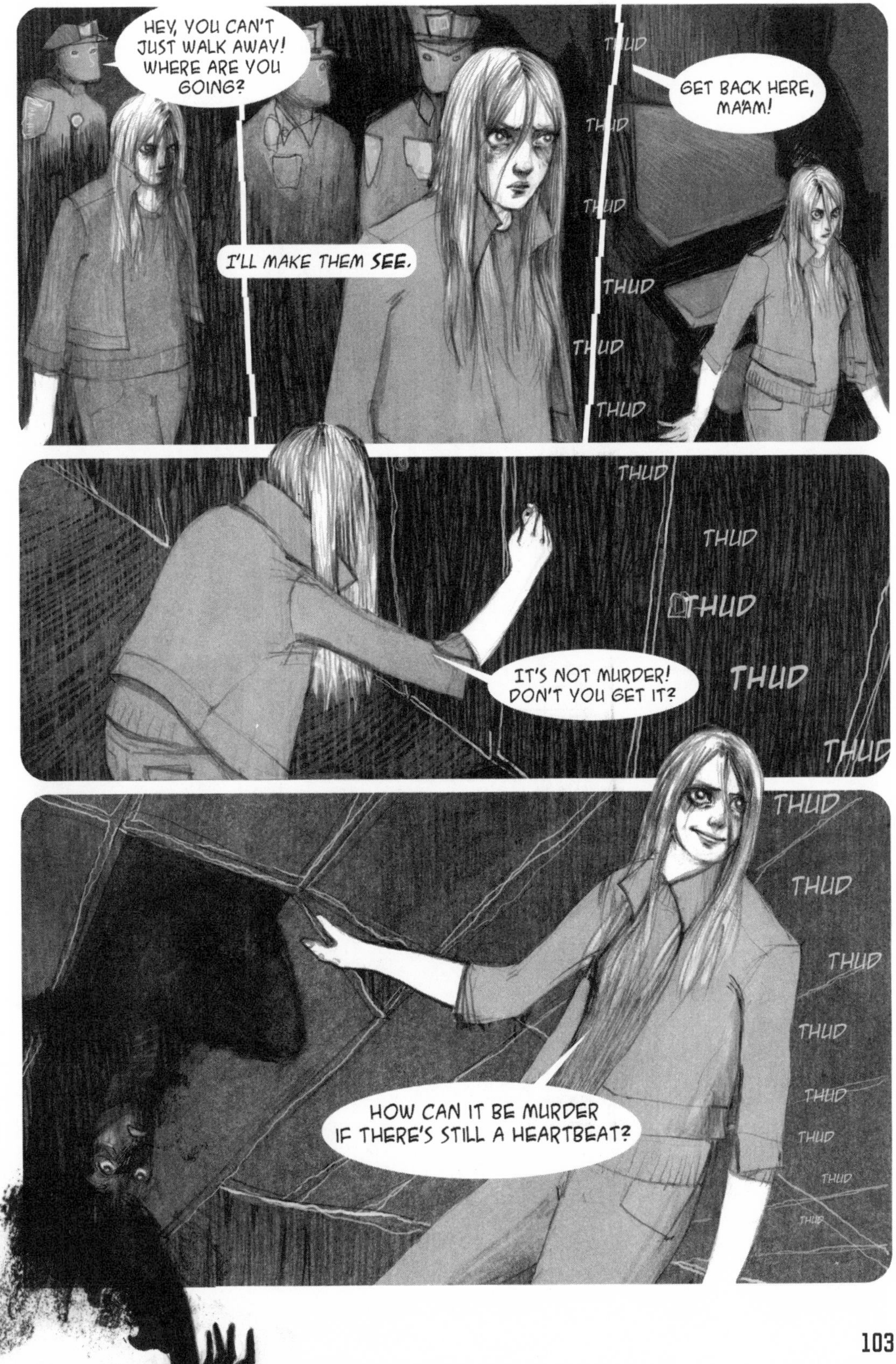
HEY, YOU CAN'T JUST WALK AWAY! WHERE ARE YOU GOING?
I'LL MAKE THEM SEE.
THUD
THUD
THUD
THUD
THUD
THUD
GET BACK HERE, MA'AM!
THUD
THUD
THUD
THUD
IT'S NOT MURDER! DON'T YOU GET IT?
THUD
THUD
THUD
THUD
THUD
THUD
THUD
THUD
THUD
HOW CAN IT BE MURDER IF THERE'S STILL A HEARTBEAT?

THE MASQUE OF THE RED DEATH

Adapted by Adam Prosser
Art by Erik Rangel

Written several years after a global pandemic of cholera had decimated populations around the world, this story delivers some poetic justice to those who would use their privileged status to avoid tragedy while doing nothing to save those less fortunate.

Prospero, the hedonistic and selfish protagonist who is determined to party while the outside world suffers, is unlike many of Poe's lead characters in that he is unsympathetic, thoroughly deserving the grotesque fate that lies in store…

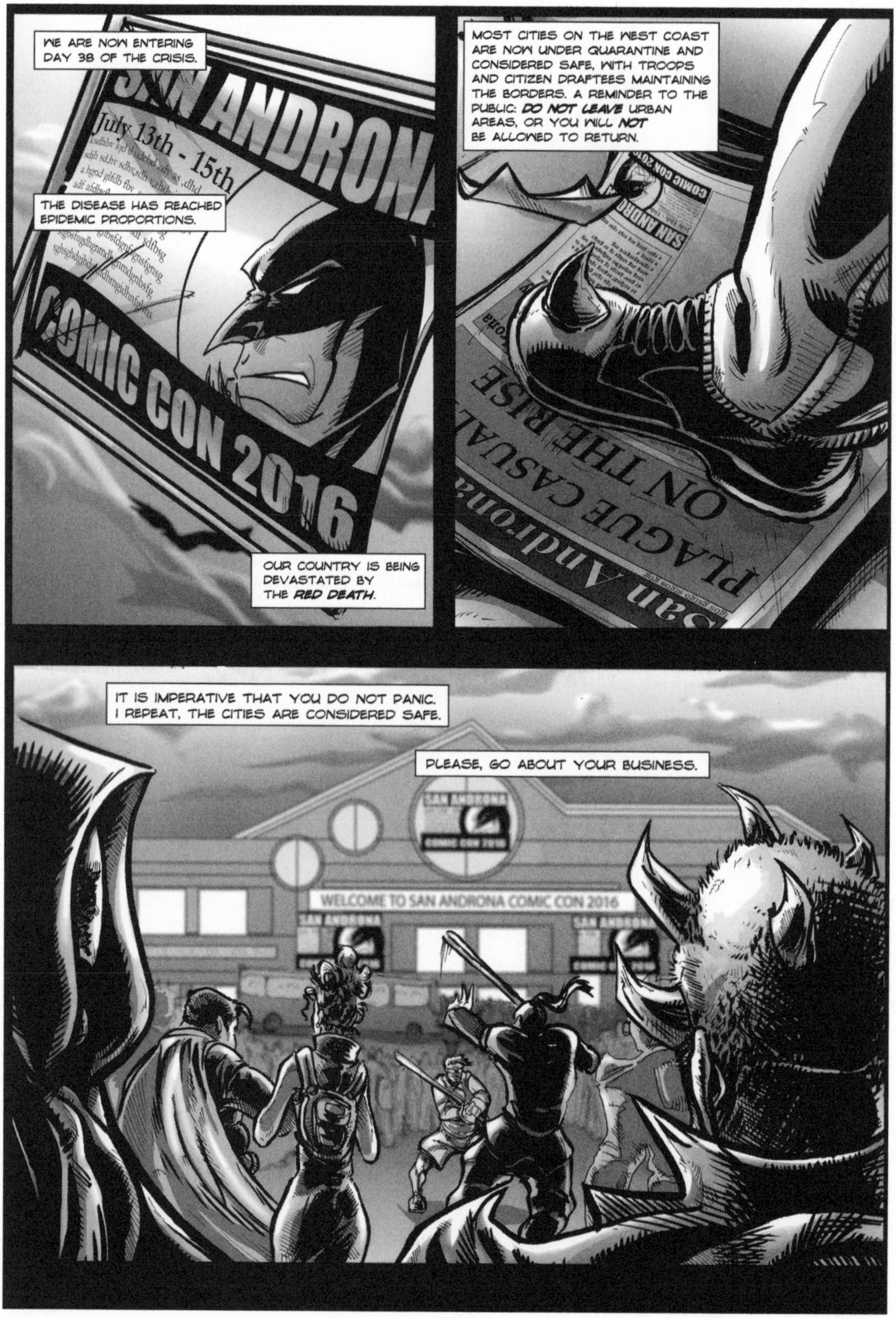
WE ARE NOW ENTERING DAY 38 OF THE CRISIS.
SAN ANDRONA
July 13th - 15th
COMIC CON 2016
THE DISEASE HAS REACHED EPIDEMIC PROPORTIONS.
OUR COUNTRY IS BEING DEVASTATED BY THE *RED DEATH*.
MOST CITIES ON THE WEST COAST ARE NOW UNDER QUARANTINE AND CONSIDERED SAFE, WITH TROOPS AND CITIZEN DRAFTEES MAINTAINING THE BORDERS. A REMINDER TO THE PUBLIC: ***DO NOT LEAVE*** URBAN AREAS, OR YOU WILL ***NOT*** BE ALLOWED TO RETURN.
San Androna
PLAGUE CASUALTIES ON THE RISE
IT IS IMPERATIVE THAT YOU DO NOT PANIC. I REPEAT, THE CITIES ARE CONSIDERED SAFE.
PLEASE, GO ABOUT YOUR BUSINESS.
WELCOME TO SAN ANDRONA COMIC CON 2016

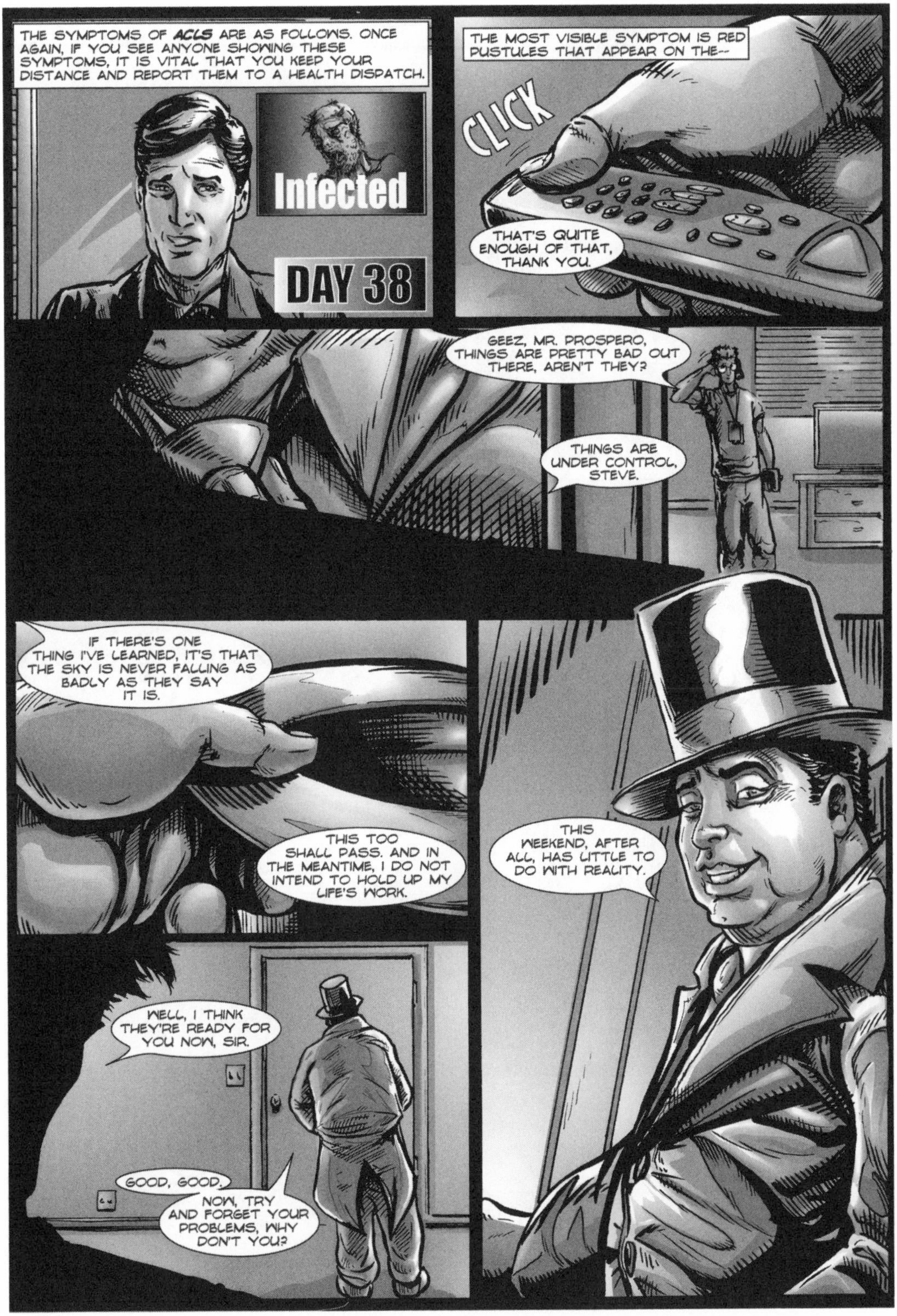
THE SYMPTOMS OF ***ACLS*** ARE AS FOLLOWS. ONCE AGAIN, IF YOU SEE ANYONE SHOWING THESE SYMPTOMS, IT IS VITAL THAT YOU KEEP YOUR DISTANCE AND REPORT THEM TO A HEALTH DISPATCH.
Infected
DAY 38
THE MOST VISIBLE SYMPTOM IS RED PUSTULES THAT APPEAR ON THE--
CLICK
THAT'S QUITE ENOUGH OF THAT, THANK YOU.
GEEZ, MR. PROSPERO, THINGS ARE PRETTY BAD OUT THERE, AREN'T THEY?
THINGS ARE UNDER CONTROL, STEVE.
IF THERE'S ONE THING I'VE LEARNED, IT'S THAT THE SKY IS NEVER FALLING AS BADLY AS THEY SAY IT IS.
THIS TOO SHALL PASS. AND IN THE MEANTIME, I DO NOT INTEND TO HOLD UP MY LIFE'S WORK.
THIS WEEKEND, AFTER ALL, HAS LITTLE TO DO WITH REALITY.
WELL, I THINK THEY'RE READY FOR YOU NOW, SIR.
GOOD, GOOD.
NOW, TRY AND FORGET YOUR PROBLEMS, WHY DON'T YOU?

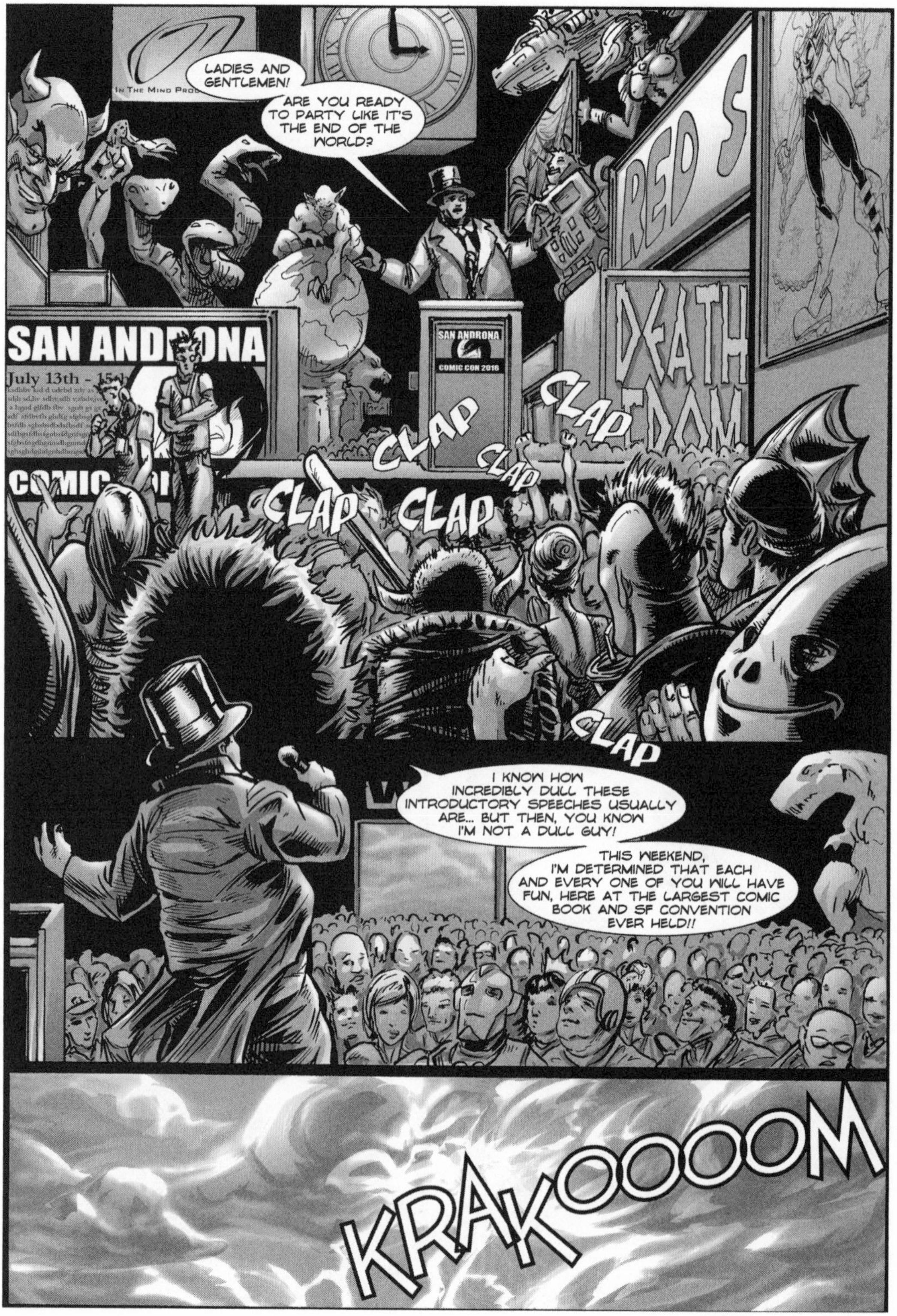
LADIES AND GENTLEMEN!
ARE YOU READY TO PARTY LIKE IT'S THE END OF THE WORLD?
SAN ANDRONA
July 13th - 15th
SAN ANDRONA COMIC CON 2016
DEATH
CLAP
CLAP
CLAP
CLAP
CLAP
CLAP
I KNOW HOW INCREDIBLY DULL THESE INTRODUCTORY SPEECHES USUALLY ARE... BUT THEN, YOU KNOW I'M NOT A DULL GUY!
THIS WEEKEND, I'M DETERMINED THAT EACH AND EVERY ONE OF YOU WILL HAVE FUN, HERE AT THE LARGEST COMIC BOOK AND SF CONVENTION EVER HELD!!
KRAKOOOOM

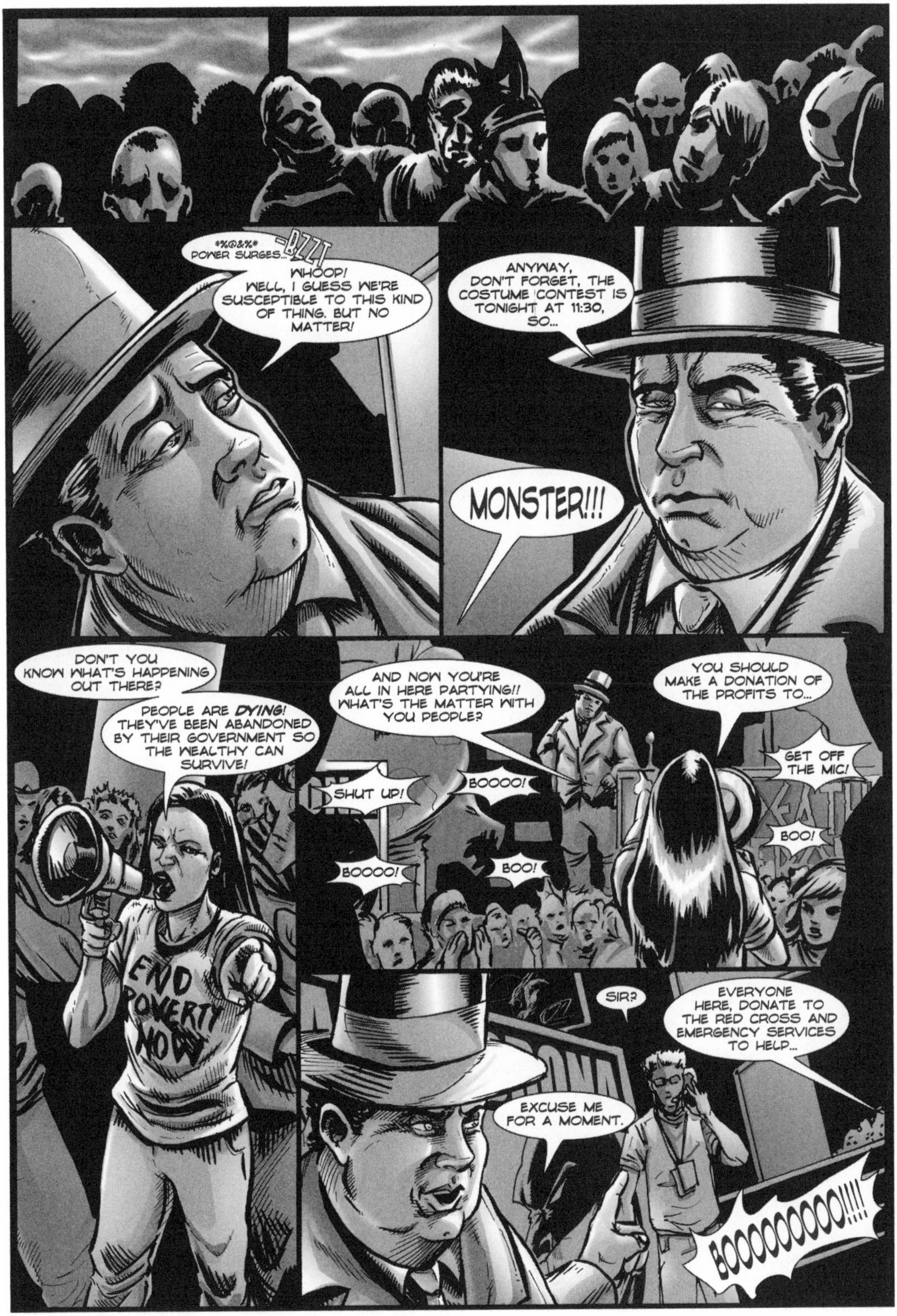
$%@&%* POWER SURGES...
-BZZT
WHOOP! WELL, I GUESS WE'RE SUSCEPTIBLE TO THIS KIND OF THING. BUT NO MATTER!
ANYWAY, DON'T FORGET, THE COSTUME CONTEST IS TONIGHT AT 11:30, SO...
MONSTER!!!
DON'T YOU KNOW WHAT'S HAPPENING OUT THERE?
PEOPLE ARE DYING! THEY'VE BEEN ABANDONED BY THEIR GOVERNMENT SO THE WEALTHY CAN SURVIVE!
END POVERTY NOW
AND NOW YOU'RE ALL IN HERE PARTYING!! WHAT'S THE MATTER WITH YOU PEOPLE?
YOU SHOULD MAKE A DONATION OF THE PROFITS TO...
SHUT UP!
BOOOO!
GET OFF THE MIC!
BOO!
BOOOO!
BOO!
SIR?
EVERYONE HERE, DONATE TO THE RED CROSS AND EMERGENCY SERVICES TO HELP...
EXCUSE ME FOR A MOMENT.
BOOOOOOOOO!!!!

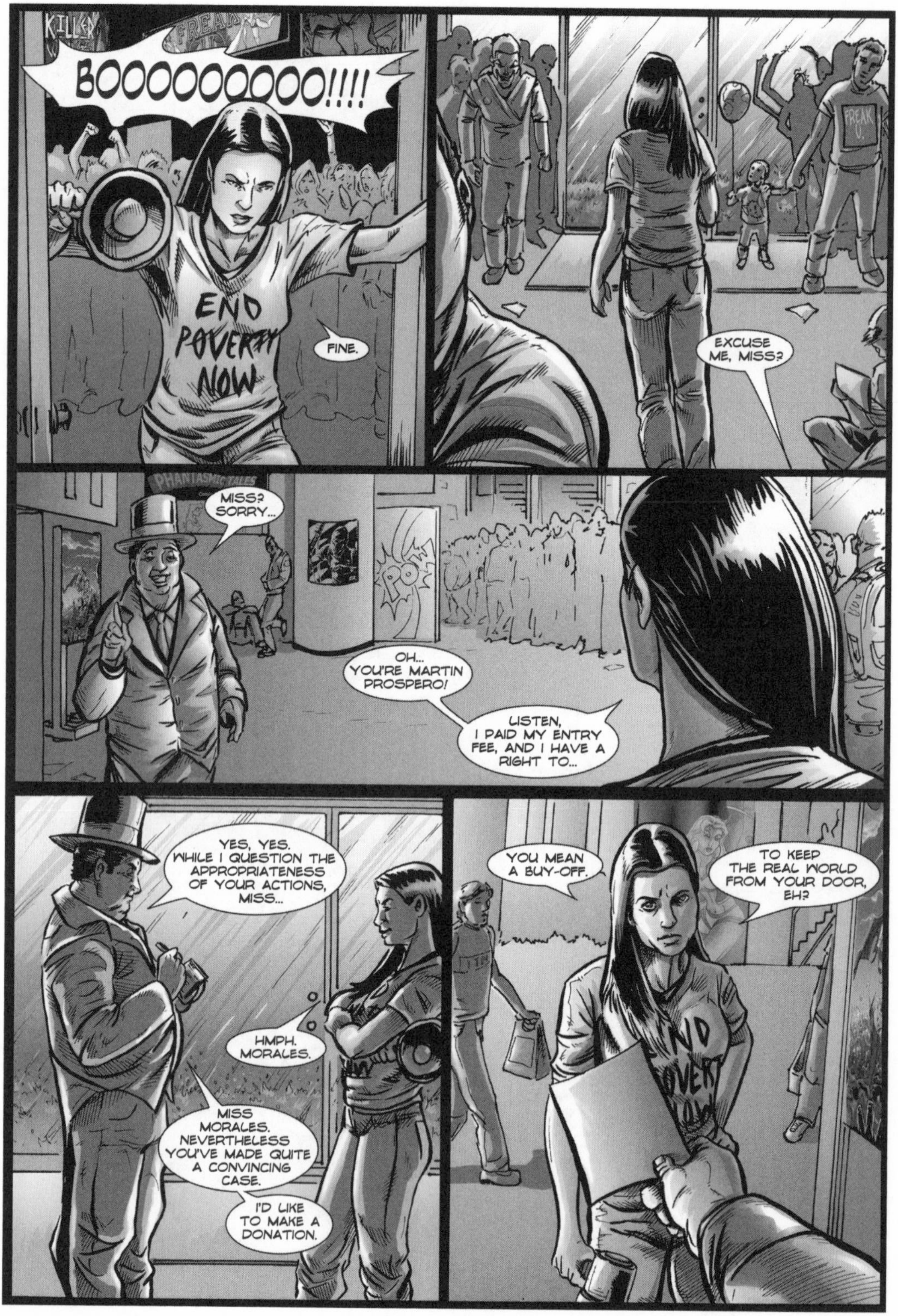
KILLER
FREAK
BOOOOOOOOO!!!!
END POVERTY NOW
FINE.
FREAK U.
EXCUSE ME, MISS?
PHANTASMIC TALES
MISS? SORRY...
POW
OH... YOU'RE MARTIN PROSPERO!
LISTEN, I PAID MY ENTRY FEE, AND I HAVE A RIGHT TO...
YES, YES. WHILE I QUESTION THE APPROPRIATENESS OF YOUR ACTIONS, MISS...
HMPH. MORALES.
MISS MORALES. NEVERTHELESS YOU'VE MADE QUITE A CONVINCING CASE.
I'D LIKE TO MAKE A DONATION.
YOU MEAN A BUY-OFF.
TO KEEP THE REAL WORLD FROM YOUR DOOR, EH?

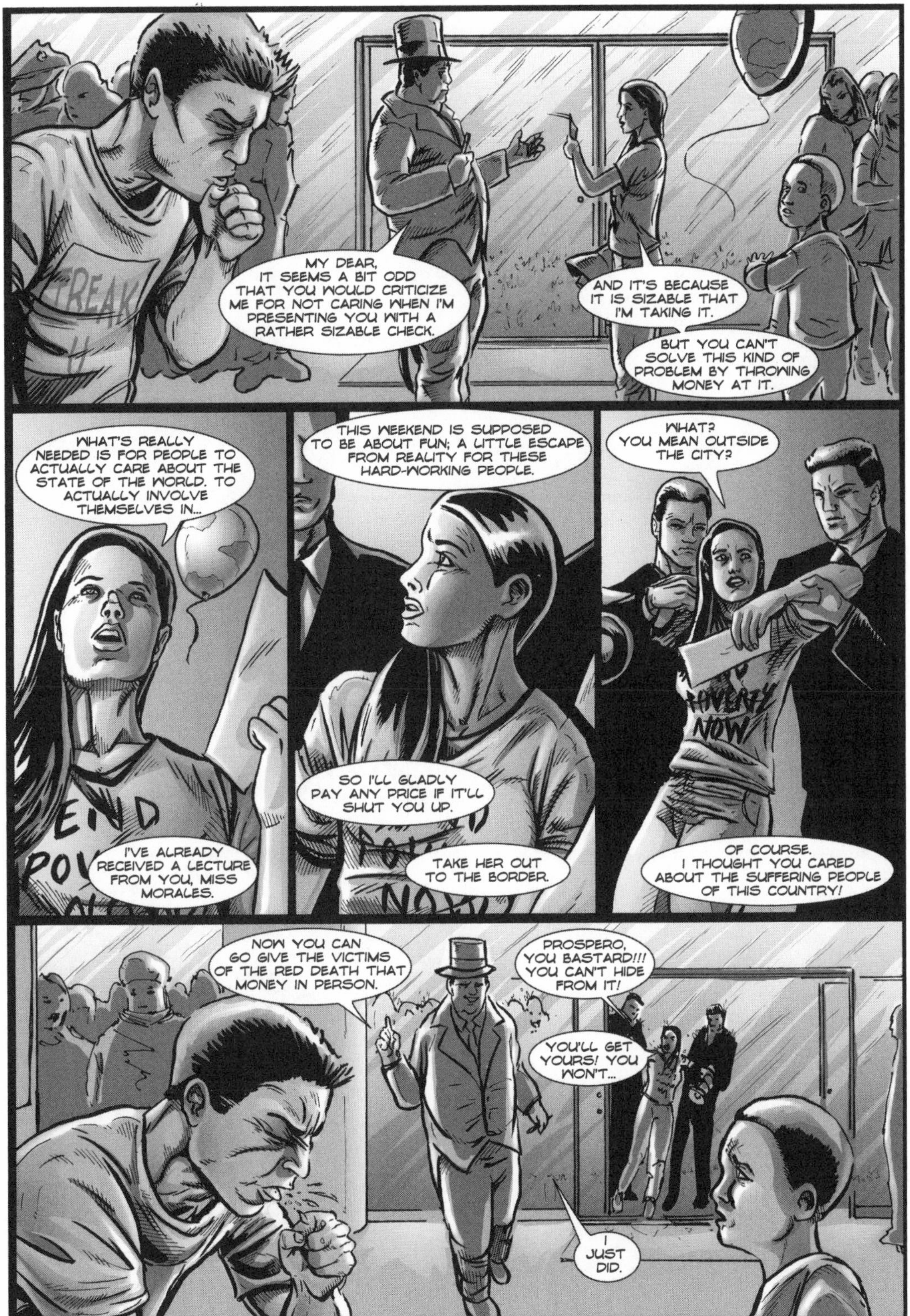
MY DEAR, IT SEEMS A BIT ODD THAT YOU WOULD CRITICIZE ME FOR NOT CARING WHEN I'M PRESENTING YOU WITH A RATHER SIZABLE CHECK.
AND IT'S BECAUSE IT IS SIZABLE THAT I'M TAKING IT.
BUT YOU CAN'T SOLVE THIS KIND OF PROBLEM BY THROWING MONEY AT IT.
WHAT'S REALLY NEEDED IS FOR PEOPLE TO ACTUALLY CARE ABOUT THE STATE OF THE WORLD. TO ACTUALLY INVOLVE THEMSELVES IN...
I'VE ALREADY RECEIVED A LECTURE FROM YOU, MISS MORALES.
THIS WEEKEND IS SUPPOSED TO BE ABOUT FUN; A LITTLE ESCAPE FROM REALITY FOR THESE HARD-WORKING PEOPLE.
SO I'LL GLADLY PAY ANY PRICE IF IT'LL SHUT YOU UP.
TAKE HER OUT TO THE BORDER.
WHAT? YOU MEAN OUTSIDE THE CITY?
OF COURSE. I THOUGHT YOU CARED ABOUT THE SUFFERING PEOPLE OF THIS COUNTRY!
NOW YOU CAN GO GIVE THE VICTIMS OF THE RED DEATH THAT MONEY IN PERSON.
PROSPERO, YOU BASTARD!!! YOU CAN'T HIDE FROM IT!
YOU'LL GET YOURS! YOU WON'T...
I JUST DID.

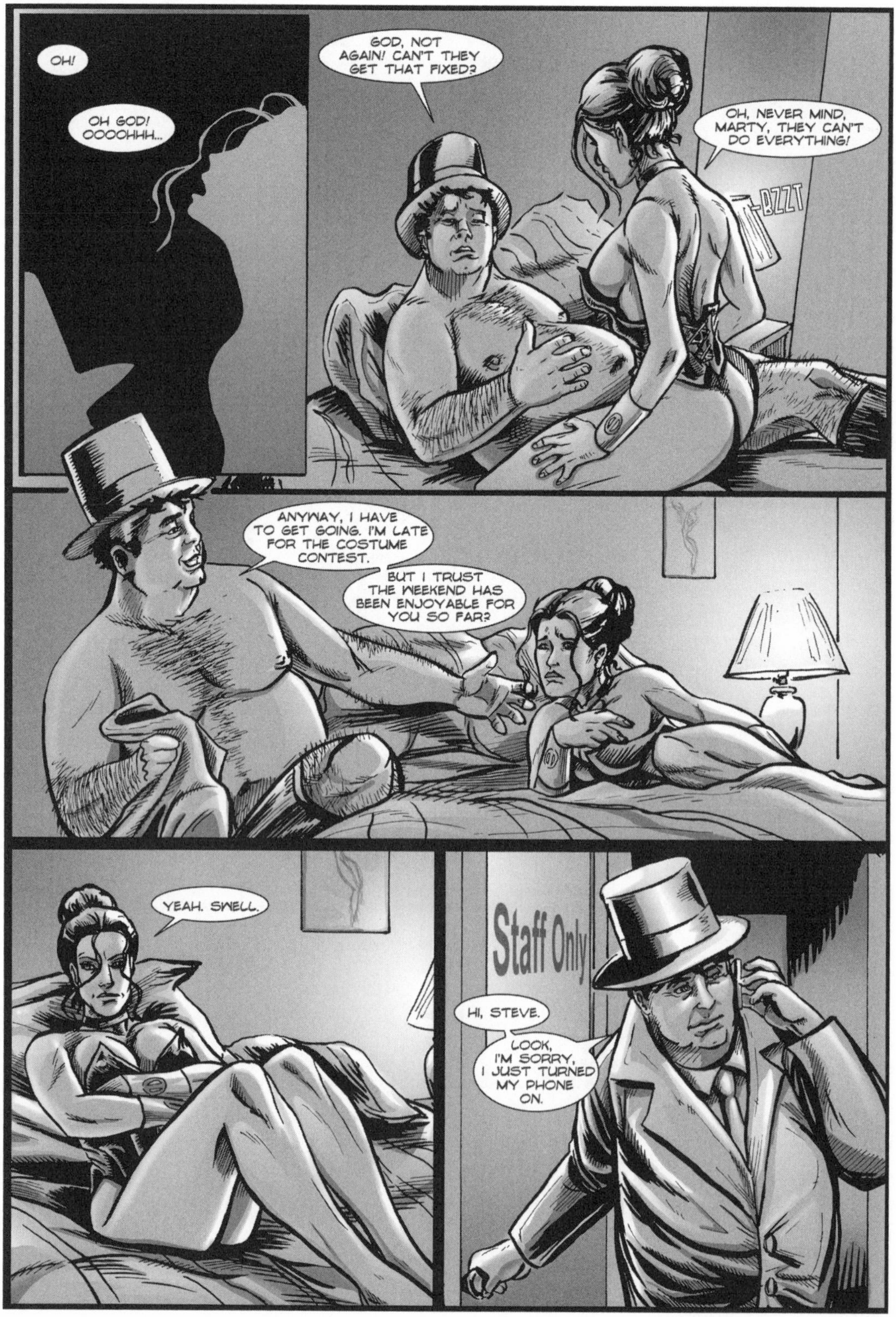
OH!
OH GOD! OOOOHHH...
GOD, NOT AGAIN! CAN'T THEY GET THAT FIXED?
OH, NEVER MIND, MARTY, THEY CAN'T DO EVERYTHING!
-BZZT
ANYWAY, I HAVE TO GET GOING. I'M LATE FOR THE COSTUME CONTEST.
BUT I TRUST THE WEEKEND HAS BEEN ENJOYABLE FOR YOU SO FAR?
YEAH. SWELL.
Staff Only
HI, STEVE.
LOOK, I'M SORRY, I JUST TURNED MY PHONE ON.

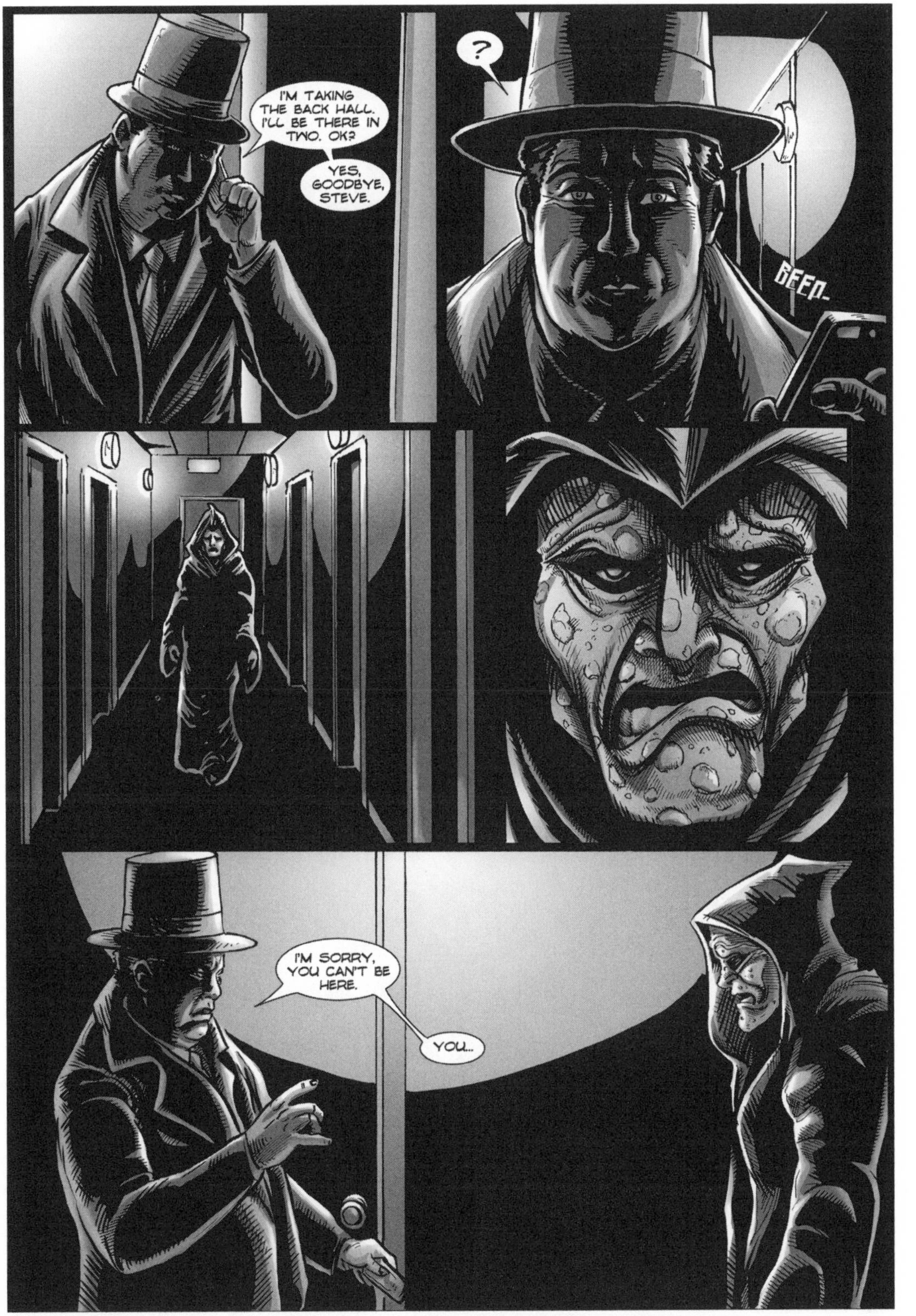
I'M TAKING THE BACK HALL. I'LL BE THERE IN TWO. OK?
YES, GOODBYE, STEVE.
?
BEEP..
I'M SORRY, YOU CAN'T BE HERE.
YOU...

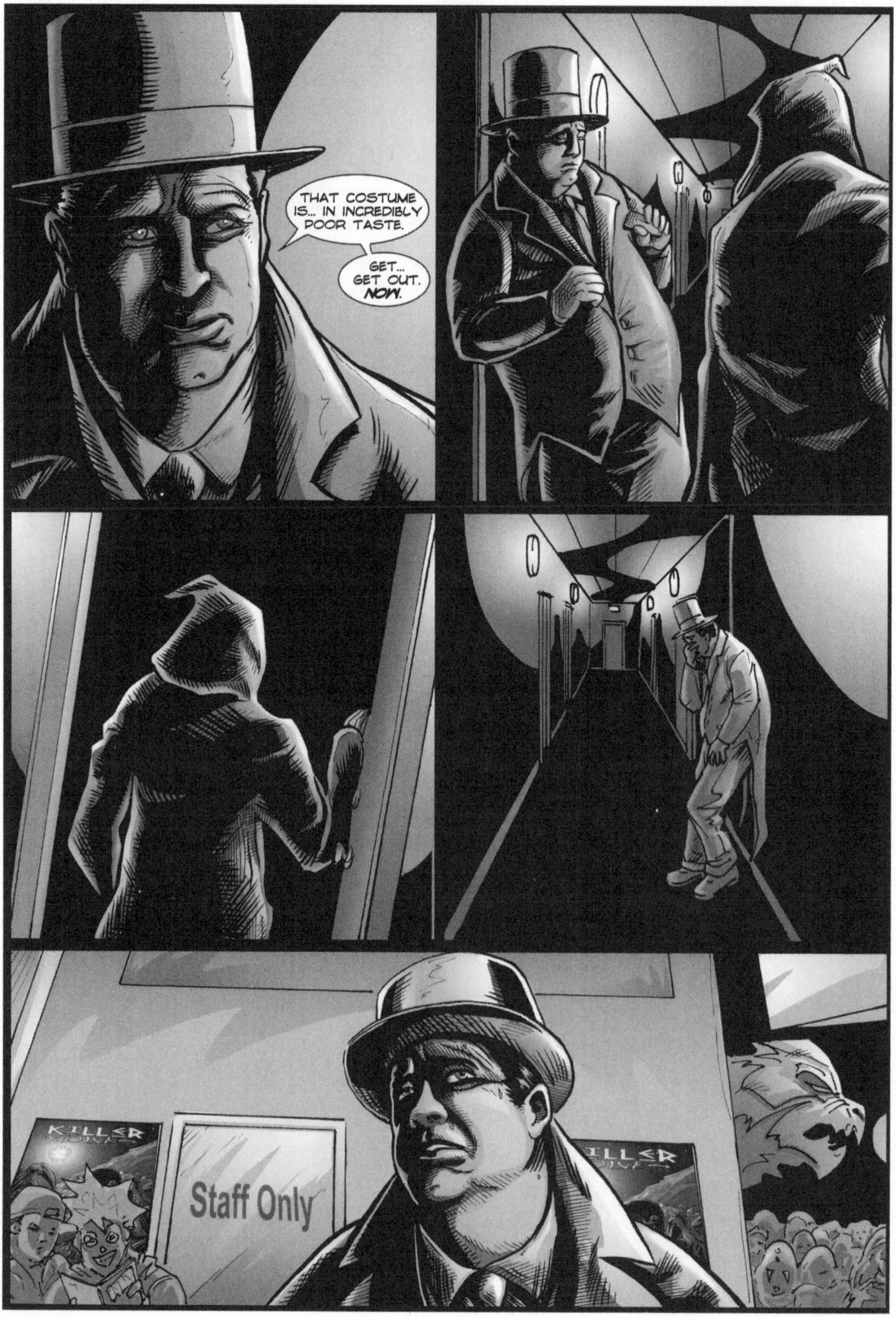
THAT COSTUME IS... IN INCREDIBLY POOR TASTE.
GET... GET OUT. NOW.
KILLER
Staff Only
KILLER

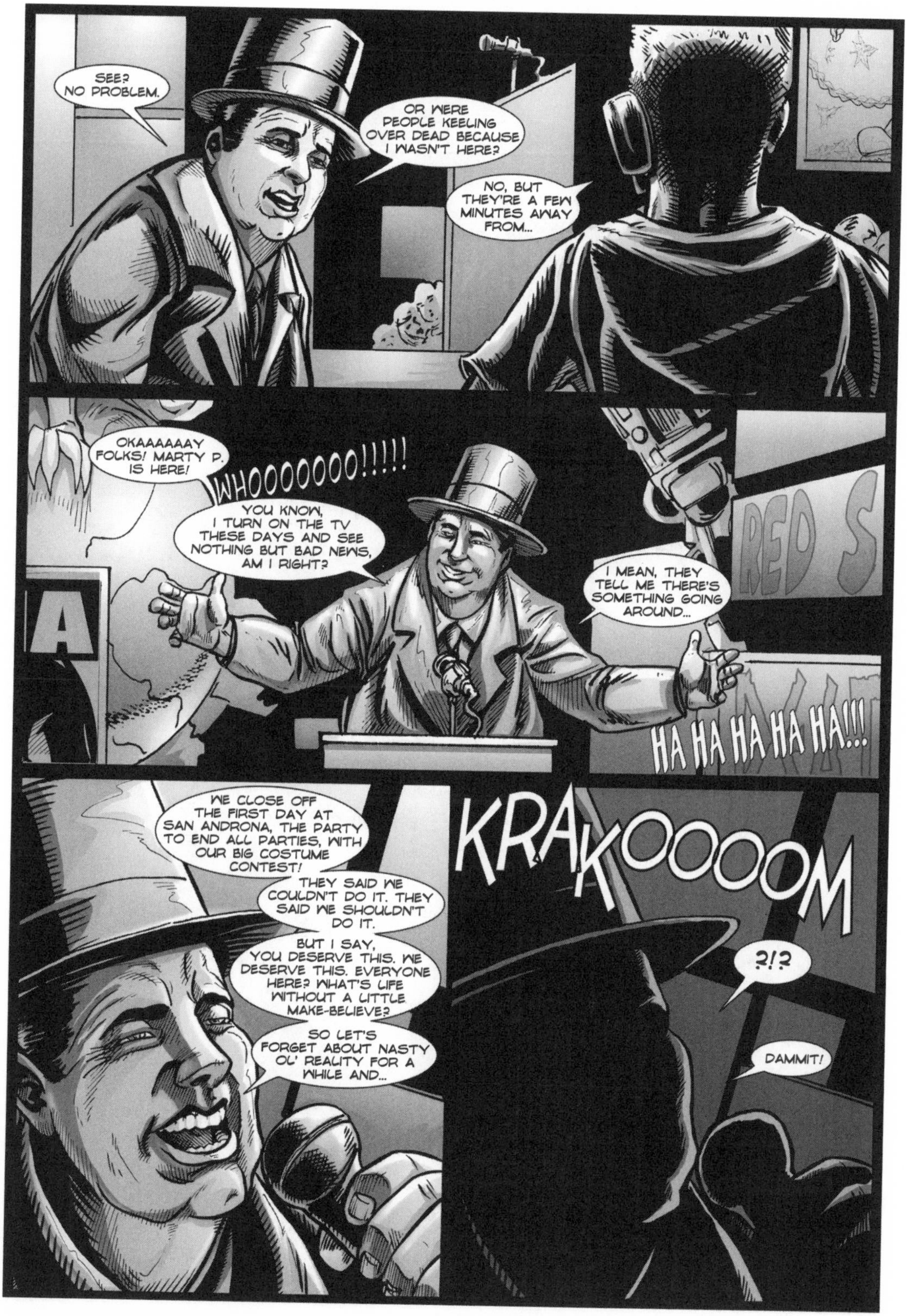
SEE? NO PROBLEM.
OR WERE PEOPLE KEELING OVER DEAD BECAUSE I WASN'T HERE?
NO, BUT THEY'RE A FEW MINUTES AWAY FROM...
OKAAAAAAY FOLKS! MARTY P. IS HERE!
WHOOOOOOO!!!!!
YOU KNOW, I TURN ON THE TV THESE DAYS AND SEE NOTHING BUT BAD NEWS, AM I RIGHT?
RED S
I MEAN, THEY TELL ME THERE'S SOMETHING GOING AROUND...
HA HA HA HA HA!!!
WE CLOSE OFF THE FIRST DAY AT SAN ANDRONA, THE PARTY TO END ALL PARTIES, WITH OUR BIG COSTUME CONTEST!
THEY SAID WE COULDN'T DO IT. THEY SAID WE SHOULDN'T DO IT.
BUT I SAY, YOU DESERVE THIS. WE DESERVE THIS. EVERYONE HERE? WHAT'S LIFE WITHOUT A LITTLE MAKE-BELIEVE?
SO LET'S FORGET ABOUT NASTY OL' REALITY FOR A WHILE AND...
KRAKOOOOM
?!?
DAMMIT!

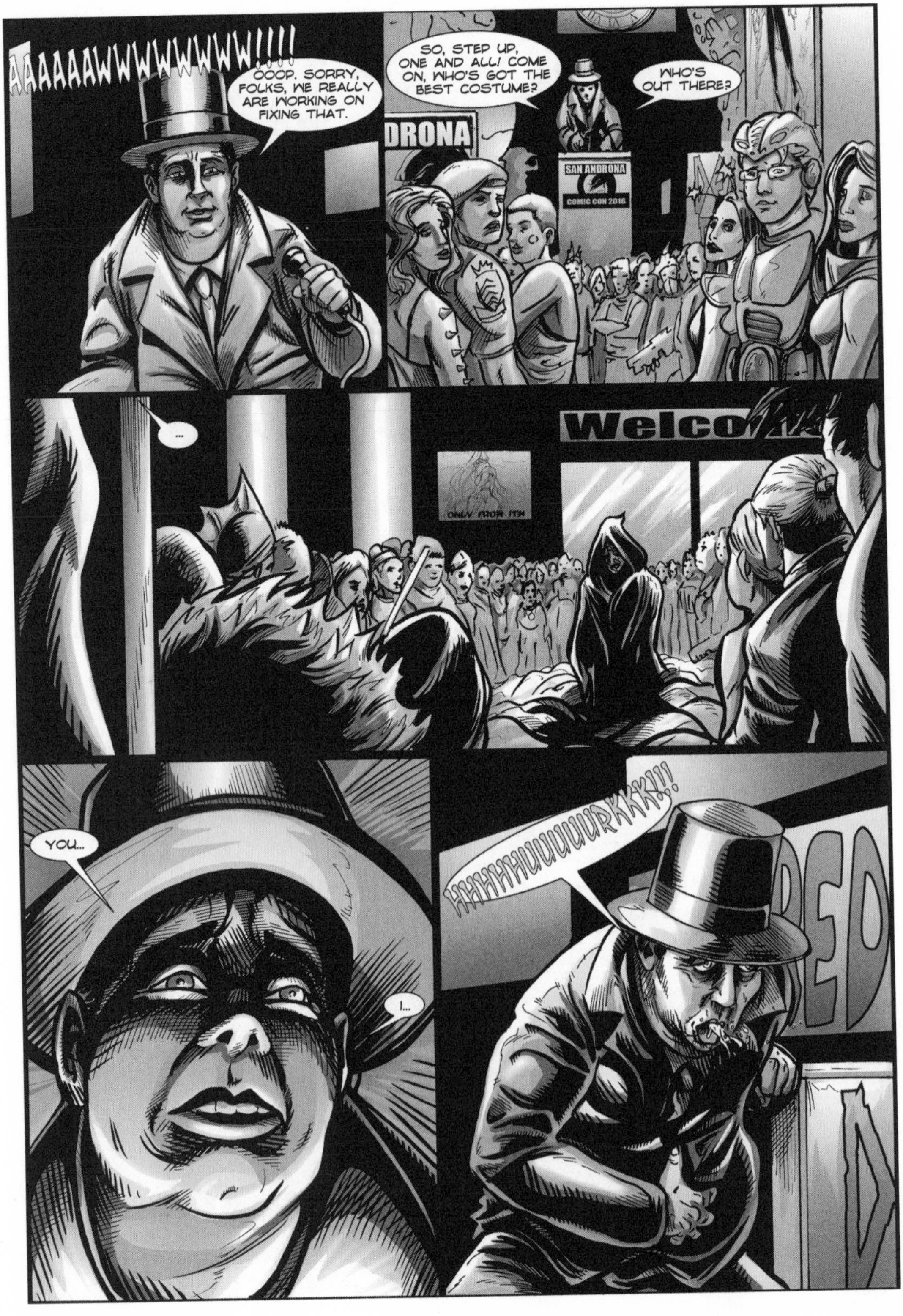
AAAAAAWWWWWWWW!!!!
OOOP. SORRY, FOLKS, WE REALLY ARE WORKING ON FIXING THAT.
SO, STEP UP, ONE AND ALL! COME ON, WHO'S GOT THE BEST COSTUME?
WHO'S OUT THERE?
DRONA
SAN ANDRONA
COMIC CON 2016
...
Welco
YOU...
I...
HHHHHUUUUURKKK!!!

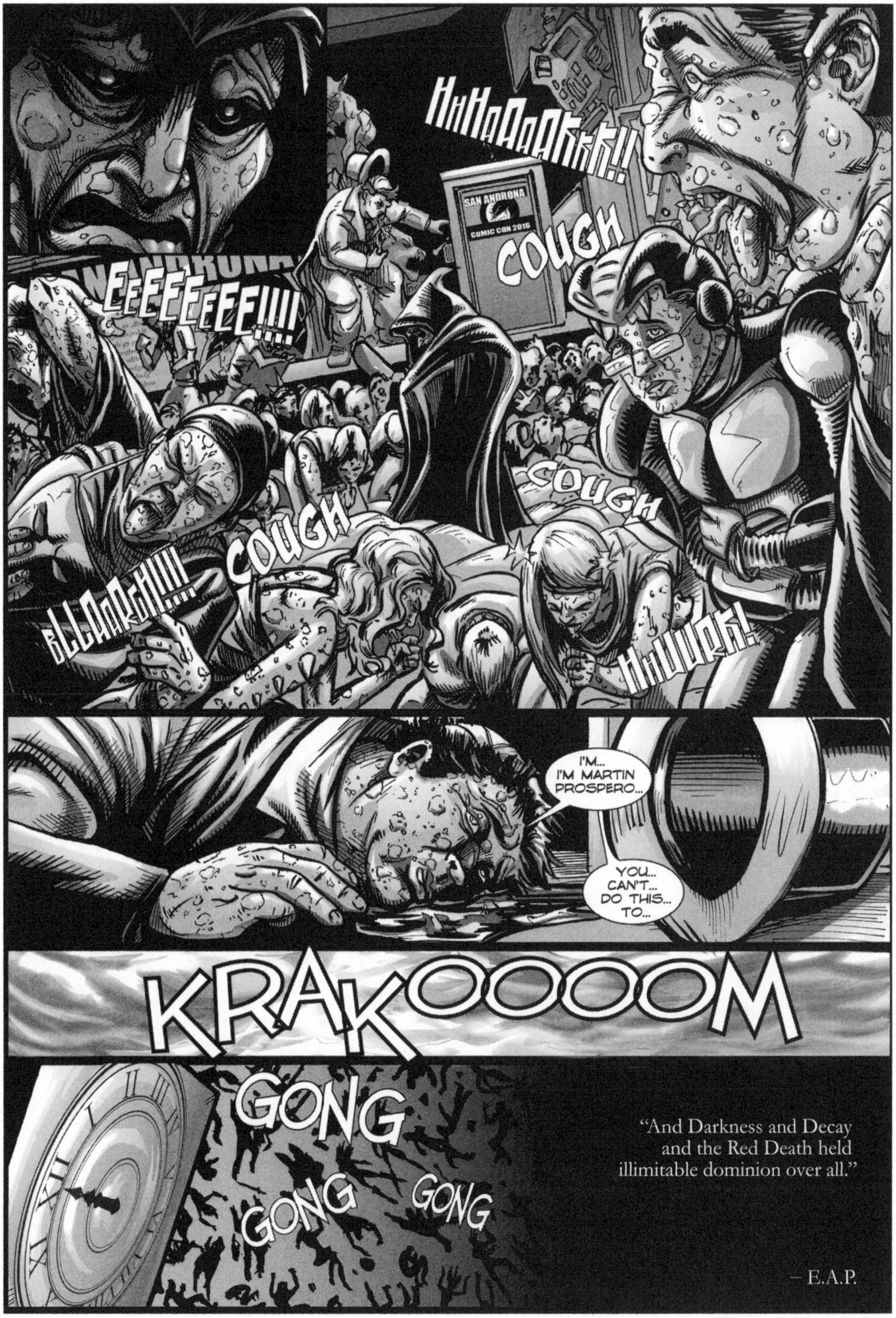
HHHAAAAKKK!!
SAN ANDRONA COMIC CON 2016
COUGH
EEEEEEEE!!!!!
COUGH
COUGH
BLLAARGH!!!!
HHUURK!
I'M... I'M MARTIN PROSPERO...
YOU... CAN'T... DO THIS... TO...
KRAKOOOOOM
GONG
GONG GONG
"And Darkness and Decay and the Red Death held illimitable dominion over all."
– E.A.P.

Facts in the case of

Edgar Allan Poe

January 19th 1809 - October 7th 1849

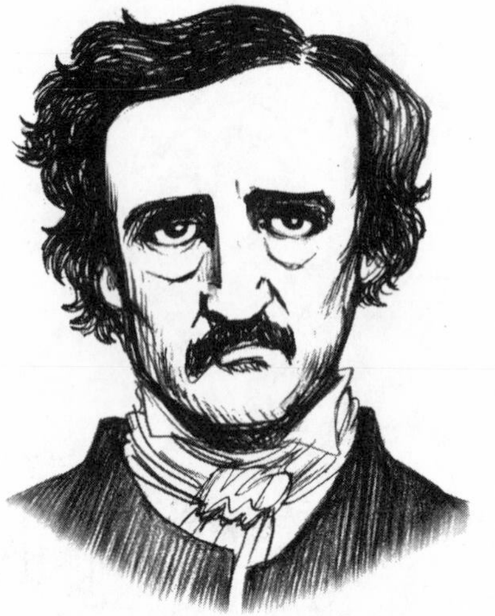

Think you know Poe?

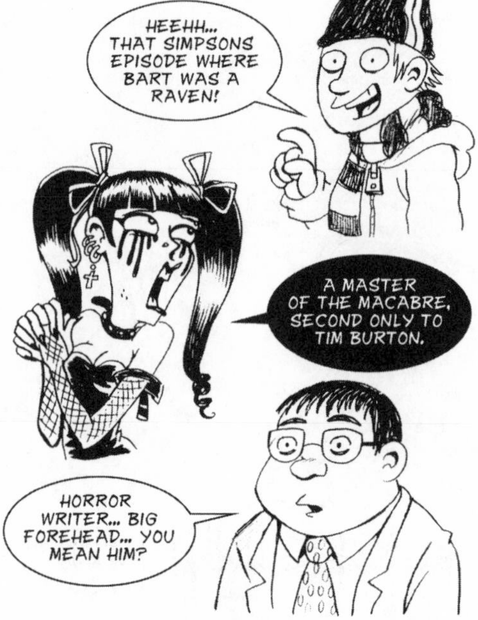
HEEHH... THAT SIMPSONS EPISODE WHERE BART WAS A RAVEN!
A MASTER OF THE MACABRE, SECOND ONLY TO TIM BURTON.
HORROR WRITER... BIG FOREHEAD... YOU MEAN HIM?

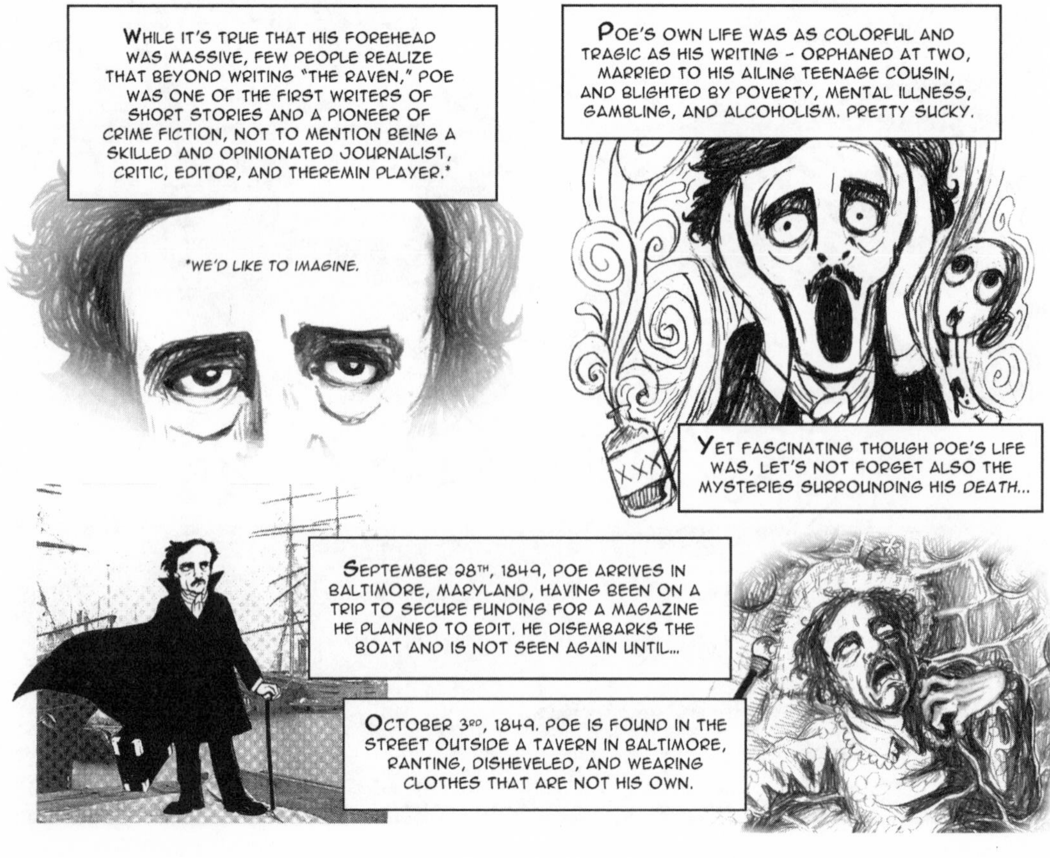
WHILE IT'S TRUE THAT HIS FOREHEAD WAS MASSIVE, FEW PEOPLE REALIZE THAT BEYOND WRITING "THE RAVEN," POE WAS ONE OF THE FIRST WRITERS OF SHORT STORIES AND A PIONEER OF CRIME FICTION, NOT TO MENTION BEING A SKILLED AND OPINIONATED JOURNALIST, CRITIC, EDITOR, AND THEREMIN PLAYER.*
*WE'D LIKE TO IMAGINE.
POE'S OWN LIFE WAS AS COLORFUL AND TRAGIC AS HIS WRITING - ORPHANED AT TWO, MARRIED TO HIS AILING TEENAGE COUSIN, AND BLIGHTED BY POVERTY, MENTAL ILLNESS, GAMBLING, AND ALCOHOLISM. PRETTY SUCKY.
YET FASCINATING THOUGH POE'S LIFE WAS, LET'S NOT FORGET ALSO THE MYSTERIES SURROUNDING HIS DEATH...
SEPTEMBER 28TH, 1849, POE ARRIVES IN BALTIMORE, MARYLAND, HAVING BEEN ON A TRIP TO SECURE FUNDING FOR A MAGAZINE HE PLANNED TO EDIT. HE DISEMBARKS THE BOAT AND IS NOT SEEN AGAIN UNTIL...
OCTOBER 3RD, 1849. POE IS FOUND IN THE STREET OUTSIDE A TAVERN IN BALTIMORE, RANTING, DISHEVELED, AND WEARING CLOTHES THAT ARE NOT HIS OWN.

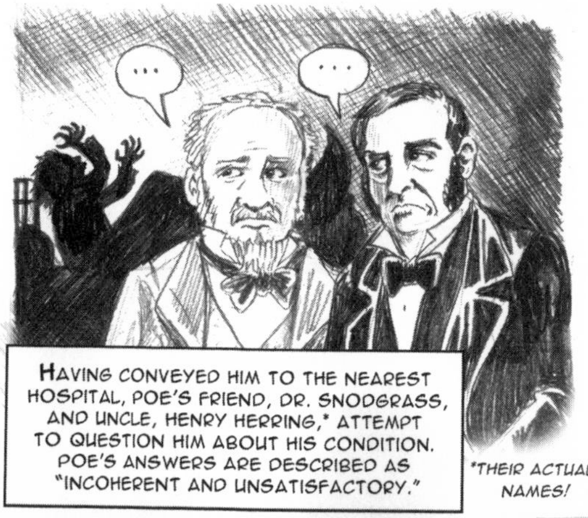
...
...
HAVING CONVEYED HIM TO THE NEAREST HOSPITAL, POE'S FRIEND, DR. SNODGRASS, AND UNCLE, HENRY HERRING,* ATTEMPT TO QUESTION HIM ABOUT HIS CONDITION. POE'S ANSWERS ARE DESCRIBED AS "INCOHERENT AND UNSATISFACTORY."
*THEIR ACTUAL NAMES!

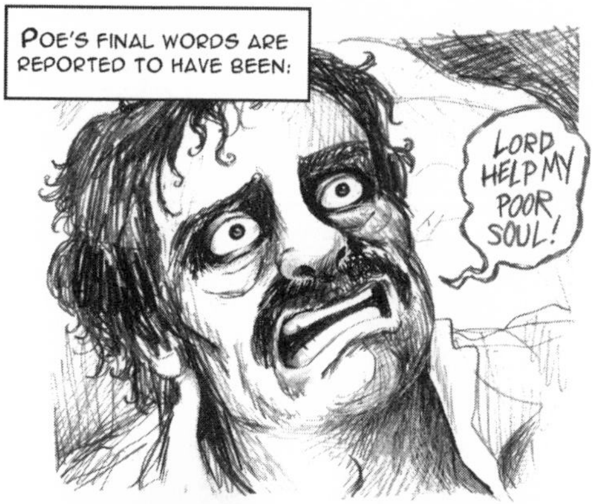
POE'S FINAL WORDS ARE REPORTED TO HAVE BEEN:
LORD HELP MY POOR SOUL!

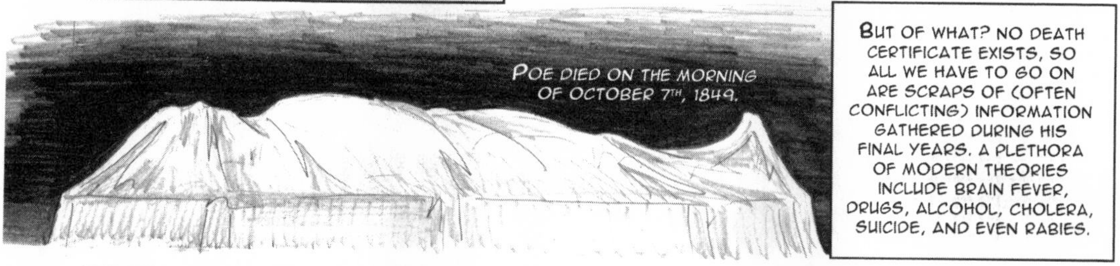
POE DIED ON THE MORNING OF OCTOBER 7TH, 1849.
BUT OF WHAT? NO DEATH CERTIFICATE EXISTS, SO ALL WE HAVE TO GO ON ARE SCRAPS OF (OFTEN CONFLICTING) INFORMATION GATHERED DURING HIS FINAL YEARS. A PLETHORA OF MODERN THEORIES INCLUDE BRAIN FEVER, DRUGS, ALCOHOL, CHOLERA, SUICIDE, AND EVEN RABIES.

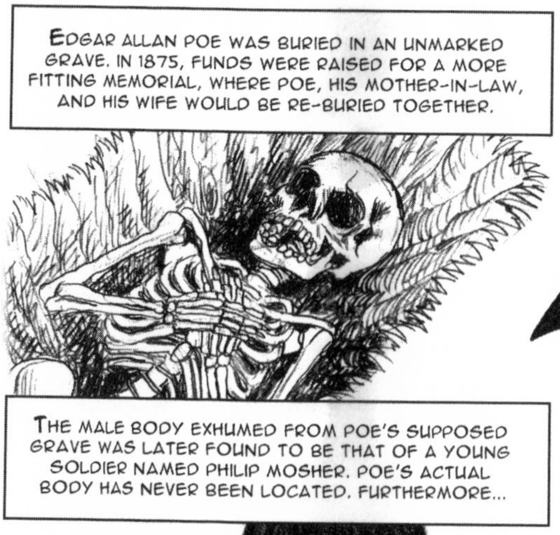
EDGAR ALLAN POE WAS BURIED IN AN UNMARKED GRAVE. IN 1875, FUNDS WERE RAISED FOR A MORE FITTING MEMORIAL, WHERE POE, HIS MOTHER-IN-LAW, AND HIS WIFE WOULD BE RE-BURIED TOGETHER.
THE MALE BODY EXHUMED FROM POE'S SUPPOSED GRAVE WAS LATER FOUND TO BE THAT OF A YOUNG SOLDIER NAMED PHILIP MOSHER. POE'S ACTUAL BODY HAS NEVER BEEN LOCATED. FURTHERMORE...

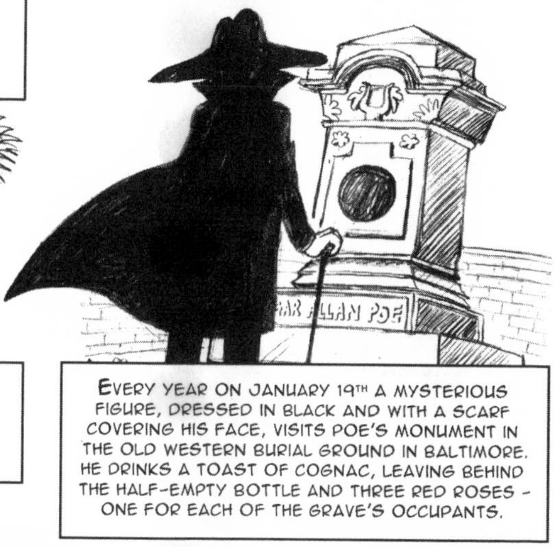
GAR ALLAN POE
EVERY YEAR ON JANUARY 19TH A MYSTERIOUS FIGURE, DRESSED IN BLACK AND WITH A SCARF COVERING HIS FACE, VISITS POE'S MONUMENT IN THE OLD WESTERN BURIAL GROUND IN BALTIMORE. HE DRINKS A TOAST OF COGNAC, LEAVING BEHIND THE HALF-EMPTY BOTTLE AND THREE RED ROSES - ONE FOR EACH OF THE GRAVE'S OCCUPANTS.

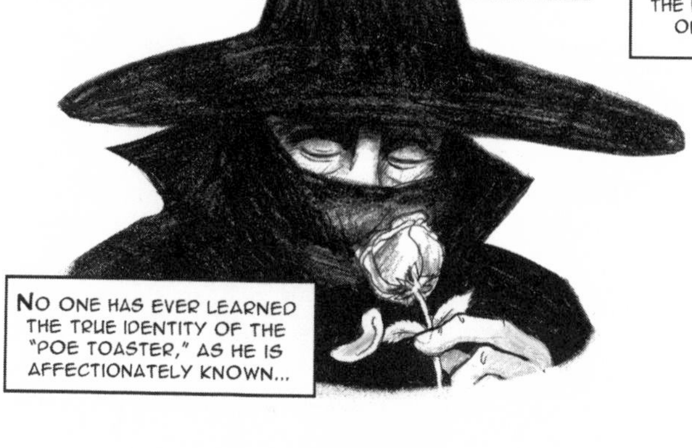
NO ONE HAS EVER LEARNED THE TRUE IDENTITY OF THE "POE TOASTER," AS HE IS AFFECTIONATELY KNOWN...

"The boundaries which
divide Life from Death are
at best shadowy and vague.
Who shall say where the one ends,
and where the other begins?"

Edgar Allan Poe,
The Premature Burial (1844)